# Beyond South Asia

# Beyond South Asia

India's Strategic Evolution and
the Reintegration of the Subcontinent

## NEIL PADUKONE

B L O O M S B U R Y

NEW YORK • LONDON • NEW DELHI • SYDNEY

**Bloomsbury Academic**
An imprint of Bloomsbury Publishing Inc

| | |
|---|---|
| 1385 Broadway | 50 Bedford Square |
| New York NY | London |
| 10018 | WC1B 3DP |
| USA | UK |

**www.bloomsbury.com**

**Bloomsbury is a registered trade mark of Bloomsbury Publishing Plc**

First published 2014

**Library of Congress Cataloging-in-Publication Data**
Padukone, Neil.
Beyond South Asia: India's strategic evolution and the reintegration of the subcontinent/Neil Padukone.
pages cm
Includes bibliographical references and index.
ISBN 978-1-62892-252-3 (paperback) – ISBN 978-1-62892-253-0 (hardback)
1. India–Foreign relations–1947–1984. 2. India–Foreign relations–1984– 3. India–Foreign relations–South Asia. 4. South Asia–Foreign relations–India. 5. South Asia–Economic integration. 6. India–Strategic aspects. 7. South Asia–Strategic aspects. I. Title.
DS448.P25 2014
327.54–dc23
2014010315

ISBN: HB: 978-1-6289-2253-0
PB: 978-1-6289-2252-3
ePub: 978-1-6289-2254-7
ePDF: 978-1-6289-2255-4

Typeset by Deanta Global Publishing Services, Chennai, India
Printed and bound in the United States of America

*For my family: Nina, Maitreya,*
*and Pia Padukone and Ajji.*
*Thank you for giving me the world.*

# Contents

**PART FOUR** South Asian Threat Perceptions
and Regional Integration 139

**PART FIVE** Conclusion 181

# Acknowledgments

It's become a cliché to say that a book would not be possible without a great number of people. But having gone through the process now, it's become clear how true that is: ideas, information, the motivation to keep going when you're beset by inertia, and—everything, really—are a product of the company you're blessed with. And though I take sole responsibility for this work, it truly would not be possible without the kindness and assistance of so many.

Gen. Ved Malik made a generous bet on a young scholar, and deserves the greatest credit for putting the notion of this book into my mind. Brig. Gurmeet Kanwal and Dr Bharat Karnad are two brilliant and pioneering minds of Indian strategic thought that encouraged me from the get-go, and without whom I would have never made it to India in the first place.

Matt Kopel and the team at Bloomsbury—including insightful anonymous reviewers—made this sometimes daunting journey a certified, and now attained destination. Thank you to all of the generous folks I interviewed, spoke with, read, and heard from—many of whom are cited herein, but many of whom preferred to remain anonymous. The American Center of New Delhi, the Harvard University library system, Google, and especially the New York Public Library made it possible for me to access hundreds of important resources without breaking the bank.

My great appreciation goes to Sunjoy Joshi, Sudheendra Kulkarni, Samir Saran, Lt. Gen. Patankar, Surendra Singh, Saeed Naqvi, Wilson John, Niranjan Sahoo, M. K. Rasgotra, Deba Mohanty, Lydia Powell, Baljit Kapoor, Satish Misra, R. Swaminathan, Dhaval Desai, Nisha Verma, and everyone at the Observer Research Foundation for unfettered access to their brilliant minds. Ambassadors Shyam Saran, Nick Burns, and Rick Inderfurth, have adroitly advanced India-US cooperation by leaps and bounds, and showed me both kindness and encouragement from the start. Deepa Ollapally, Prem Shankar Jha, Parag Khanna, Adam Ellick, Bharati Chaturvedi, P. R. Chari, Ashley Tellis, Stephen Cohen, Robin Wright, Suzanne DiMaggio, Stanley Weiss, Rajesh Rajagopalan, and Rick Ponzio have paved some very important roads by walking.

I was lucky to study with the late James Rosenau, who shed light on a sea change in global politics 20 years before the rest of the world opened its eyes to it. Nitin Pai and Lt. Col. Peter Garretson are today's oracles, anticipating what happens in the world months if not years before. Maya Chadda, David Alton, and Leon Fuerth have been generous intellectual, professional, and personal mentors that have guided me—and quietly, much of the world—through thick and thin; thank you so much for your unstinting warmth, encouragement, and examples.

Kaustav Chakrabarti and Hemant Nair were intellectual soundboards, and interlocutors in long email rants, that have become close friends. Rajeswari Rajagopalan is a brilliant analyst who's been a dear friend, stalwart ally, and supportive mentor since the first day I wandered confusedly through Delhi.

Colin Christopher, thank you for always having an open ear and mind, and belly laugh to share, and for always posing the unasked question. Deepti Sharma manages to keep me upbeat even in the worst of times. Jessica Jean-Francois inspires me just by being who she is. Namita Kallianpurkar has been a dear friend through decades of ups and downs.

Dina Magaril, Eli Blumm, Sam Yoo, Ben Silverman, Christine Fang, Samantha Lomeli, Saroj Sedalia, Gitanjali Prasad, Faizan Jawed, Sheetal Auntie and Rahul Uncle, Chitraj Singh, Vishal Gadhavi, Shivani Khatau, Shruti Chandhok, Hannah Schafer, Molly Rosner, Gauri Goyal, Megha Rajagopalan, Charles Loi, Uri Ferruccio, Shweta and Priya Savoor, Isa Mirza, J. J. Hurvich, Lauren Lyons, and many others I can't list here—you know who you are—make my world a much, much brighter place.

Reuben Stern, Matt Polazzo, and Deborah White, though I was just one of many who sat in your Stuyvesant High School classrooms so long ago, you ignited a deep passion for international relations and public policy that has continued through today; credit for so much of what I have done is owed to you.

Shrinath and Jyoti Savoor, thank you for opening your home and hearts to me, and making me realize how unhesitatingly wonderful family is. Gery and the Molnars, the Blumms, the Katis, the Nadkarni and Padukone clans, have been family even without the name or proximity.

Rohit Mitter lives the verses of Kharaqani by reflexively caring for anyone who walks through his door. Dharana Rijal's brilliance, love, and encouragement always raised me up and pushed me forward, even from half a world away. Evan Faber, Zach Hindin, and Justin Zorn: thank you for always providing equal—and large—doses of laughs, love, and inspiration.

My dear Anamma, the late Vrinda Padukone's quiet, profound insights taught us to appreciate beauty even in the subtle and never underestimate the value of anything. My Ajju, Prabhashankar Padukone's ocean of humor, wisdom and consistent optimism always bring smiles to everyone's faces. My Ajja, the late Sanjiv Nadkarni lived his life with a vigor and tireless zeal that was both absolutely humbling and inspiring. And my Ajji, Nalini Nadkarni's love, concern, and resulting motivation and efficiency are *literally* unparalleled—her chutzpah inspires me every day. In fact, it was my incredible Ajji who made the connections that helped get me to India in the first place!

Geopolitics, the subject of this book, is often understood as a contest for control of the earth. With their path-breaking examples, unrelenting love and enduring support, slogging to make sure I had both the best opportunities and the biggest laughs, kicks in the butt when I needed them the most, warm smiles and big hugs even after coming home late with tired eyes, and wise guidance, I've been absolutely blessed with a family that have always put the world at my fingertips and made me feel like it's mine for the taking (to say nothing of the roof over my head from where I wrote most of this text). As Tupac Shakur wrote in homage to his family, "there's no way I can pay you back. But the plan is to show you that . . . you are appreciated." In one tiny, tiny way, Nina, Maitreya, and Pia Padukone, and Ajji, this book is dedicated to you.

# List of Acronyms

APF – Armed Police Force
BJP – Bharatiya Janata Party
BRO – Border Roads Organization
Btu – British Thermal Unit
CENTO – Central Treaty Organization
CBI – Central Bureau of Investigation
CBM – Confidence-Building Measure
CIA – Central Intelligence Agency
CPI – Communist Party of India
CPI (M) – Communist Party of India
   (Marxist)
CPN (M) – Communist Party of Nepal
   (Maoist)
CTBT – Comprehensive Test Ban Treaty
DMK – Dravida Munnetra Kazhagam
FDI – Foreign Direct Investment
FII – Foreign Institutional Investor
FMCT – Fissile Material Cutoff Treaty
GDP – Gross Domestic Product
GNP – Gross National Product
GCC – Gulf Cooperation Council
HuJI – Harakat-ul-Jihad-ul-Islami
ITBP – Indo-Tibetan Border Police
IAS – Indian Administrative Service
IB – Intelligence Bureau
IM – Indian Mujahideen
INC – Indian National Congress
IPI – India-Pakistan-Iran
IPKF – International Peace-Keeping Force
ISI – Inter-services Intelligence
IWT – Indus Water Treaty
JeI – Jamaat-e-Islami
JuD – Jamaat-ud-Dawa
LeT – Lashkar-e-Taiba
LNG – Liquefied Natural Gas
LPG – Liquefied Petroleum Gas

LTTE – Liberation Tigers of Tamil Eelam
LWE – Left-Wing Extremism
MEA – Ministry of External Affairs
MFN – Most Favored Nation
MHA – Ministry of Home Affairs
MOU – Memorandum of Understanding
NAM – Non-Aligned Movement
NATO – North Atlantic Treaty Organization
NCTC – National Counter-Terrorism Center
NDA – National Democratic Alliance
NEFA – Northeastern Frontier Agency
NNC – Naga National Council
NPT – Nuclear Nonproliferation Treaty
NSG – National Security Guards
NWFP – Northwestern Frontier Province
ONGC – Oil and Natural Gas Corporation
PLA – People's Liberation Army
PLAN – People's Liberation Army Navy
PRC – People's Republic of China
R&AW – Research & Analysis Wing
SAARC – South Asian Association for
   Regional Cooperation
SAFTA – South Asian Free Trade
   Agreement
SEATO – Southeast Asia Treaty
   Organization
SIMI – Student Islamic Movement of India
SLOC – Sea Line of Communication
TAPI – Turkmenistan-Afghanistan-
   Pakistan-India
Tcf – Trillion cubic feet
TTP – Tehreek-e-Taliban Pakistan
UN – United Nations
UNSC – United Nations Security Council
UPA – United Progressive Alliance
USD – United States Dollars

# PART ONE

# Introduction

# 1

# Introduction

In the years since 11 September 2001, American-led wars have flared in Afghanistan and Iraq. Energy and commodities trade have skyrocketed in the Persian Gulf. A political awakening has poured youth into the streets of the Arab world. Economic growth has changed the course of Southeast Asia, sectarian conflicts within Islam have spilled into the streets of the Muslim world and beyond, and China has become an economic heavyweight that threatens to challenge the US-led order in much of the world.

In a widely acclaimed book that made the rounds and influenced decision-makers in Washington, D.C., and other capitals, author Robert Kaplan refers to the Indian Ocean as the "nexus of world power and conflict in the coming years." It is here, he writes, "where the five-hundred-year reign of Western power is slowly being replaced by the influence of indigenous nations . . . and where a tense dialogue is taking place between Islam and the United States." It is the Indian Ocean where "the fight for democracy, energy independence, and religious freedom will be lost or won, and it is here that American foreign policy must concentrate if America is to remain dominant in an ever-changing world."[1] Perhaps paying Kaplan heed, the administration of US President Barack Obama announced, in late 2011, a "strategic pivot" of US armed forces to Asia.

At the very center of this meeting ground lies the Republic of India. With the world's second largest population, India sits in the middle of the Indian Ocean, astride the Dharmic, Islamic, Western, and Confucian worlds, uniting thousands of languages and cultures within a single nation, while facing profound challenges reconciling the modern with the traditional in the largest democratic system of government on earth. Perhaps most consequentially for much of the rest of the world, India has come to be seen as a "rising power" in

---

[1] Robert Kaplan, *Monsoon: The Indian Ocean and the Future of American Power*. New York: Random House, 2010.

global politics, stemming from its massive economic growth after the 1990s, its detonation of a nuclear bomb in 1998, and military and strategic expansion since.

As Ashley Tellis of the Carnegie Endowment for International Peace, and one of the key architects of the political realignment between the United States and India, writes, "The record thus far amply substantiates the claim that India will be one of Asia's two major ascending powers. It is expected that the Indian economy could grow at a rate of 7 to 8 percent for the next two decades. If these expectations are borne out, there is little doubt that India will overtake current giants."[2] The United States' National Intelligence Council writes, in its *Global Trends: 2025*, that "No other countries are projected to rise to the level of China or India . . . and none is likely to match their individual global clout."[3]

At the same time, the Indian Ocean and South Asian regions are and, for decades, have been mired in conflict. As the 2011 killing of Osama bin Laden in the Pakistani town of Abbottabad demonstrated, the Afghanistan-Pakistan border region that has come to be called "AfPak" is also the epicenter of global Islamist terrorism.[4] With over 1.13 billion people—which include a third of the world's poor, the population that lives on less than one dollar a day—living in a tropical, equatorial region, India is ground zero for the consequences of climate change. Arguably a third of both Indian and Pakistani territory is "stateless," outside the direct reign of national capitals and often under the control of local militants or insurgents that oppose those capitals. In Pakistan, this is due to various Islamist militants affiliated with the Taliban movement; in India, the Naxalite or Left-Wing Extremism (LWE) movement has afflicted nearly a third of the country's administrative districts. Meanwhile, India and Pakistan have been locked in a decades-long cycle of nuclear-tipped conflict; four hot wars and dozens if not hundreds of skirmishes between the two South Asian countries have captured the world's attention, leading many to refer to the Indian subcontinent as "the world's most dangerous place."

How New Delhi interacts with this geographic and emerging political space will have profound consequences for the twenty-first-century world, not to mention India and South Asia themselves. Yet, while much has been said of the world's view of India, there is little in the public domain on India's

[2]Ashley J. Tellis, "The United States and South Asia," Testimony before the House Committee on International Relations, 14 June 2004; Ashley Tellis, "India as a New Global Power: An Action Agenda for the United States," Carnegie Endowment for International Peace, July 2005.
[3]C. Thomas Fingar, "Global Trends 2025: A Transformed World," National Intelligence Council, Directorate of National Intelligence, November 2008.
[4]Rohan Gunaratna and Khuram Iqbal, *Pakistan: Terrorism Ground Zero*. Chicago: University of Chicago Press, 2011.

view of the world. In fact, many Indians lament about what they see as their country's lack of strategic vision or culture.[5] Foreign observers, particularly in the United States, have also spoken of a lack of a strategic or planning culture in India, including a reactivism in strategic, military, and economic matters. Some attribute this to institutional squabbles within and inertia among the bureaucracies of the Indian state, particularly those responsible for national defense and security policy: the Ministry of External Affairs, Ministry of Defense, the Home Ministry and Ministry of Finance, and even technocratic institutions such as the Defense Research and Development Organization.[6]

The key, path-breaking study of Indian strategic culture since India's independence from Great Britain in 1947, George Tanham's "Indian Strategic Thought," argued that this deficit was partly because of a uniquely Indian worldview rooted in the legacy of Hinduism and Vedic philosophy.[7] Tanham argued that, in contrast to many western traditions that emphasize a Manichean (good vs. evil) and messianic (linear) perspective, the Indian worldview was rooted in Dharmic philosophy, which emphasizes fatalism, the cyclical evolution of events, and nonlinearity. Given this idea of nonlinearity, despite a long history of intellectual and scientific exploration, Indian empires and civilizations rarely kept written documents of their own history, seeing it as inconsequential to an unpredictable future. The effect of this, Tanham argued, was a discounting of strategic vision and planning even in modern Indian governance.[8]

Yet this critique is based largely on the paucity of *official* Government of India documents that specifically articulate the country's strategic interests, vision, and tactics. In fact, the contours of India's strategic evolution from the time of independence in 1947, as Tanham goes on to concede, have been shaped by a number of ideas, historical perceptions, and geostrategic factors, and continue to evolve in the face of global shifts.

This of course poses the question: if existing factors gave rise to goals, and goals gave way to strategies, why, then, hasn't the Indian government publicly articulated these plans? Indeed this is a challenge that proponents of strategic planning face the world over: does planning require a single "grand" strategy to guide actions? As an Indian defense secretary once said before

---

[5]This is a view taken mostly in Op-Ed pieces in the mainstream English media. Its proponents include, but are not limited to, K. Subrahmanyam, Kanti Bajpai, Mohan Guruswamy, and Brahma Chellaney.
[6]P. R. Chari, "National Security and Defense Strategy," presentation at Conference on India's Strategic Environment and Defense Policies, Observer Research Foundation and National Bureau of Asian Research, New Delhi, 23–25 April 2009.
[7]George K. Tanham, "Indian Strategic Thought: An Interpretive Essay," RAND, 1992.
[8]There were additional elements to Tanham's exploration that will be addressed in subsequent chapters.

the Parliamentary Standing Committee on Defense, "all the elements of the doctrine are well known and have been incorporated from our constitution downwards. . . . There have been policy pronouncements by Ministers in Parliament. So, our national security doctrine is well known and *the absence of a written document . . . does not create any confusion or lack of clarity in this matter. I . . . accept that we do not publish it as a document as such.*"[9]

Official pronouncements or even articulation may have two key consequences. On the one hand, formal pronouncements make public one's aims, setting a certain standard for what is to be expected from a country. This can be enabling, in that it provides a vision for ultimate goals and thus parameters on how those goals must be brought about, empowering those responsible for the execution of a strategy to work concertedly toward its realization.

But this public articulation can also be restrictive. If these aims, particularly in the arena of national security and statecraft, go against those of another party or country, they (perhaps unnecessarily) set the stage for adversarial relations with that party. If one country's strategy, for example, aims for the weakness of another country, the latter would certainly not be pleased to hear it. In the realm of diplomacy and statecraft, in which the goal is to maintain security and stability within one's own borders, public and even official antagonism—which may result from public pronouncements of intentions—may be unnecessary and even counterproductive. Indeed, a key tenet of statecraft, as defined as far back as the Maurya Empire of 250 B.C.E., whose key strategist was Kautilya, the author of the famed Indian text on strategic thought, the *Arthashastra* (science of administration), is secrecy (*gupti*).[10]

Meanwhile, any ostensible disconnect between internal vision and aims, and what is professed, can be a source of power in national affairs: India's first prime minister, Jawaharlal Nehru, was widely perceived as an idealist in world affairs, advocating non-alignment, global disarmament, and international cooperation—a perception that earned him many supporters around the world. But in reality, Nehru "practiced hard *realpolitik*," seeing morality as nothing more than "an instrument of state policy. He . . . had little compunction in saying one thing and doing another," according to senior Indian defense analyst Bharat Karnad.[11]

---

[9]Quoted in Ali Ahmed, "Clarifying India's Strategic Doctrine," *IDSA Comment*, 25 October 2010, available at www.idsa.in/idsacomments/ClarifyingIndiasStrategicDoctrine_aahmed_251010, emphasis added.

[10]Radha Kumud Mookerji, *Chandragupta Maurya and his Times*. Delhi: Motilal Banarsidass Publications, 1966, pp. 77–8.

[11]Bharat Karnad, "India First," Seminar, No. 519, November 2002; See also Bharat Karnad, *Nuclear Weapons and Indian Security: The Realist Foundations of Strategy*. New Delhi: Macmillan Press, 2002. The realist foundations behind Nehru's strategic thinking are explored further in Chapter 1.

On the other hand, public articulation of one's strategic interests reduces flexibility—particularly in cases in which it is better that the parameters of a strategic doctrine not be followed precisely or rigidly. By prioritizing certain goals or tactics over others, a strategy can neglect some of the negative ramifications of following the decided course, as well as sacrificing the benefits of alternative courses of action. One of the paramount global goals of our era, economic growth through industrialization, for example, often comes at the expense of environmental security.

Yet, spoken or unspoken, flexible or rigid, there are always goals, visions, and assumptions that undergird the actions of people and nations. This was the case with ancient Indian empires—as the existence of the Arthashastra attests—all the way through to the British Raj, and particularly during the life of the Indian Republic, the largest nation-state that was formed in the wake of the independence of the subcontinent from Britain. Understanding this worldview and its underlying assumptions will enable observers to make sense of and manage the emerging changes in what has come to be called the "Asian century."

This book follows the course of India's strategic evolution from independence to the present day. It aims to represent the author's understandings of New Delhi's strategic worldview, particularly that emanating from the Prime Minister's Office, the Ministry of Foreign Affairs, the Ministry of Defense, the Indian Armed Forces, business community, and research institutions that host scholars, former officials, and others affiliated or formerly affiliated with these governing institutions.

At times the analysis follows a "realist" perspective, at others a more "liberalist" and even "constructivist" perspective; at certain points, culture, individuals, history, and governing institutions are emphasized, at others geography, military balance, or economics are emphasized. This is not owed to a lack of analytical rigor or intellectual consistency, but because of an effort to stay true to the factors that drive and have driven India's strategic perspective at different junctures in history. This is done with the foremost intention of conveying and relaying, while also providing a critical analysis.

# The Strategy of a Nation

Of course, the strategic worldview of a "country" necessarily follows a statist perspective—one that emanates from a country's capital whose sovereignty extends to certain defined, though possibly contested, national borders. Such a perspective may clash not only with other countries, but also with other parties within the same country. The revisionist historian Howard Zinn,

for example, argued that "there is a *pretense* that there really is such a thing
as a" nation-state,

> subject to occasional conflicts and quarrels, but fundamentally a community
> of people with common interests. . . . Nations are not communities and
> have never been. The history of any country, presented as the history of
> a family, conceals fierce conflicts of interest (sometime exploding, most
> often repressed) between conquerors and conquered, masters and slaves,
> capitalists and workers, dominators and dominated in race and sex.[12]

This is a dilemma of the modern disciplines of political science, government,
and international relations, which, even as they acknowledge additional
super-state and substate entities and processes, their first point of reference
remains the nation-state. Even revisionist historians who deride the notion
and hegemony of the nation-state affirm its importance in analysis. This in turn
comes down to a question of the "legitimacy" of the governing authority.

India's process of nation building in the twentieth century, and the
development of New Delhi's "legitimacy" over that geographic space, was
arguably a response to (and thus a product of) British colonialism. British
Prime Minister Winston Churchill famously argued that without external
British influence, India would never have been a country at all—that "India
is merely a geographical expression. It is no more a single country than the
Equator."[13] Many of the "conflicts of interest" to which Zinn refers are rooted
in geography, culture, and history, in addition to more local issues of hierarchy
and power.

In the case of India, the evolution of these "conflicts of interest" has, for
better or worse, been central to the development of New Delhi's strategic
worldview. New Delhi has based many of its decisions on either opposing
or even harnessing these conflicts. Moreover, from before the time of
independence, foreign policy was largely shaped, influenced, and discussed
by Jawaharlal Nehru and his coterie of trusted advisors. Even today, national
strategy remains largely elite-controlled in both the Congress and Bharatiya
Janata Parties; foreign policy is largely undiscussed and of little consequence
to the majority of voters in regional and state politics and even in national
elections. Having conceded all of these points, this book uses the words
"India" and "New Delhi" to be coterminous with the prevailing thinking in

---

[12]Howard Zinn, *A People's History of the United States: 1492-Present.* New York: Harper Collins,
2010, pp. 9–10.
[13]Quoted in Shashi Tharoor, *India: From Midnight to the Millennium and Beyond.* New Delhi:
Penguin Books, 2012, p. 8.

the halls of the national capital, and as representative of the "interests" of the nation-state of India.

# Beyond South Asia

Based on 4 years of research in South Asia and the United States, which included field interviews with Indian officials and serving and retired bureaucrats from the Indian military, police, and civil service, Indian activists, political analysts and observers, journalists, and businesspersons, and their foreign counterparts, and analyses of primary and secondary documents and news and scholarly reports from within South Asia and without, this book explores the evolution of India's strategic worldview: how New Delhi has interpreted, framed, and acted on its national security and foreign policy perspective, and how that perspective has played out within the subcontinent and without.

The book divides the subject into three sections. The first section discusses the rise, implementation, and ultimate failure of India's "Monroe Doctrine," which directed Indian strategic thought in the decades following independence. Arising from the legacy of imperial Britain's strategic outlook for a united South Asia, geopolitical compulsions associated with the Indian subcontinent's specific topography, and a nationalist understanding of Indian history that came with certain political-economic narratives and objectives, India's Monroe Doctrine had two key goals in mind. The first was for India to keep the subcontinent internally united by denying the autonomous tendencies of its South Asian neighbors; the second was to disallow extra-regional powers a presence in the region. The strategy ultimately backfired, hastening the involvement of the United States and China in the subcontinent and contaminating relations with the rest of the countries of South Asia, who resisted strategic and even economic cooperation with India, often violently.

The second section describes the factors that are causing a shift in New Delhi's strategic worldview today, namely the opening of New Delhi's markets to foreign investment, the ensuing need to access new markets and energy resources abroad, and the imperative of countering China's emerging military strategy. These shifts are compelling India to look beyond South Asia for its strategic needs. In doing so, India has established itself in a number of new theaters: through a "Look East" policy in Southeast Asia and the South China Sea; a "Look West" policy in the Persian Gulf, Middle East and Africa; a "New Silk Road" in Central and West Asia; a defense realignment from its western coast, adjacent to Pakistan, to India's borders with China in the north, naval eastern command in the Bay of Bengal, and the southern Indian Ocean; and a supposedly "natural alliance" with the United States.

The third section analyzes and anticipates how this strategy is affecting India's South Asian neighbors and New Delhi's relations with them. In order to access markets and resources beyond South Asia, limit China's involvement in the region, and maintain stability in the subcontinent, New Delhi is seeking greater conciliation with its regional neighbors. Moving from a position of domineering confrontation to one of greater accommodation in South Asia, India's evolving strategic doctrine aims to contribute to the stabilization of the region and to set the foundations for the economic reintegration of the subcontinent.

# PART TWO

# India's Monroe Doctrine

# 2

# Indian Geopolitical Strategy

## The Strategic Unity of South Asia

Nearly 50 million years ago, after breaking off of eastern Africa, the Indian subcontinent was pushed northward and crashed into and became grafted onto southern Asia. The collision of the tectonic plates not only produced the Himalayan Mountains, but also defined the Indian subcontinental plate as its own distinct geographic region, attached to but distinct from the rest of the continent of Asia.[1]

As a result, the peninsula that is called "South Asia" today is essentially one geographic and strategic unit. The contours of this unit include (i) the Arabian Sea to the west; (ii) the Bay of Bengal to the east; (iii) the Indian Ocean to the South; (iv) in the northwest, the Makran, Kirthar, Suleiman, Hindu Kush, Pamir, and Karakoram mountain ranges that extend from modern Baluchistan to northern Kashmir-Xinjiang; (v) and in the north, the Himalayan range that divides South Asia from the Tibetan Plateau, and extends east to (vi) the Rakhine mountain range of northern and western Myanmar in the northeast. These features define a strategically cohesive unit that, despite minor excursions and incursions through the northwest or by sea, has remained relatively insular and insulated over many centuries.

The "center" of this unit is the Indo-Gangetic Plain, the "Indian heartland" that extends from northwestern Punjab (in modern Pakistan) in the west to Bengal in the east, and the southern Himalayan foothills in the north to the Yamuna River and in the south. The Indo-Gangetic Plain is irrigated by three major river systems—the Indus, the Ganges, and the Brahmaputra—as well as two seasonal rain patterns—the southwest and northeast monsoons—that

---

[1]Douwe Van Hinsbergen, et al., "Greater India Basin hypothesis and a two-stage Cenozoic collision between India and Asia," *Proceedings of the National Academy of Sciences*, 2012, no. 109, vol. 20, pp. 7659–64.

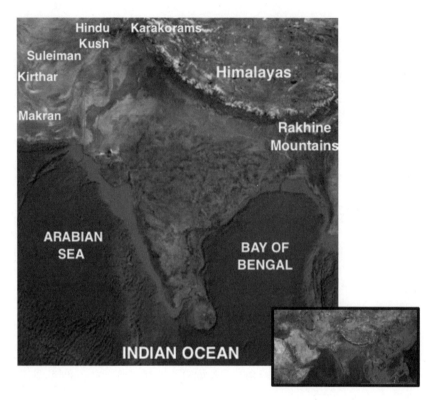

**FIGURE 2.1** *Topography of the Indian subcontinent—adapted from Google Maps.*

have made the Plain one of the most fertile and densely populated (and at one point one of the richest) regions of the world.

   To the northwest of this "unit," Central Asia had long been "India's door to the outside world."[2] In the past, both invaders and traders used the Central Asian route to access the Indo-Gangetic Plain. According to historian Romila Thapar,

> the passes in the northwest mountains . . . were less snow-bound than those of the higher Himalaya and therefore more frequently used. These included the Bolan, Gomal and Khyber passes. The fertile Swat Valley formed another route, as did the Hunza and Upper Indus Valley. . . . These passes

---

[2] "Northern India has always had a Central Asian character too. . . . The history of Tibet, parts of Xinjiang, Afghanistan, and the land north of the Amu Darya has been intertwined with that of the Indo-Gangetic plains . . ." Rajiv Sikri, "Connectivity with Central Asia: Economic and Strategic Aspects," in *Connectivity Issues in India's Neighborhood*, Asian Institute of Transport Development, 2008, p. 128.

were used so frequently that it is incorrect to project the north-western mountains as barriers. They were corridors of communication.[3]

To the north, the Himalayas and the Tibetan Plateau provide the most formidable barrier between South Asia (India) and China. The Himalayas are an almost impermeable barrier between the subcontinent and the Tibetan Plateau, and likewise, Tibet was a physical and cultural buffer between South Asia and mainland, Han China to the east[4] for centuries. This buffer kept direct trade or military contacts between South Asia and Han China to a minimum. One instance of land invasion was in 649 C.E., when a Chinese Buddhist monk organized a group of 7000 Nepali horsemen, Tibetan warriors, and Chinese soldiers and invaded the Gangetic plain.[5] But any land-based Sino-Indian contact that did permeate these barriers was not sustained over long periods; cultural diffusion (i.e. of Buddhism) took centuries and percolated through Tibet, and Silk Road trade either trickled over the Rakhine or came to India through the northwest, modern Kashmir and Central Asia. Another, more circuitous line of communication between Han China and the subcontinent was the Southeast Asian sea route, which was also used by both traders and Buddhist scholars.[6] Regardless, political and military contacts between the two were minimal.

To India's south, east, and west, the Indian Ocean has been a perennial strategic and economic buffer, opportunity, and vulnerability. For centuries, trade between western India and East Africa and the Arabian Peninsula and between southeastern India and Southeast Asia was conducted on a small scale via shipping lanes on the Arabian Sea and Bay of Bengal, respectively. But notwithstanding some military adventures of the Tamil Chola Dynasty into Southeast Asia, India's historical maritime pursuits—particularly of a military nature—had been relatively insignificant. With improved technologies, however, European companies used the same bodies of water to colonize the Indian subcontinent.

Since then, the Indian Ocean and peninsula have become hubs in maritime trade, at the center of: (i) *The Persian Gulf*, which hosts nearly 66 percent

---

[3]Romila Thapar, *Early India: From the Origins to AD 1300*. Berkeley, CA: University of California Press, 2004, p. 40.

[4]"Han" China refers to the geographic and cultural segment of the People's Republic of China east of the fertile 15-inch Isohyet that bisects the PRC. A majority of the PRC's population—and nearly all of the ethnic "Han"—reside east of this line, forming the Chinese "heartland." See, for example, Ray Huang, *China: A Macro History*. Armonk, NY: M. E. Sharpe, 1997, Chapter 3.

[5]John Keay, *China: A History*. London: Harper Press, 2008, cited in Nitin Pai, "Secure Under the New Himalayas," *Pragati: The Indian National Interest*, 6 January 2012.

[6]See, for example Prabodh Chandra Bagchi, *India and China: A Thousand Years of Cultural Relations*, Second Edition. Calcutta: China Press, 1950.

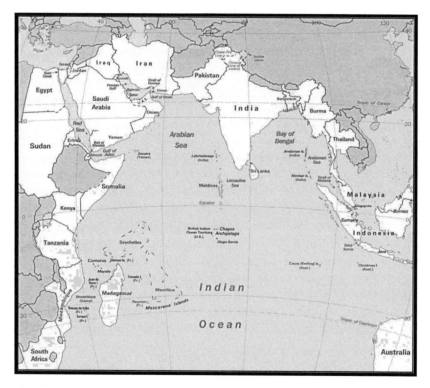

**FIGURE 2.2** *Indian Ocean region—US National Geospace Intelligence Agency, coordinate systems analysis branch.*

and 35 percent of the world's proven petroleum and natural gas reserves, respectively. About 40 percent of the world's petroleum products pass through the Strait of Hormuz, while 70 percent pass through the whole Indian Ocean[7]; (ii) The maritime gateway to the *Caucasus and Caspian Sea*, which are estimated to contain about "250 billion barrels of recoverable oil, boosted by more than 200 billion barrels of potential reserves. That's aside from up to 328 trillion cubic feet of recoverable natural gas"[8]; (iii) Land access to *Central Asia*, where Turkmenistan has proven oil reserves of between 546 million and 1.7 billion barrels and natural gas reserves of approximately 71 trillion cubic feet (Tcf); Uzbekistan contains 594 million barrels of proven oil reserves and natural gas reserves of 66.2 Tcf; while Kazakhstan has between

---

[7]Charles Esser, Persian Gulf Oil and Gas Exports Fact Sheet, Energy Information Administration, US Department of Energy, March 2002, available at http://www.eia.doe.gov/cabs/pgulf2.html, accessed 12 March 2009.
[8]John Daly, "Central Asia's Energy Chessboard," *World Politics Review*, 19 November 2009.

9 and 40 billion barrels of oil reserves and 65–100 Tcf of natural Gas;[9] (iv) the *Gulf of Aden and Suez Canal*, and thus the quickest water route to the Mediterranean Sea of Europe; (v) the *Strait of Malacca*, with its access to Southeast Asia and the South China Sea, and; (vii) the *Cape of Good Hope* at South Africa, with southern access to the Atlantic.

Despite this centrality, India's location at the center of the Indian Ocean has also been a source of autonomy. The only countries with the naval capacities to challenge India have been extra-regional: the British Empire and perhaps, after World War II, the United States, which assumed control of the Diego Garcia naval base in the central Indian Ocean.[10]

The partition of South Asia in 1947 had a profound effect on the geostrategic and economic reality of the Indo-Gangetic Plain. The original plan for the partition of the subcontinent was based solely on demographics—the existence of large Muslim populations—that resulted from historical, cultural, and political, rather than geographic factors. The new nation-states of the region were based only marginally on geographic structures.[11] The resultant regions were the northwestern mass of the subcontinent (modern Pakistan) as well as the Ganges River Basin (East Pakistan, today's Bangladesh). While the southern portion of India's border with Pakistan is bounded by the Thar Desert (which, in contrast to other deserts like the Sahara, is comprised of loose, shifting sand that is not easily traversable by vehicular traffic) and by swamps in Gujarat and southern Rajasthan,[12] the fertile northern Indian plain

---

[9]Langdon D. Clough, "Energy profile of Central Asia," in Cutler J. Cleveland (ed.), *Encyclopedia of Earth: 2008*, last revised 4 September 2008; available at http://www.eoearth.org/article/Energy_profile_of_Central_Asia

[10]In 1960 the atolls, previously part of Mauritius, were transferred to the United Kingdom, which engaged in a mass expulsion of the local population (mainly African and Indian laborers that had been brought by French colonists in the eighteenth century) in order to turn it into a Naval Base. In 1971, the base was turned over to joint US-UK management.

[11]Robert Kaplan, among others, argues that the modern nation-state of Pakistan is "the very geographical . . . embodiment of all the Muslim invasions that have swept down into India throughout its history," and carries the geographic legacy of the Mughal Empire, which he claims was based in the northwest of the subcontinent. (Robert Kaplan, "What's Wrong With Pakistan?," *Foreign Policy*, July/August 2012). Yet the Mughal capital was in Delhi, in modern day India, and its rule extended east to Bengal, and south to Hyderabad. Moreover, the population transfer of nearly 15 million people between India and West Pakistan in the wake of partition demonstrates that this geographic section was not so demographically neat; had it been so, the politics of partition, population exchange, and the creation of the western Radcliffe Line separating India and Pakistan would not have been so contentious.

[12]The Pakistani Army discovered the difficulty of traversing this territory during the battles of Charwa and Chawinda in 1965 and the Battle of Longewala in 1971, in which even Pakistan's technically superior tanks were at a loss due to the loose earth. John Pike, "Pakistan Army Order of Battle - Corps Sectors," Global Security, 20 May 2009, available at http://www.globalsecurity.org/military/world/pakistan/army-orbat-corps-aor.htm

is bisected by Pakistan at Punjab. Meanwhile, land access to Afghanistan, Iran and Central Asia, via the mountainous corridors of the northwest, has since fallen within Pakistani territory.

To the east, cutting into the Ganges River delta, an independent Bangladesh makes it such that access to the more mountainous states of northeast India is reliant on the Siliguri Corridor or "Chicken's Neck" in West Bengal, the narrow space between Bangladesh and Nepal that is just kilometers away from the international borders with Bhutan and China.

The Chinese invasion and occupation of Tibet in 1950, meanwhile, altered the situation in India's north, bringing the People's Republic of China (PRC) and its military, the People's Liberation Army (PLA) to India's doorstep: the Tibetan Plateau. While the Himalayan barrier has remained intact, there are a number of mountain passes over which interaction is possible.

These include the Tawang Pass in the northwest corner of Arunachal Pradesh, and Aksai Chin in eastern Kashmir, which was part of the *Princely State of Kashmir and Jammu,* constituted by the British Indian government in the early nineteenth century. From the 1950s, Aksai Chin has been administered by the government of the PRC, which sought to use Aksai Chin to connect its newly acquired territories of Tibet and Xinjiang via the China Highway 219 road link.

With partition, the "strategic unity" of the subcontinent was broken.[13] Since independence, these geopolitical factors, as well as its leaders' understanding of the subcontinent's history have shaped many of India's strategic aims.

# Indian Geopolitics

Geographic structures also have implications at more local levels—river systems, mountain ranges, natural trade and transport corridors, region-specific industries (and industry-specific regions) provide both opportunities for and threats to the integration of the country. The subcontinent's river systems include (a) The **Indus River System** of the northwest, the tributaries of which have their origins in Tibet and eastern Kashmir, wind through Kashmir into the Punjab, Sindh (in today's Pakistan), and then feed into the Arabian Sea; (b) The **Ganges River System** of north-central India, which starts at the central border between north India and Tibet, comes down through the Indo-Gangetic Plain, is fed by Nepal's major rivers (the Koshi, Gandaki, Karnali), and ultimately joins the Brahmaputra in Bangladesh, which empties into the Bay of Bengal;

---

[13]See, for example, George Friedman, "The Geopolitics of India: A Shifting, Self-Contained World," Stratfor, 16 December 2008, available at http://www.stratfor.com/analysis/20081215_geopolitics_india_shifting_self_contained_world

(c) The **Brahmaputra** of the northeast, 40 percent of which starts as the Yarlung-Tsampo in southern Tibet, winds south to Arunachal Pradesh, where it is expanded by glaciers and monsoon rainwater, extends into the valley of Assam, and joins the Ganges at Bangladesh and empties into the Bay of Bengal; (d) the **Narmada** in western-central India, which has its origins in Madhya Pradesh, flows eastward toward the Narmada Basin between the valley formed between the Satpura and Vindhya mountain ranges, across the tri-border region between Madhya Pradesh, Maharashtra, and Gujarat, and then empties from Gujarat into the Gulf of Khambat; (e) The **Godavari**, which starts in the Nashik region of northwestern Maharashtra, flows west across the Deccan Plateau and into Andhra Pradesh, from where it flows into the Bay of Bengal at Yanam; (f) The **Krishna River system**, with its source at Mahabaleshwar in Maharashtra, extends across Maharashtra, northern Karnataka, irrigates the relatively dry Deccan Plateau, and reaches the Bay of Bengal at Hamasaladeevi, which, combined with local rains, make the Delta extremely fertile. The Krishna and Godavari deltas give Andhra Pradesh its reputation as "India's Rice Bowl"; and finally (g) the **Kaveri River system**, which begins in southern Karnataka and makes its way to eastern Tamil Nadu.

The smaller, internal mountain ranges within the subcontinent include the Vindhya and Satpura ranges in western-central India; the Aravalli range in Rajasthan and Madhya Pradesh; the Ghats that straddle the eastern and western coasts of the peninsula; and the Deccan and Chota Nagpur plateaus in central and eastern India, respectively.

These geographic features have affected the sociopolitical development of the subcontinent over the centuries. The waters from the Indus and Ganges River Systems have made the northern Indian plain (modern Punjab to Bengal) one of the most fertile regions of the world, and accordingly one of the most populous. The Vindhya and Satpura mountain ranges, along with the Narmada River, are said to be the key divisions between the political-cultural entities of "north" and "south" India that have persisted over centuries. The Rakhine Mountains of Myanmar that taper into northeast India effectively bound much of that region—starting at southern Meghalaya and moving east to the Myanmar border—from West Bengal and even the Brahmaputra Valley in western Assam. The Thar Desert of Rajasthan, an arid, infertile region bounded in the east by the Aravalli mountain range, segregates Rajasthan from central India.

With these minor exceptions, South Asia has no barriers of the scale of the Himalayan Mountain ranges that would serve as major obstacles to *internal* communication, transport, or invasion. As a result, South Asian history has been colored by two seemingly opposing phenomena: (i) an array of diverse cultures defined by local geographic features, often centered on urban areas irrigated by river basins, and (ii) impermanent political divisions due to easily

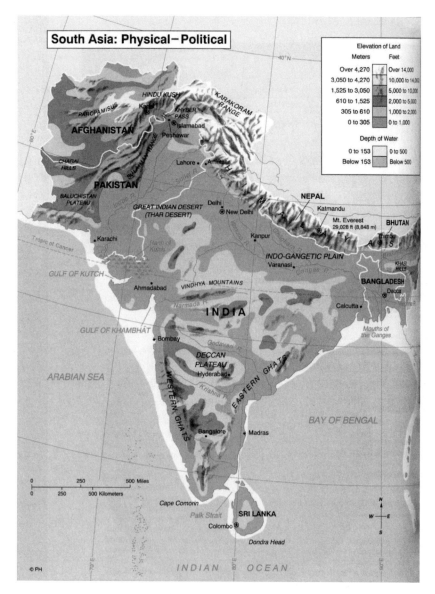

**FIGURE 2.3** *Topographic Map of South Asia—From Wikimedia commons.*

traversable geographic features that enabled both invasion and cultural diffusion: few political entities in South Asia have remained intact for more than a few centuries.

The internal geography of the subcontinent has given the region a highly decentralized political culture, such that Indian history has been colored with a number of local cultures—Punjabi, Gujarati, Tamil, Bengali, Assamese—that, over centuries, have been under the control of diverse and geographically dissimilar political configurations; no political boundary within the subcontinent has remained the same for more than a few centuries as different local kingdoms fought one another for control of land.[14] Even when under the control of a single empire, the Indian subcontinent retained its decentralized political culture: a raja or shah (king) would govern a locality, and be part of a federated empire controlled at the larger level by a Maharaja or Shahanshah (Great King or "King of Kings") in what was a system of layered, shared sovereignty over a large terrain.[15] For example,

> The Tughlaq dynasty ruled much of the subcontinent for most of the fourteenth century . . . [and] divided their domain into 25 provinces. When Tughlaq power disintegrated . . . many of the satraps of the provinces under Tughlaq suzerainty declared themselves sovereign rulers, and a host of regional sultanates . . . and independent kingdoms [came into being], such as. . . . Malwa, Gujarat, Bengal, Jaunpur. From the late sixteenth century the Mughals . . . reinstated a Delhi-based empire. . . . But they too organized their vast and heterogeneous domain into numerous provinces (*subahs*). Akbar, the great Mughal monarch . . . established 15 new provinces . . . from Kabul to Bengal and Kashmir to the Deccan. . . . The British conquest and colonization of India generated its own internal borders—the Bengal, Bombay, and Madras "presidencies" (huge administrative jurisdictions) evolved distinct identities and policies and even had separate armies until 1895. The patchwork of several hundred "princely states" of various sizes and populations that the British created through the nineteenth century, governed by vassal Indian rulers who acknowledged British "paramountcy" eventually covered nearly half of the subcontinent's land area.[16]

It was this very division that enabled foreigners to take political and military control over the subcontinent in the past. As Hindu kings fought among one another, Greek, Afghan, Turkic, and Mughal raiders were able to take advantage of the disunity to subdue the subcontinent. The Europeans (and British in particular) were also able to use "divide and conquer" tactics, playing Mughals and local Muslim rulers against Hindus, and Hindu kings

---

[14]See, for example, Stephen P. Rosen, *Societies and Military Power: India and Its Armies*. Ithaca, NY: *Cornell University Press*, 1996.

[15]Lloyd I. Rudolph and Susanne H. Rudolph, "Federalism as State Formation in India: A Theory of Negotiated and Shared Sovereignty." *International Political Science Review* 31, 5 (2010): 557.

[16]Sumantra Bose, *Transforming India: Challenges to the World's Largest Democracy*. Cambridge, MA: *Harvard University Press*, 2013, pp. 287–8.

against one another—ultimately placing the subcontinent under their control.[17] This understanding of subcontinental geography and history gave the first strategic planners of independent India two key strategic goals: (i) keeping the subcontinent internally united, and (ii) denying extra-regional powers access to the region.[18]

To accomplish the first aim, India had to go through a process of both nation and state building. A number of pan-Indian bureaucracies were left over by the British Raj, facilitating the transition. These included institutions such as the pan-Indian Indian administrative service (IAS), Indian military, and even railway system, which served to bind the country administratively. Democratic, federalized, linguistic-state based governance, meanwhile, ensured the local management of affairs, while cultural institutions such as a centralized media and common historical and nationalist narratives served to keep the country internally cohesive.

Prime Minister Nehru's socialist-influenced economy was an economic means of accomplishing both strategic aims.[19] A centralized economy would unify the country economically (and, he hoped, politically). Meanwhile, recognizing that Britain's control over India started with the British East India Company, and was thus economic as well as political, Nehru decided that a closed economy would disallow outsiders from controlling Indian assets and compromising Indian autonomy. The area denial strategy would be furthered by the development of a strong Navy, which had earlier enabled the British to deny other powers regional access. India also remembered that even with a small foothold in the region (the northwest in the case of the Mughals and Bengal for the British), outside powers have been able to take on the majority of the region.[20]

It would not have been quite as difficult to ensure against the development of such footholds in a completely united South Asia; given the natural boundaries of the subcontinent, a united, secure South Asia could pool its resources to

---

[17]For an early Indian nationalist rendering of Indian history see, for example Jawaharlal Nehru, *The Discovery of India.* Oxford: Oxford University Press, 1946; and K. M. Panikkar, *A Survey of Indian History.* Bombay: Asia Publishing House, 1966. For an analysis of the role of history in influencing Indian strategic thought, see George K. Tanham, "Indian Strategic Thought: An Interpretive Essay," RAND, 1992.

[18]Nehru, for example, argued, "the fact remains that we cannot tolerate any foreign invasion from any foreign country in any part of the Indian sub-continent." Quoted in Leo E. Rose, *Nepal: Strategy for Survival.* Berkeley, CA: University of California Press, 1996, p. 185.

[19]This is not to deny, of course, the influence of Nehru's personal inclinations toward Fabian Socialism on his economic and political decisions for India.

[20]K. M. Panikkar, *India and the Indian Ocean: an essay on the influence of sea power on Indian history*, London: George Allen&Unwin, 1946; James R. Holmes, Andrew C. Winner, and Toshi Yoshihara, *Indian Naval Strategy in the Twenty-first Century.* London: Routledge, 2009.

fortify its northwestern flank from invasion, while accessing Central Asia for trade or, if need be, for military excursions.[21] An internally secure South Asia could then devote more of its resources to develop a Navy to protect the region from maritime offenses.

But by the time of independence, hundreds of Princely States, which had been protectorates of the British, abounded throughout the subcontinent and were on the verge of regaining their political autonomy. While encouraged to choose between India and Pakistan, they were also allowed to remain independent. From India's perspective, this latter option would mean being able to provide those footholds to foreign powers once again. These regions included Junagadh in Gujarat, Hyderabad on the Deccan Plateau, Kashmir in the northwest, and Travancore in Kerala, among 565 such Princely States throughout South Asia.

As home minister and deputy prime minister, Sardar Vallabhai Patel launched a diplomatic charm offensive across India to convince the local rulers of the Princely States to join the Indian Union to ensure against internal discord. In hundreds of cases, Sardar Patel was able to convince the local royalty to accede their territory to the Indian union in exchange for keeping their personal wealth, which might otherwise have been nationalized.[22]

But where diplomacy failed, democracy was tried: in Muslim-ruled, Hindu-majority Junagadh, a plebiscite was held resulting in the accession of the region into India.[23] (Pakistanis later argued that this democratic logic ought to have applied to Hindu-ruled, Muslim-majority Jammu and Kashmir as well). And where democracy did not work, force was brought in: the Muslim Nizam of the Hindu-majority State of Hyderabad in the center of the subcontinent sought to remain independent, but New Delhi sent in armed forces to forcibly annex the territory.[24]

Despite these efforts, by 1948 the subcontinent was partitioned into more than eight administratively and geographically distinct entities: India, (West) Pakistan; East Pakistan (later Bangladesh); Nepal; Sri Lanka; Bhutan; the Princely State of Kashmir; and Sikkim, which later acceded to India in 1975.[25] These were autonomous of New Delhi—and thus able to provide footholds

---

[21]The Central Asian plains have historically been relatively barren, so their limited economic utility made military occupation undesirable for most Indian empires.

[22]Ramachandra Guha, *India After Gandhi: The History of the World's Largest Democracy*. New York: Harper Collins, 2007, Chapter 3.

[23]Larry Collins and Dominique LaPierre, *Freedom at Midnight*. New York: Simon and Shuster, 1976.

[24]V. P. Menon, *The Story of the Integration of the Indian States*. New York: Macmillan, 1956.

[25]The internal division of the Republic of India into linguistic and cultural states (provinces), of course, compounded this fear.

for outsiders or even to challenge New Delhi directly—and made it such that India could not rely on geography alone for its territorial defense. So India's objective of "unity" required a wider purview.

What has been variously called a "Pax India"[26] and "India's Monroe Doctrine"[27]—and even the "Indira Doctrine" and the "Rajiv Doctrine," after the two Indian prime ministers who were said to have enforced it most pronouncedly—had a single goal in mind: to *keep the subcontinent internally united by denying the autonomous tendencies of India's smaller South Asian neighbors, particularly if they involved granting extra-regional powers a presence in South Asia.*[28]

## The Realities of Geopolitics

Attaining these goals, however, quickly proved difficult; despite India's intentions of insulating the subcontinent from the broader world, the Cold War between the United States and Soviet Union quickly took root in South Asia, while the internal dynamics of the subcontinent—in which local groups, rulers, and cultures sought their own autonomy—would rear their head within the new Indian Republic.

Understanding India's political leadership of much of the third world and its geostrategic position in the center of the Indian Ocean—even fearing that India could threaten American trade in the Indian Ocean—the United States sought India's assistance in the coming Cold War. Even before independence, Nehru had earned a reputation as a major statesman of the global anti-colonial movement with the Indian National Congress (INC). This was solidified with the March 1947 Asian Relations Conference in New Delhi, and again at the 1955 Asian-African Conference in Bandung, Indonesia. In this role, the Americans thought, India could influence the decisions of the newly independent colonies of the "Third World" to join either the American or the Soviet bloc.

But Nehru was extremely skeptical both of the United States, thinking of it as a postwar Great Britain (replete with global navy) that would recolonize

---

[26]George Tanham, Indian Strategic Culture. *The Washington Quarterly*, 15, 1 (Winter 1992): 129–42.

[27]Sunanda Datta-Ray, "India's Monroe Doctrine," *The Sunday Statesman*, 2 August 1987; Devin T. Haggerty, "India's Regional Security Doctrine." *Asian Survey*, 31, 4 (April 1991): 351–63; James R. Holmes and Toshi Yoshihara, "Strongman, Constable or Free-Rider? India's 'Monroe Doctrine' and Indian Naval Strategy." *Comparative Strategy*, 28, 4 (September 2009): 332–48; Bhabani Sen Gupta, "The Indian Doctrine," *India Today*, 31 August 1983, p. 20.

[28]In fact, many Indian nationalist leaders assumed that the Pakistan project would fail and the country would rejoin India within a matter of years.

India, and of the unbridled free-market Capitalism that America was offering, seeing it as unjust domestically and imperialistic abroad. With that in mind, Nehru kept his distance from the United States, and instead formed the socialism-inclined "non-aligned" movement (NAM).

The NAM—which Nehru initiated with Ghana's Kwame Nkrumah, Indonesia's Sukarno, Yugoslavia's Josip Broz Tito, and Egypt's Gamal Abdul Nasser—sought to place third-world solidarity, decolonization, and anti-imperialism at the center of India's foreign policy. Yet, as K. Subrahmanyam, the chief postindependence Indian strategist, put it, nonalignment was always meant to be the practice of realpolitik cloaked in idealism. Applied to the subcontinent, nonalignment reinforced India's "Monroe Doctrine": external (particularly western) powers would have no role in the affairs of South Asia, which would be India's domain. And accordingly, the first decade of Indian independence saw New Delhi keeping equal distance from Washington and Moscow, accepting food and development aid from, and maintaining cordial political relations with both.

Yet the first few years of India's independence saw uncertainty in the application of this doctrine, even within India. Notably, there was large-scale opposition to and agitation against some key aspects of Nehru's vision of independent India. Across swaths of West Bengal, Assam, Indian Punjab, Delhi, and Bombay, refugees from the lands that became Pakistan had to be reintegrated into the new India. Large refugee camps housing millions of migrants were set up, with little certainty about what their fate might be.

Right-wing Hindu fundamentalists sought to establish a "Hindu Rashtra" or nation, in which the rights of non-Hindu minorities, notably Muslims, would be curtailed. Inspired by the success of Mao Tsetung in China in 1949, left-wing Communists hoped to bring about a proletariat revolution that would spread throughout the country. In addition to the tumult of the refugee-filled lands, border regions in India's northeast, northwest, and far south—including many tribal areas and kingdoms that had remained within the British Raj only uneasily—were uncomfortable with their presence under New Delhi's rule.

Even within those provinces of India that had histories of territorial incorporation within a broader Indian state, their internal composition and autonomy within the new Indian Union came into question. Religious minorities, linguistic groups, economic and social minorities (such as *dalits*, formerly regarded as "untouchables", and *adivasis* or tribals), and others all sought occupational quotas within the emerging governing systems—the Constituent Assemblies and Parliaments—and even independent states within the Indian territorial union and without. Even the question of which language Indians would speak with one another was up for debate, with some proposing highly Sanskritized Hindi, in a nod to the Hindu origins of much of the country's population, others proposing Hindustani, the mix of Sanskritized Hindi and Persianized Urdu spoken by a majority of north Indians irrespective of religion, and even English, so that South Indians who had no connection to Hindi or Hindustani would not be excluded. T. T. Krishnamachari of Madras encapsulated the sentiments of many of the minorities within India's nation-building process: "this kind of intolerance makes us fear that the strong center which we need, a strong center which is necessary, will also mean the enslavement of people who do not speak the language," literal and proverbial, "of the center."[29]

Many of these tensions were peacefully settled in the Constituent Assembly, the street (via peaceful protest), the courtroom, or by the 1950 constitution, which articulated the development of a federalized country that would leave some autonomy with individual states. This proved insufficient in 1953, when New Delhi was compelled by popular pressure to create a state for speakers of the Telugu language: Andhra Pradesh. The victory of the Telugu movement inspired others—including the Sikh speakers of Punjabi and speakers of Gujarati—to agitate for language-based statehood, resulting in the States Reorganization Commission that restructured India into provinces determined more by language.[30]

Yet many of these tensions would not be resolved so easily. The Naga Hills, then located in the state of Assam and adjacent to India's border with Burma, East Pakistan, and China, vehemently opposed New Delhi's control. The Naga population straddled the Rakhine Mountains, with nearly half residing in Burma. In the wake of independence, the Naga National Council (NNC) sought to retain the autonomy they had enjoyed under the British, and many factions even sought an independent nation of their own. Even Nehru was skeptical of the ability of even the pluralist, diverse Indian Republic to fully absorb and integrate a culture as different from the Indian mainstream as that of the Naga tribals. By the middle of the 1950s, these political contests turned into a large-scale guerrilla war by the NNC and counter-insurgency by the Indian Army, with ordinary Naga citizens caught in the middle of what were perceived to be overhanded tactics by both sides.[31] A ceasefire was signed in 1963, granting autonomy to a new province—within the Indian Union—of Nagaland. Similar conflicts would break out, far from the eye of

---

[29]Frank Anthony, *Constituent Assembly Debates: Official Report*. New Delhi: Lok Sabha Secretariat, 1988.
[30]Maya Chadda, *Ethnicity, Security, and Separatism in India*. New York: Columbia University Press, 1997, pp. 71–6.
[31]Charles Chasie and Sanjoy Hazarika, "The State Strikes Back: India and the Naga Insurgency," East-West Center, Policy Studies, No. 52, 2009.

the Indian mainstream, in other parts of the northeast: Manipur, Tripura, and southern Bihar.

Further south, the INC party received electoral challenges from Tamil Nadu's Dravida Munnetra Kazhagam (DMK) party, and perhaps more formidably, from Kerala's Communist Party of India (CPI). The CPI was a member of the Communist International, a vehicle for the Soviet government in Moscow, so the sweeping of the Kerala Legislative Assembly by the CPI, under the leadership of E. M. S. Namboodiripad, was a surprise and setback for Nehru's INC at the center. Moreover, the CPI's leadership enacted educational and economic reforms that Kerala's Nair community and powerful Christian establishment, which had traditionally supported Congress, deemed threatening. The situation degenerated into strikes and protests from activists of all parties, and attacks on civilians by the CPI-led police. The unrest compelled—largely for political reasons emanating from New Delhi's Monroe Doctrine—Prime Minister Nehru to invoke President's Rule in 1959, topple the elected government, and install a New Delhi- (and Congress Party-) appointed Governor to administer the state.[32]

To India's north, the mountainous, landlocked Nepal, Bhutan, and then independent Sikkim, remained dependent on New Delhi by virtue of economic needs and geography, while the government of Sri Lanka was comfortable under India's security umbrella in the immediate years after independence.[33] Pakistan, the other independent nation in South Asia, however, rejected India's twin strategic goals first by simply being autonomous: its very existence was the result of an effort by the Muslim League to gain political independence for a large section of the subcontinent.

Yet this unpleasant political dynamic became even more contaminated, and bilateral relations turned decidedly hostile. Soon after partition, Pashtun rebels based in Pakistan invaded the independent Princely State of Kashmir, a Muslim-majority region ruled by the Hindu king Hari Singh, in an effort to inspire a popular uprising. Hari Singh called upon New Delhi to intervene against Pakistan, in exchange for Kashmiri accession to India.[34] What ensued was the first Indo-Pakistan War in 1948, after which Pakistan ruled the area of Kashmir west and north of the Line of Control (Azad Kashmir and Gilgit-Baltistan) and

---

[32]Ramachandra Guha, *India After Gandhi: The History of the World's Largest Democracy*. New York: Harper Collins, 2007, pp. 275–80.

[33]Rohan Gunaratna, "Sri Lanka, A Lost Revolution? The Inside Story of the JVP," Institute of Fundamental Studies, 1990.

[34]The history of the first Indo-Pakistan war and its origins remains shrouded in politics, with Indian accounts generally maintaining that the Pashtun rebels were in fact agents of the Pakistani military, while Pakistani accounts argue that the Pashtuns were autonomous agents that were simply responding to the calls of local Kashmiris seeking freedom from Indian influence.

India administered the remaining areas (Jammu, the Kashmir Valley, and Ladakh, while maintaining *de jure* control over Aksai Chin).

To the north, a border war with China in 1962 forced a militarily unprepared India to seek defense equipment from abroad, breaking India's insistence on (defense) industrial self-reliance. China, meanwhile, developed a close political-military relationship with Pakistan, a further blow to India's regional objectives. China's presence in South Asia also broadened India's own strategic purview, and raised the bar on Indian defense investment.

More conflict between India and Pakistan followed. In April 1965, emboldened by the Indian defeat at China's hand, Pakistani leaders sought to take control over another disputed territory: the Rann of Kacch, a large patch of desert marshes between Indian Gujarat and Pakistani Sindh that was rich with natural gas. The incident involved over 1,347 border and ceasefire violations by Pakistan that were ultimately resolved by the British High Commissioner in Delhi. Pakistan's relative successes in that incident, however, further encouraged Gen. Ayub Khan, the military president of Pakistan, to undertake Operation Gibraltar, another effort to infiltrate 30,000 Pakistani troops, disguised as locals, into Indian-administered Kashmir to foment an insurgency against Indian control. The incident escalated into a large-scale war between the Indian and Pakistani militaries, with three to four thousand casualties on both sides.[35] Although there was no change in the borders, the conflict was largely seen as an Indian victory.

In 1971, political tensions between Islamabad and Bengali East Pakistan erupted into violence. Rawalpindi, West Pakistan's military headquarters, launched a massive crackdown on East Pakistan, sending millions of refugees pouring into India's northeastern states and West Bengal. New Delhi responded first by providing training and military support to the Mukti Bahini, the Bengali rebels, and later by intervening militarily in the civil war. The war resulted in an Indian military victory and the detachment of East Pakistan from the West, thereby creating the new nation of Bangladesh.

The 1971 war with Pakistan was the decisive factor in India's relationship with the Cold War world. Toward the end of that conflict, the United States sent its battleship, the USS *Enterprise*, to the Bay of Bengal in a vain attempt to ward off an Indian onslaught of East Pakistan. Seeing this (potentially nuclear) American-Pakistani-Chinese threat, and seeking an ally that, because of geographic distance and the lack of a blue water navy, would not be able to put satellite status on it, India established the 1971 Indo-Soviet Treaty of Peace, Friendship and Cooperation, effectively putting India into the Soviet

---

[35]B. C. Chakravorty, *History of the Indo-Pak War: 1965*, History Division, Ministry of Defence, Government of India, 1992.

camp. By 1974, India tested its own "peaceful nuclear device" in response to both the 1964 Chinese nuclear test as well as the American entry into the Bay of Bengal.

In 1975, Indira Gandhi extended her strategic doctrine domestically. On the heels of the war with Pakistan, the 1973 Arab oil embargo, and most notably, allegations of corruption within the Indira Gandhi government over electoral fraud, Gandhi declared a state of emergency in India. The 21-month period of Emergency Rule that lasted from June 1975 to March 1977 granted Gandhi the power to rule by decree, suspend elections, restrict the media, curtail civil and political liberties, ban and jail political opposition, and even enact a draconian forced sterilization program to try to curtail population growth. The Emergency was independent India's longest foray away from democratic governance. The Janata Party coalition that took over when elections were held in 1977, however, foundered when ideological and political divisions brought the coalition apart in 1980.[36]

Further afield, a number of events in the Middle East (West Asia) in 1979 ultimately had a profound effect on the subcontinent: the US-brokered peace between Egypt and Israel essentially brought Egypt into the western camp against the Soviets; the Iranian Islamic Revolution, in which a Shi'ite Islamist government toppled a US-backed regime; and the November seizure by Islamist militants of the Grand Mosque in Mecca, as a result of which the Saudi government began to emphasize its Islamist credentials elsewhere in the world. Fearing a loss of its influence in the Muslim world and an Iranian-style Islamic revolution in Afghanistan that would spread to its own Muslim republics in Central Asia, the Soviet Union invaded Afghanistan in December 1979, bringing the Soviet Union to Pakistan's immediate north.

In response, the United States increased its own presence in South Asia; along with Saudi Arabia, the United States began funding a Pakistan-managed Afghan Mujahideen insurgency to fight the Soviet Union in Afghanistan. Through the 1980s, billions of dollars of US military aid were sent to Pakistan (including a number of F-16 fighters that had little value in an insurgency campaign but which served to increase Pakistan's conventional security vis-à-vis India), Pakistan's then nascent nuclear weapons program continued without any meaningful American opposition (and with Chinese assistance), and a massive guerrilla training infrastructure was established along the Pakistan-Afghanistan-Kashmir border. This guerrilla-training infrastructure would also be used to mount sub-conventional operations against India.

---

[36] Paul R. Brass, *The Politics of India Since Independence*. Cambridge, MA: Cambridge University Press, 1994, pp. 40–50. G. G. Mirchandani, *320 Million Judges*. New Delhi: Abhinav Publications, 2003, pp. 98–126.

Indeed, as a result, one of India's most tender political sensitivities was reignited. India's border region of Punjab, adjacent to Pakistan, hosted most of India's Sikh population, which had earlier agitated for its own independent nation of "Sikhistan" and later for its own state of Punjab—in contrast with Hindu-majority but Punjabi-speaking Haryana, which was broken off of greater Indian Punjab in 1966. But by the end of the 1970s, Sikhs in Punjab had begun a larger scale insurrection against what was perceived as New Delhi's mismanagement—including the dissolution, by the center, of the Punjab legislature in October 1983.[37] The uprising became a massive insurgency, replete with terrorist acts, that Prime Minister Indira Gandhi tried to quell by invading the Golden Temple in 1984, the Sikh holy site that many of the insurgents had occupied. The insurgents responded in kind. Sikh Khalistani rebels received training by Pakistan's Inter-Services Intelligence (ISI) agency in some of the same guerrilla infrastructure that had been set up in Pakistan's northwest. Soon after, Prime Minister Gandhi was assassinated by her two Sikh bodyguards.

India's reaction to these regional tidings was a doubling down of its Monroe Doctrine. In 1986, India's Research and Analysis Wing (R&AW) opened the CIT-X and CIT-J desks to carry out terrorist attacks in Karachi and support anti-Islamabad insurgents in Baluchistan.[38] The Indian Army launched the largest post–World War II military mobilization in the world, Operation Brasstacks, which involved the amassing of over 400,000 troops along the Rajasthan-Sindh border over 5 months in 1986–87. Both of these demonstrations of force were attempts to deter Pakistan from its support for Indian domestic insurgencies.[39] In Operations Chequerboard and Falcon of 1986, India amassed a number of troops along the northeastern border with China, while it deployed its army in a number of internal conflicts within India, particularly Nagaland, Assam, Punjab, and later Kashmir.

The 1980s saw a massive increase in India's military expenditures, supplied largely by the Soviet Union and financed by deficit spending.

In 1987, approximately 20 per cent of all the arms exported to Third World countries were sold to India. . . . From 1982–87, Indian defense expenditures rose by 50 percent. The 1987/88 defense budget alone increased by

---

[37]Harnik Deol, *Religion and Nationalism in India: The Case of the Punjab*. New York: Taylor and Francis, 2000, p. 106.

[38]B. Raman, *The Kaoboys of R&AW: Down Memory Lane*. New Delhi: Lancer Publishers, 2008.

[39]"It seems fairly evident that Operation Brasstacks must have at least in part been intended to signal India's willingness to initiate a conventional response to [Pakistan's support for] the sub-conventional war in Punjab." Praveen Swami, *India, Pakistan, and the Secret Jihad*. London: Routledge, 2007.

23 percent from the previous year, which had in turn increased by an unplanned 16 percent. From 3 percent of GNP over the 1960s and 70s, defense expenditures moved closer to 5.5 percent during the late 1980s.[40]

Prime Minister Rajiv Gandhi sought a major overhaul of the Indian military, purchasing MiG-29s, T-90s, and submarines, even leasing a Charlie class nuclear submarine from the Soviet Union. New Delhi also purchased the Mirage 2000 fighter from France, diesel submarines from Germany, and howitzers from Sweden.[41] This hardware was deployed in a number of regional military operations, including Operation Meghdoot of 1984, in which the Indian Army captured the Siachen Glacier along the line-of-control with Pakistan; and the 1987 intervention of an Indian Peace-Keeping Force in Sri Lanka, in large part to supplant the influence of American, Pakistani, and Israeli mediators in that country's civil war.

Throughout South Asia, where New Delhi sought to impose its supremacy, India was vehemently resisted. The people and governments of the subcontinent's smaller nations—Nepal, Bangladesh, and Sri Lanka in particular—opposed New Delhi's efforts to collaborate, economically integrate or "strategically bandwagon" with the regional capitals. Pakistan, meanwhile, would go one step further by maintaining actively hostile relations against India, going so far as to break the second pillar of India's Monroe Doctrine by inviting countries like China and the United States to sustain a presence in the region. The "strategic unity" that India sought to impose on the post-independence subcontinent would be lost.

---

[40]Chris Smith, *India's ad hoc Arsenal: Direction of Drift in Defense Policy?* New York: SIPRI and Oxford University Press, 1996.

[41]"A corruption scandal centered on the Swedish guns from the Bofors Company contributed to Rajiv Gandhi's defeat in the 1989 general elections." Stephen P. Cohen and Sunil Dasgupta, *Arming without Aiming: India's Military Modernization*. Washington, D.C.: Brookings Institution Press, 2010, p. 11.

# 3

# Big Brother, Little Brother: India's Small Neighbors

## Nepal

Geography and politics condition Nepal's existence as an independent state. Nepal is a composite of three key geographic factors that affect its cultural, political, and economic life: (i) the Himalayan Mountains (or Parbat) that lie adjacent to Tibet in the north, which have long been more of a barrier than a means of communication, and which are culturally influenced by Tibet; (ii) the Terai or Madhesh, the marshy upper edge of the Indo-Gangetic Plain, which covers much of Nepal's south; and (iii) the hill region, or pahar, which lies between the former two and is the valley that hosts the urban centers, the country's agricultural base, and the majority of the country's population.

In the north, there are about 18 passes between Nepal and Tibet, the most prominent being Kerong and Kuti, which is about 14,000 feet high, while the others are higher and remain snowbound for much of the year.[1] Meanwhile, Nepal's four key rivers (part of the Ganges River System) flow from the glaciers of the north into the southern plains and onward into India, irrigating much of the southern plain, only 20 percent of which are cultivable, but whose agriculture provides nearly 40 percent of Nepal's GDP and 80 percent of its employment.[2]

Until the early twentieth century, Nepal was able to retain contact with—and even military control over trade routes to and land in—Tibet through the

---

[1]Leo E. Rose, *Nepal: Strategy for Survival*. Berkeley, CA: University of California Press, 1971, p. 242.
[2]Andrea Matles Savada, "Nepal: A Country Study: Agriculture," Government Printing Office, United States Library of Congress, 1991, available at http://countrystudies.us/nepal/These numbers remain steady as per the CIA World Factbook of 2010, available at https://www.cia.gov/library/publications/the-world-factbook/geos/np.html

mountain passes of what is now Sikkim, over which it had political influence. (Since the late 1700s, when it came under the influence of both China and the British Raj, however, Sikkim has been politically autonomous from, but culturally integrated with the Kathmandu Valley). Largely because British Imperial troops were unable to subdue Nepali guerrillas in the nineteenth century, Nepal remained politically independent of British India. Accordingly, the British were compelled to keep Nepal as a buffer zone between India and Tibet, a strategic practice that India retained after independence. Regardless, its land-locked geography makes Nepal economically reliant on the Indo-Gangetic plain, which also connects to Kolkata, the closest seaport, for international trade. This bifurcated geography gives Nepal two seemingly paradoxical goals: (1) integrate with India and the Indo-Gangetic Plain in order to remain economically viable, (2) retain a sufficient level of political autonomy from India to resist dominance.

In the wake of the 1950 Communist Chinese seizure of Tibet, and fearing an extension of communist influence to (and even occupation of) Nepal, the governments of India and Nepal signed the 1950 Agreement of Peace and Friendship, which aimed to secure the geographically induced status quo. India would continue to facilitate Nepal's economic viability, through a largely open and porous border over which Nepalis and Indians could migrate and trade, free of visas or tariffs. International trade (with third nations) would also have to go through India, largely for geographic reasons. Moreover, the treaty ensured that New Delhi retained influence over Nepal's foreign and defense policies: Kathmandu could not take international actions or defense-oriented policies without consulting Delhi, and each would have to inform the other about actions taken regarding regional security.[3]

The 1954 Kosi Agreement and the 1959 Gandak Agreement established mechanisms for water management between Nepal and India. All four major rivers of Nepal (the Mahakali, Karnali, Gandaki, and Kosi) and five minor tributaries (Babai, West Rapti, Bagmati, Kamala, and Kankai) flow from northern Nepal into India. These rivers provide 47 percent of the overall river flow in the Ganges basin, and 71 percent of its glacial flow, with the rest coming from groundwater aquifers.[4] Both water agreements essentially gave the lower riparian (India) the majority of the benefits: while

---

[3]"Treaty of Peace and Friendship between the Government of India and the Government of Nepal," Signed at Kathmandu on 31 July 1950, full text available at http://untreaty.un.org/unts/1_60000/3/9/00004432.pdf

[4]Ajaya Dixit, Pradeep Adhikari, and Rakshya Rajyashwori Thapa, "Nepal: Ground Realities for Himalayan Water Management," in *Disputes Over the Ganga: A Look at Potential Water Related Conflicts in South Asia.* Kathmandu: Panos Institute South Asia, 2004, pp. 159–92.

India would finance the construction of a border barrage to manage floods, only the 29,000 acres of land in Nepal that was *used* for the barrage itself would benefit (even though it had the capacity to irrigate 1.5 million acres of Nepali land), while India would retain control over the remainder.[5] Although some of the more contentious provisions were altered in the 1960s, Nepali grievances remained over the simple fact that India would still control the Nepali land over which waters flowed in order to benefit its downriver states (namely India's Bihar), while Nepal would receive few of the irrigation benefits. However, many of the planned Indian-funded projects ultimately never even came to fruition.[6]

But regional events of the 1970s led to a rise of Nepali insecurity and the beginning of a sea change in Indo-Nepali relations. The secession of Bangladesh, abetted by India, in the 1971 war with Pakistan; the Indian nuclear test of 1974; a pro-Chinese Naxalite insurgency in West Bengal, just adjacent to the Nepali border; as well as the absorption of Sikkim as an Indian state in 1975, raised Nepali fears of being subsumed by India.

The absorption of Sikkim had a particularly pronounced effect on Nepali threat perceptions. The tiny Himalayan kingdom's geostrategic importance was ensured by the Nathu La pass that served as a primary geographic link between South Asia and the Tibetan plateau, which had historically enabled Nepali traders and invaders to occupy and retain political control over a great deal of southern Tibet. In fact, it was this potential that compelled India to seek Sikkim's integration into the Indian Union: as popular protests against the Sikkimese monarchy unfurled, New Delhi feared that China could use the instability to claim Sikkim as a part of southern Tibet and annex it. Delhi preemptively sent in Reserve Police to quell the situation, and held a referendum that abolished the Sikkimese monarchy and turned the territory into an Indian state.

Yet for centuries, the Kingdom of Sikkim had been under Kathmandu's influence, and had been politically integrated into the Nepali Kingdom. When ethnic Nepali-majority Sikkim was assimilated into India in 1975, Kathmandu felt it was a bad omen. In response, Nepali King Birendra Bikram Shah Dev proposed a reorganization of its own Treaty of Peace and Friendship with India, and that Nepal be recognized as a "Zone of Peace," in which Indian

[5]Medha Bisht, "Revisiting the Kosi Agreement: Lessons for Indo-Nepal Water Diplomacy," *IDSA Comment*, 22 September 2008, available at http://www.idsa.in/idsastrategiccomments/RevisitingtheKosiAgreement_Medha%20Bisht_220908
[6]Dwarika N. Dhungel, "Historical Eye View," in Dwarika N. Dhungel and Santa B. Pun (eds), *The Nepal-India Water Relationship: Challenges*. Springer Science + Business Media B.V., United Kingdom, 2009.

influence in Nepal would lessen, and China would be kept as a possible counterweight.[7]

The proposal received support from a number of countries in the nonaligned movement. But India's response was lukewarm: "if the king's proposal did not contradict the 1950 treaty and was merely an extension of nonalignment, it was unnecessary; if it was a repudiation of the special relationship, it represented a possible threat to India's security and could not be endorsed."[8]

Tension increased over the next decade, during which India and Nepal had a few spats over trade and transit. But push came to shove in 1988, when the Nepali government sought a nominal agreement with the Chinese government over the acquisition of Chinese weaponry through the Kathmandu-Kodari road to Tibet, which China had begun constructing in the 1960s. India saw the arms purchase (about which Kathmandu did not inform New Delhi) as Kathmandu's attempt to forge a military relationship with Beijing in violation of the 1950 Treaty. In response, India enacted an economic blockade on Nepal, closing all but two of the 17 transit routes between the countries.[9] The worsening economic condition put domestic pressure on the Nepali monarchy, which was forced to back down in its dealings with China and implement a parliamentary democracy.

The new democratic government (still presided over by a monarchy) maintained cordial relations with India during the first part of the 1990s. Despite the induction of a Nepali Congress-led democracy, a political crisis among the largely left-leaning members of the coalition broke out. By 1996, a Maoist guerrilla insurgency was launched by the Communist Party of Nepal (Maoist) or CPN (M) cadres, which targeted government institutions in western Nepal, later spreading throughout many of the rural parts of the country. In June 2001, Prince Dipendra, the heir to the Nepali thrown, murdered the Nepali Royal family before killing himself, in a monarchic crisis that further threatened the legitimacy of the monarchy itself. King Gyanendra took the throne in the wake of the killings, and constituted the Armed Police Force (APF) to suppress the Maoist insurgency. But when the APF failed to quell the instability, the Royal Nepal Army was also inducted to the fighting, raising the scale of violence and bringing about greater popular resistance to the India-backed monarchy.

---

[7] J. P. Anand, "Nepal's Zone of Peace Concept and China." *China Report*, 13, 1 (1977): 6–10; Uma Kant Sharma, "The Peace Zone Concept and its Utility in Nepalese Foreign Policy." *Journal of Political Science*, 7, 1 (2004): 44–50.

[8] James Heitzman and Robert L. Worden (eds), *India: A Country Study*. Washington, D.C.: Government Printing Office for the Library of Congress, 1995.

[9] John Garver, "China-India Rivalry in Nepal: The Clash over Chinese Arms Sales." *Asian Survey*, 31, 10 (October 1991): 956–75.

By 2006, the CPN (M) had gained military and political control of much of Nepal, and a democratic revolution toppled the monarchy, bringing a Maoist political coalition to power. The rise of the Maoists in Nepal irked Delhi in two ways: through their guerrilla campaign, the Nepali Maoists maintained close tactical links with their Indian counterparts, the Naxalites and other Left-wing Extremists, in Indian West Bengal, Chattisgarh, and through the northeast.[10] And as part of their aim of retaining autonomy from India, the Maoists remained politically close to Beijing.[11] As of the early 2010s, however, a political crisis has handicapped the Maoists' ability to govern; having only a plurality of the popular vote, rather than a full majority, the Maoists have been unable to enact their agenda, rewrite a new constitution, or even keep a prime minister for extended periods. Maoist parties have fragmented further into opposing groups, while their armed guerrilla wings have slowly been incorporated into the Nepali military.

Meanwhile, since 2000, Indian agencies have alleged that the Terai region of southern Nepal has been used as a launching pad for Pakistani ISI Agency attacks on India. A "secret report" revealed in June 2000 that the ISI was using the open border of the Terai to infiltrate counterfeit Indian rupees into the north Indian economy; to organize Nepali politicians and citizens to help Pakistani organized crime syndicates (such as Dawood Ibrahim's "D Company") smuggle persons and materiel across the Indian border; and to "radicalize," through networks of Lashkar-e-Taiba (LeT) and Harakat-ul-Jihad-ul-Islami (HuJI) madrassas, the Muslims living in southern Nepal in order to infiltrate and assist terrorist attacks within India.[12]

At the same time, India's fear of China has also become more prominent in Nepal. Although the Himalayan Mountains were once a fairly decisive boundary between Nepal and China, economic growth in Tibet and Chinese concerns about the political activities of the Tibetan diaspora in Nepal have brought Beijing closer to Kathmandu. Although the Himalayas preclude any major Chinese military force from being deployed in Nepal, good roads could "prevent India from using its ultimate sanction of economic blockade

---

[10]Yubaraj Ghimire, "Nepal Maoists say they will back Indian Maoists," Indian Express, 27 June 2010; Krishna Hachhethu, "Maoist Insurgency in Nepal: An Overview," in P. V. Ramana (ed.), The Naxal Challenge: Causes, Linkages, and Policy Options. New Delhi: Pearson-Longman, 2008, pp. 136–62.

[11]Nihar Nayak, "Nepal: New 'Strategic Partner' of China?," IDSA Comment, 30 March 2009, available at http://www.idsa.in/idsastrategiccomments/NepalNewStrategicPartnerofChina_NNayak_300309; Abanti Bhattacharya, "China and Maoist Nepal: Challenges for India," IDSA Comment, 23 May 2008, available at http://www.idsa.in/idsastrategiccomments/ChinaandMaoistNepal_ ABhattacharya_230508

[12]The 78-page Indian intelligence report, titled "Pakistan's Anti-India Activities in Nepal," was revealed in Harinder Baweja, "The Kathmandu Nexus," India Today, 12 June 2000.

on Kathmandu." If China were able to supply the essential goods that Nepal receives from India—particularly petrol, diesel, and kerosene—New Delhi's unilateral leverage over Kathmandu would be limited.[13]

Indo-Nepali relations are stuck in a cycle of distrust: As India sees it, Nepal is a mere buffer state, either cowering in fear of Indian might, or ungratefully biting the hand that feeds it by enabling China or Pakistan access to its land to undertake "anti-India activities."[14] Yet according to Nepali views, India is a domineering "big brother" that uses its geographic influence over Kathmandu to restrain Nepali development and maintain New Delhi's exclusive hegemonic control.[15] Any Nepali efforts to seek alternatives to Indian hegemony, including political ties with Beijing, are fiercely resisted by New Delhi, which maintains control over Nepal's closest maritime port, Kolkata.

## Sri Lanka

Sri Lanka, as an island at the southern ridge of the Indian Ocean littoral zone, retains a geographic independence that allows Colombo to pursue a mixed policy vis-à-vis India, using New Delhi's assistance when needed, and remaining autonomous otherwise. From the time of independence, Colombo joined India in its nonaligned movement, and the two countries had the shared aim of securing the Indian Ocean in the wake of the British Empire's naval retreat.

For decades, Colombo was comfortable under India's security umbrella, and even sought New Delhi's military intervention against an insurgency by the Sri Lankan Janatha Vimukthi Peramuna (People's Liberation Front) in 1971. The ill-prepared Sri Lankan forces, which had not had combat experience since World War II, required Indian naval patrols off the coast and Indian Air Force helicopters to assist the largely police-driven counter-insurgency.[16]

By the late 1980s, however, the tide had begun to change. Beyond security and geography, the major factor that influenced Indo-Sri Lankan relations was the ethnic Tamil population that straddled India's southeastern tip in Tamil Nadu

---

[13]Rhoderick Chalmers, International Crisis Group analyst, quoted in Greg Bruno, "Nepal's Two Boulders," *Foreign Affairs*, 26 May 2010.

[14]For demonstrative Indian accounts of Nepal see, for example RSN Singh, "Nepal: The Ticking Time-Bomb," *Indian Defence Review*, 24, 2 (4 May 2009); Rajeev Sharma, "South Asia's Rectangular Triangle: Nepal, Bhutan and India," *South Asia Analysis Group*, Paper No. 4012, 31 August 2010.

[15]For a demonstrative Nepali account of Indo-Nepali bilateral relations, see Yubaraj Ghimire, "Nepal's Agony," *Seminar Magazine*, Securing South Asia, No. 517, September 2002.

[16]Rohan Gunaratna, *Sri Lanka, a Lost Revolution? The Inside Story of the JVP*. Sri Lanka: Institute of Fundamental Studies, 1990.

and extended into Sri Lanka's northeastern Jaffna province. About 3 million Tamils lived in Sri Lanka, while over 60 million lived in India.[17]

Prior to independence from the British in 1948, the largely Hindu Tamil minority had dominated the economy and civil administration of Sri Lanka. Post-independence, the mainly Buddhist Sinhala majority sought to reverse this tide; as a cliché about ethnic relations in Sri Lanka puts it, the "Sinhalese are a majority with a minority complex."[18] Numerically dominating the post-independence democratic government, the Sinhalas instituted pro-Sinhala policies and reservations at the cost of the Tamil minority; the 1956 Official Language Act, known colloquially as the "Sinhala Only Act," instituted the Sinhala language as the sole official language over English, which had previously served as a privilege to the more educated Tamil population.[19] Although the more controversial elements of the act were later resolved, the damage had been done: Tamil nationalist sentiment had been inflamed, and the Sinhala majority began to reap most of the benefits of the state.[20]

By the late 1970s, the Tamil political opposition began to organize violently; organizations such as the Tamil United Liberation Front and the Tamil New Tigers (later the Liberation Tigers of Tamil Eelam or LTTE) began to demand an independent "Tamil Eelam" or homeland in the northeast of Sri Lanka, and used violent tactics to attack both Sinhalas and moderate Tamils. Initially, New Delhi's R&AW sided with, and even provided training and logistical support to a number of Tamil militant groups. This was for a number of reasons. First, in India's 1971 war with Pakistan, Colombo had permitted Pakistani ships to refuel in Sri Lanka en route to the erstwhile East Pakistan, an act that New Delhi saw as an affront, as it empowered the Pakistani Air Force against India; R&AW support for the Tamil organizations was thus seen as retaliation against Colombo.[21] Second, the Tamil population of Indian Tamil Nadu had supported the Sri Lankan Tamil minority's aspirations for independence, compelling Indira Gandhi's Congress government in New Delhi to support the Sri Lankan Tamil groups in order to maintain Tamil Nadu's political support in the Lok Sabha. Lastly, New Delhi supported a number of both Tamil and Sinhala factions,

---

[17] "Abstract Of Speakers' Strength Of Languages And Mother Tongues," Government of India, Ministry of Home Affairs, 2001.

[18] Remarks by Prasad Kariyawasam, Sri Lankan High Commissioner to India, "Discussion on India-Sri Lanka Relations," Institute for Peace and Conflict Studies, Seminar Report # 316, 17 March 2010. The phrase was initially used by K. M. de Silva, *A History of Sri Lanka*. Berkeley, CA: University of California Press, 1981.

[19] A. Jeyaratnam Wilson, *Sri Lankan Tamil Nationalism: Its Origins and Development in the Nineteenth and Twentieth Centuries*. London: C. Hurst & Co Publishers, 2000.

[20] Murugar Gunasingam, *Sri Lankan Tamil Nationalism: A Study of its Origins*. Sydney: MV Publications, 1999, p. 108.

[21] Mohan Kaushik, "India in Sri Lankan Politics." *Strategic Analysis*, 7, 4 (July 1983) 285–290.

in order to exert control over all the parties involved, including Tamil separatists based in India.[22]

By early 1983, however, Indian involvement increased. In order to extend its "Monroe Doctrine" against American, Pakistani, and even European intervention in the region, New Delhi sought to broker a peace deal between the Sinhala government and Tamil separatist groups.[23] As *India Today* reported at the time, "it was possibly the involvement of Israeli and Pakistani advisers that annoyed New Delhi more than anything else."[24]

In July 1987, the government of Rajiv Gandhi brokered an agreement in which both sides of the Sri Lankan conflict would disarm, while New Delhi would retain increased influence over Sri Lanka's foreign relations. As part of the agreement, Colombo would "(1) consult with New Delhi about the employment of foreign military and intelligence personnel; (2) prohibit the military use of the port of Trincomalee by any country in a manner prejudicial to India's interests; and (3) review its existing agreements with foreign broadcasting organizations to ensure that their facilities are not used for any military or intelligence purposes."[25]

Colombo accepted an International Peace-Keeping Force (IPKF) to monitor a ceasefire that would disarm the recalcitrant LTTE. The LTTE, however, considered the accords to be a sell-out of its interests, and refused to disarm. The IPKF, which was staffed by nearly 100,000 members of India's three military services and paramilitary forces, found itself trying to counter a large-scale insurgency in Sri Lanka's northeast. The Force suffered massive casualties (over 1,200 dead and several thousand wounded) as a result of guerrilla attacks by the LTTE. The crippled Indian forces withdrew in September 1989, leaving Sri Lanka in a stalemate. After the failure of the IPKF, while campaigning in Tamil Nadu in 1991, Indian Prime Minister Rajiv Gandhi was killed at the hand of a suicide bomber operating under the LTTE, which feared that the IPKF would be redeployed to Sri Lanka if Gandhi came to power again.

Since then, India has kept its distance from the Colombo-LTTE conflict, not intervening when hostilities escalated through the 1990s, or when the United States, European Union, or other extra-regional powers facilitated ceasefires or peace talks. Fearing a political backlash from the Indian Tamil parties such as the DMK, the United Progressive Alliance government in Delhi, post-2004, refrained from providing Colombo with "offensive weaponry" or even taking public stances on intervention in the region.

---

[22]Mary Anne Weaver, "The Gods and the Stars," *New Yorker*, 21 March 1988, p. 50.
[23]Bhabani Sen Gupta, "The Indian Doctrine," *India Today*, 31 August 1983.
[24]Dilip Bobb, S. H. Venkatramani, and Anita Pratap, "Tackling the Tigers," *India Today*, 20 June 1987, p. 34.
[25]Devin T. Hagerty, "India's Regional Security Doctrine." *Asian Survey*, 31, 4 (April 1991): 356.

In the political realm, perhaps the most decisive era of the Sri Lankan civil war occurred in May 2009, when the Sri Lankan military bombarded a no-fire zone that had been restricted to predominantly Tamil civilians. The alleged target of this bombardment was Vellupillai Prabhakaran and the LTTE leadership, which had interspersed itself among civilians in the north. The *Times of London* and *United Nations* reported that over 20,000 civilians were killed in the safe zone, while the Sri Lankan government disputed the figure.[26] Most sources put May 2009 as the military defeat of the LTTE.[27] Behind the scenes in Colombo's war, however, was the diplomatic and logistical support of Beijing. While western governments (and even India) publicly focused on the human rights violations of the Sri Lankan Army, China continued to supply financial and military support (mainly weapons) and diplomatic cover at the United Nations, enabling Colombo to finish off its military campaign unobstructed.

Some reports even argue that, despite New Delhi's public statements calling on restraint from Colombo, the Indian Air Force and Navy in fact covertly lent naval intelligence regarding LTTE locations, military hardware, and even private diplomatic support to the Sri Lankan Army during its bombardment of the Jaffna peninsula.[28]

In the wake of the LTTE's end and broader Indian Ocean politics, India's strategic view of Sri Lanka has been tinted, again, by China. In the early 2000s, Colombo sought Indian assistance in developing its southern town of Hambantota into a deep-sea port, as well as a land link between northern Sri Lanka and south India. India rejected the proposal to develop Hambantota,[29] and the initial contract was awarded to China's Harbor Engineering Company and Sinohydro Corporation. With these developments in mind, many Indian strategists feared that Sri Lanka, and as a result the whole southern Indian Ocean littoral, was "lost" to Beijing.[30]

---

[26]"Slaughter in Sri Lanka," *The Times*, 29 May 2009; Gethin Chamberlain, "Sri Lanka death toll 'unacceptably high,' says UN," *Guardian UK*, 29 May 2009; "Sri Lanka Fighting 'killed 20,000'," Al Jazeera, 29 May 2009.

[27]Matthew Weaver and Gethin Chamberlain, "Sri Lanka declares end to war with Tamil Tigers," *Guardian UK*, 19 May 2009; Jayadeva Uyangoda, "Sri Lanka post the LTTE," India Seminar, #605, January 2010; C. Bryson Hull and Ranga Sirilal, "Sri Lanka's long war reaches climax, Tigers concede," *Reuters*, 17 May 2009.

[28]See, for example, Nitin Gokhale, *Sri Lanka: From War to Peace*. New Delhi: Har-Anand Publications, 2009.

[29]C. Raja Mohan, "India and the Changing Geopolitics of the Indian Ocean," Eminent Persons Lecture Series, *National Maritime Foundation*, India Habitat Centre, New Delhi, 19 July 2010; C. Raja Mohan, "While Delhi lets Chennai write its Lanka policy, China scripts new chapter," *Indian Express*, 2 June 2005.

[30]Brahma Chellaney, "How India lost out in Sri Lanka," *Forbes*, 10 October 2009; Sudha Ramachandran, "China moves into India's backyard," *Asia Times*, 13 March 2007.

# Maldives

While Indian troops faced no success in Jaffna in 1988, their destiny in the Maldives, to Sri Lanka's immediate southwest, was quite different. Though it had remained independent during India's colonization, the island chain nation of the Maldives had hosted a British military base on its southern Gan Island during World War II. From 1948, hoping to balance the preponderance of a larger India and economically dominant Sri Lanka, Male established itself as a protectorate of the United Kingdom. After its 1965 independence, Male successfully balanced the interests of India, the United Kingdom, the United States, and the Soviet Union, to use Maldivian territory to extend their power in the Indian Ocean. Male kept up this balancing until 1988.[31]

In November of that year, Maldivian businessman Abdullah Luthufi recruited a number of Sri Lankan Tamil militants to launch a coup against Maldivian President Maumoon Abdul Gayoom. Gayoom immediately sought India's assistance, and Rajiv Gandhi (fearing that the United States or United Kingdom would respond to Gayoom's calls for assistance faster than India) immediately dispatched 1,600 Indian paratroopers and three warships to intervene.[32] A few hundred Indian troops remained to train Maldivian security forces, and a defense relationship was established in which Male would remain under New Delhi's security umbrella in the case of threats from insurgents and "terrorists". Although established under the rule of President Gayoom, this relationship survived the 2008 democratic revolution that brought former opposition leader Mohamed Nasheed to power. As late as 2009, India had plans to develop Maldives' security infrastructure, interlinking the Maldivian islands with India's Coast Guard and coastal radar system[33]—in large part to counter China's own efforts in the Indian Ocean.[34]

Yet analysts in New Delhi have also expressed concern about a growing tide of Islamism in the Maldives. In 2010, nine Maldivian militants were arrested in Pakistan's South Waziristan, where they were training with Taliban, while the Pakistan-based Idarat Khidmat-e-Khalq, an affiliate of the LeT, established a presence in the Maldives under the auspices of conducting post-tsunami humanitarian relief.[35]

---

[31] Ravinatha Aryasinha, "Maldives, Sri Lanka and the 'India Factor'," *Himal Southasian*, March 1997.

[32] Sanjoy Hazarika, "Indian Troops End Coup in Maldives," *New York Times*, 5 November 1988.

[33] Many Pubby, "India bringing Maldives into its security net," *Indian Express,* 13 August 2009.

[34] "India eyes Maldives to counter China in Indian Ocean," Indo-Asian News Service, 20 August 2009; Siddharth Srivastava, "India drops anchor in the Maldives," *Asia Times*, 2 September 2009.

[35] Animesh Roul, "Jihad and Islamism in the Maldive Islands." Jamestown Foundation, *Terrorism Monitor*, 8, 6 (12 February 2010).

# Bangladesh

The geo-economics of Bangladesh are largely centered on water. Bangladesh lies at the delta of two major river systems—the Brahmaputra and the Ganges—a fertile region that converges into the equally marshy Chittagong Hill Tracts of the Bay of Bengal. For centuries the region was politically and economically integrated into West Bengal and even the southern Assam and Meghalaya region—an integration that was furthered by the development of industry and plantations in the 1800s. The region's fertility has made even the border areas between Bangladesh and India densely populated, and replete with arable land, abundant water, and natural gas.

The political, economic, and even cultural integration between Bengalis on both sides of the border was slowly diminished by the British in the early twentieth century, when Bengal was administratively bifurcated and electorates were separated by religion. The economic infrastructure that once connected these bi-national resources—road, rail, and river transport that linked, for example, jute plantations in east Bengal with factories in the west—remained in place after partition, but was all but removed after the 1965 war between India and Pakistan.[36]

India's assistance in the independence of Bangladesh from Pakistan—by supporting the Bengali Mukti Bahini insurgency against the Pakistani Army, and later confronting the Pakistani Military directly in the 1971 war—brought New Delhi and the new government of Sheikh Mujibur Rehman to good terms. Unfortunately for India, Bangladesh, as a small delta country adjacent to a larger neighbor, soon came under the influence of an insecurity complex. The 1975 assassination of Mujibur Rehman brought to power Ziaur Rehman, whose government saw India as a possible threat. Ziaur Rehman was more Islamist and pro-Pakistan than his predecessor, and even leaned toward China and the United States in an effort to "balance" India in the Cold War world.

Although erstwhile tension with Pakistan compelled India to terminate its transport links with Bangladesh, the potential for connectivity remains strong. Bangladesh had always been a major link between the Indo-Gangetic Plain and India's northeast states, which are now dependent on the Siliguru Corridor for access to New Delhi. Moreover, the infrastructure that can be used to transport Bangladeshi produce to India can also be used to transport the same goods to third-country markets: one potential link involves the multi-state Nepal-West Bengal-Bangladesh-northeast India route; another would traverse Bangladesh's border with Burma to create a Northeast India-Bangladesh-Myanmar link.

---

[36]Veena Sikri, "The Geopolitics of Bangladesh." *India Seminar*, 603 (November 2009).

Power generation is another potential point of convergence. The hydroelectric potential in Nepal can be extended to cover Bangladesh as well as India and Bhutan. India has also sought to develop Bangladesh's natural gas reserves, which are concentrated primarily in the Chittagong Hill Tracts and Bay of Bengal, adjacent to the maritime border with Myanmar. Indeed, Farooq Siobhan, the president of the Bangladesh Enterprise Institute estimates that full economic integration with India could increase Bangladesh's economic growth rate tremendously—from 6 to 8 percent.[37]

Despite this potential, however, mutual skepticism remains, due primarily to security concerns on both sides of the border. Migration from Bangladesh has been one particularly sour point. Ever since partition, when refugees came pouring across the border, resettling them has been a challenge for New Delhi. The Assamese were particularly perturbed by the influx of Muslim Bengali migrants, who sought both political refuge and economic opportunities, and whose presence was a sore point that contributed to insurgency in that region. The 1971 war over East Pakistan also compelled a large amount of migration into India, setting off another round of discord in eastern and northeastern India.

More recently, environmental and simple economic issues have been compelling migration across the border. Typhoons and the inundation of Bangladeshi land, as well as broader economic opportunities in India, have led thousands of Bangladeshi migrants across the border. This three million-strong migrant population has sought ration and voting cards in India, upsetting local political economies. These logistical challenges have also taken on more profound political dimensions. The Indian government has expressed concerns that border crossings have enabled militants, namely those that abet northeastern insurgencies, to seek refuge in Bangladesh while planning attacks in India. More recently, the presence in Bangladesh of the HuJI, a Pakistan-based Islamist militant group, has been particularly disturbing for India and even Bangladeshi society.

Another irritant in the relationship has been the management of water resources from the Meghna, Brahmaputra, and Ganges rivers. The delta of the three rivers carries great potential for fresh water storage (through barraging) and hydroelectricity generation. Questions over water rights—which parties in which countries can control and have access to what—however, have restricted the development of any major water-sharing infrastructure at the border.[38]

---

[37]Personal Communication with Farooq Sobhan, Former Bangladeshi Ambassador to China and India, and President, Bangladesh Enterprise Institute, 16 January 2011; See also "Trying to be good neighbors," *The Economist*, 10 December 2009.

[38]Stephen Brichieri-Colombi and Robert W. Bradnock, "Geopolitics, Water and Development in South Asia: Cooperative Development in the Ganges-Brahmaputra Delta." *The Geographical Journal*, 169, 1 (March 2003): 43–64.

Perhaps the most important reason that Indo-Bangladeshi economic integration has remained so low, even after the independence of Bangladesh from Pakistan, is due to issues of geopolitics. Bangladesh, as a smaller country, fears a loss of autonomy if it "bandwagons" with India in the strategic and even economic realms. From New Delhi's perspective, Bangladeshi political parties are bifurcated into those that seek enhanced integration with India and emphasize their "Bengali" identity (namely the Awami National League) and those that seek to balance India and emphasize their "Bangladeshi" and Muslim identity (namely, the Bangladesh Nationalist Party and its Islamist affiliates such as the Jamaat-e-Islami).

Likewise, the country's international relations oscillate between support for, and skepticism of India. The skepticism has manifested in the resistance to investments by Indian companies to invest in Bangladesh—such as Tata's development of Bangladeshi natural gas fields—and perhaps more poignantly in Dhaka's attempts to "balance" India with other countries, such as Pakistan and particularly China. Relations between Beijing and The Bangladesh Army in particular are reputedly strong, with a majority of the Army's weaponry and weapons systems coming from China.

> In 2006, China supplied 65 artillery guns and 114 missiles and related systems. Most of the tanks (T-59, T-62, T-69, and T-79), a large number of armored personnel carriers (APCs), artillery pieces and small arms and personal weapons in the Bangladesh Army are of Chinese origin. . . . The Bangladeshi Navy is largely made up of Chinese-origin platforms. These include the 053-H1 Jianghu I class frigates with 4 x HY2 missiles, Huang Feng class missile boats, Type-024 missile boats, Huchuan and P-4 class torpedo boats, Hainan class sub chasers, Shanghai class gun boats and Yuchin class LCUs. The BNS Khalid Bin Walid has been retrofitted with HQ-7 SAM from China. . . . Over the years, China has delivered F7 and Q5 fighter aircraft and PT 6 Trainers to the Bangladesh Air Force.[39]

China's efforts to develop Chittagong port into a listening station and potential naval base—adjacent to its current listening post in Myanmar's Coco Islands—place Dhaka at a central node of China's maritime strategy, irking New Delhi, which fears that Dhaka may grant China basing rights in Chittagong, which China has agreed to develop into a military base.[40]

---

[39]Vijay Sakhuja, "China-Bangladesh Relations and the Potential for Regional Tensions." Jamestown Foundation, *China Brief*, 9, 15 (23 July 2009).
[40]Mukul Devichand, "Is Chittagong one of China's 'string of pearls'?," *BBC News*, 17 May 2010; Ananth Krishnan, "China Offers to Develop Chittagong Port," *The Hindu*, 15 March 2010.

# 4

# Paired Minorities: The Fraught Relationship with Pakistan

## Geopolitics?

Throughout their six decades of existence, the relationship between India and Pakistan has been a textbook case of political hostility. From the outset, debates about whether both countries should even exist plagued the relationship, with Pakistan seeking to separate from what was an imminently independent Indian Republic. This was clear not just in the political realm—with debates and conflicts between the INC and the Muslim League—but later on, in the strategic arena, through political and violent conflicts over which territories would fall in which country, from Junagadh to Hyderabad, Punjab to East Bengal, the Indus River System itself, and of course the lingering issue of Kashmir.

But more structural, ingrained issues also contributed to conflict between the two countries. Geography is one. Throughout history, the entity that dominated the entire Indo-Gangetic Plain, the most fertile, populous, and strategically significant section of the peninsula, would have political control over the majority of the subcontinent. This included the Guptas, Mauryas, Mughals, and British. Because it is one geographic unit, lasting stability in northern India had been reliant on the political cohesion of, or at least the suzerainty of a single entity in, the entire plain. Since partition divided the plain at Punjab, many have argued that conflict between the two main components of the subcontinent—India and Pakistan—is inevitable.[1]

---

[1] See, for example, George Friedman, "The Geopolitics of India: A Shifting, Self-Contained World," *Stratfor*, 16 December 2008; Robert Kaplan, "What's Wrong With Pakistan?," *Foreign Policy*, July/August 2012; Rajesh Rajagopalan, "Neorealist Theory and the India–Pakistan Conflict—I." *Strategic Analysis*, 22, 9 (December 1998): 1261.

The sheer imbalance between the size and power of the two countries is reason enough to cause insecurity. Even in plain geographic terms, the differences are stark. The diverse topography of India—vast coastlines, numerous river systems, mountains, some coal and petroleum deposits, fertile land, and so on—accounted for a relative abundance of natural resources. Meanwhile the "moth-eaten" land that became (west) Pakistan, to use the country's founder, Muhammad Ali Jinnah's own words,[2] received the waters of the Indus River System only *after* they passed through India; only one-fifth to one-fourth of its land was arable, while the remainder was largely mountainous[3]; and the major cities of West Pakistan (Lahore, Karachi, Peshawar, and later Islamabad), based around the Indus river, were nearly adjacent to the border with India, and thus easily vulnerable to attack from India. Indeed, Pakistan had very few geographic resources to start with. In other strategic terms, the following table gives a sample of how hulking India appears when compared to Pakistan.

| | India | Pakistan |
|---|---|---|
| Land Mass (square miles) | 1,236,085 | 307,374 |
| Population | 1,237,000,000 | 179,000,000 |
| 2009 nominal GDP (USD)[4] | 1,235,975,000,000 | 166,515,000,000 |
| Military expenditures (USD)[5] | 24,716,000,000 | 4,217,000,000 |
| Total number of troops[6] | 4,514,300 | 1,480,000 |

The imbalance of resources might not have made conflict inevitable. But the paradigm through which both countries viewed their international relations

---

[2] Quoted in Z. H. Zaidi (ed.), *Quaid-e-Azam Mohammad Ali Jinnah Papers*, National Archives of Pakistan, Ministry of Culture, Government of Pakistan and Oxford University Press, 1993.
[3] Some natural gas reserves exist in Pakistan's western Baluchistan province.
[4] World Economic Outlook Database, International Monetary Fund, April 2010.
[5] "The SIPRI Military Expenditure Database: Year 2008", Stockholm International Peace Research Institute, 2009, available at http://milexdata.sipri.org/result.php4
[6] Anthony Cordesman and Martin Kleiber, "Asian Conventional Military Balance in 2006: Overview of major Asian Powers," Center for Strategic and International Studies, 2006, available at http://csis.org/files/media/csis/pubs/060626_asia_balance_powers.pdf

was offensive realism.[7] According to that paradigm, in order to ensure its own security, a state must maximize its power (particularly when compared to others); influence and power are defined in hard terms: economic might, military expenditures, weapons systems, and the ability to inflict damage on others; and there ought to be a *balance of power* in the system.

To balance India's might, Pakistan had three options, according to the realist conception: (i) bandwagoning, or joining along with India in order to avoid being attacked and to share the benefits of India's power; (ii) internal balancing, or building up Pakistan's own "power" base to counter India; and (iii) external balancing, joining forces with third parties in order to keep outside pressure on India so that it would not attack Pakistan.

Bandwagoning is usually the most preferred option for any country, because doing so requires that the fewest resources be diverted toward the active resistance of an opponent. And in fact, geography—mainly the shared Indus River System and Indo-Gangetic Plain—would otherwise lead Pakistan toward economic integration, and thus a bit of strategic "bandwagoning" with New Delhi, which controls most of the plain. But Pakistan has, from the beginning, vehemently resisted this choice for a number of reasons.

One reason was that Pakistan (which included Bangladesh at the time of independence) was geographically more autonomous than the small, landlocked and mountain-bound countries of Bhutan, Nepal, and at the time, Sikkim, that India surrounded. Pakistan could physically connect with countries like Iran, Afghanistan (and from there, Central Asia), Myanmar and the Bay of Bengal via East Pakistan, and after the 1948 war in which it gained control of northern Kashmir, to Xinjiang Province and the PRC through the Karakoram pass. Not to mention, Pakistan had a 1,046 km-long coastline,[8] and in Karachi it had a port with a rich history of trade and maritime activity. With its size, coastline, and extra-regional access, Pakistan, more than other countries in South Asia, was *able* to resist bandwagoning with India—to resist Indian hegemony, as it was seen.

But perhaps the most important reason that Pakistan resisted bandwagoning with India was the unresolved question of the two countries' identities. Pakistan was founded on the "two-nation theory," which stated that Hindus and Muslims

---

[7] Itty Abraham, "Towards a Reflexive South Asian Security Studies," in Marvin G. Weinbaum and Chetan Kumar (eds), *South Asia Approaches the Millennium: Reexamining National Security*. Boulder, CO: Westview Press, 1995, pp. 17–40. See also Ali Ahmed, "Towards Détente in South Asia," *South Asian Journal*, 27 (January–March 2010): 133–142.

[8] CIA World Factbook: Pakistan, US Central Intelligence Agency, 19 August 2010, available at https://www.cia.gov/library/publications/the-world-factbook/geos/pk.html

were two irreconcilably different nations, and thus could not live peaceably in a democracy ruled by a Hindu majority.[9] The very purpose of partition was to give the Muslims of South Asia political independence from the supposed domination of "Hindu" India. If the new Islamic nation had simply bandwagoned with India and lost its autonomy, its very reason for being would be gone.

Thus rejecting the "bandwagon" option, Pakistan instead looked to balance against India using both methods: internal and external balancing. In the 1950s, about 4 percent of Pakistan's Gross National Product (GNP) was devoted to defense, and since then, that number has not gone below 5 percent, reaching a high of 6.28 percent in 1975.[10]

# The Idea of Pakistan[11]

Yet Pakistan's efforts to balance India internally were also tied to questions of its own national identity. From the start, the very "idea" of Pakistan was unclear. When campaigning for an independent Pakistan, Muhammad Ali Jinnah and his Muslim League purposely kept the notion of "a nation for South Asia's Muslims" unclear in order to drum up as broad a support base as possible for an independent country among the Muslims of British India. As Stephen Cohen writes,

> because he had to weld together disparate elements of the Indian Muslim community, Jinnah's arguments were deliberately vague. This vagueness brought both strength and weakness to the Pakistan movement, enabling it to muster support for independence and opposition to Hindu domination [across a wider spectrum of the Muslim populace], but not to build a consensus on the kind of state Pakistan was to become.[12]

---

[9] There were, of course, other factors that led to the formation of Pakistan. For example, Muhammad Ali Jinnah sought to use the "Pakistan question" as a way to gain leverage against the Indian National Congress rather than create a separate nation-state; Great Britain wanted to create a buffer state between India (and the Arabian Sea) and the Soviet Union to give the western bloc greater strategic depth in the emerging Cold War; and Jawaharlal Nehru resisted compromise with the Muslim League, initially dismissing it as a fringe group with little backing, though it later came to win massive electoral support. All these factors ultimately influenced the creation of "The Islamic Republic of Pakistan".

[10] Based on figures in US Arms Control and Disarmament Agency, *World Military Expenditures and Arms Transfers, 1966–1975*. Washington, D.C.: US Government Printing Office, 1976, pp. 33, 43.

[11] This section title is a reference to a book that explores the idea of Pakistani identity in its state formation and international relations, namely Stephen Philip Cohen, *The Idea of Pakistan*. Washington, D.C.: Brookings Institution Press, 2004.

[12] Stephen Philip Cohen, *The Idea of Pakistan*. Washington, D.C.: Brookings Institution Press, 2004, p. 29.

Specifically, the role of Islam in the proposed country's public life and in governance was never specifically articulated or conceptualized. Nor, beyond opposition to Hindu domination,[13] was the basis of unity among the diverse Muslims that would make up the new country; Pashtuns, Punjabis, Baluchis, Sindhis, Muhajirs (Urdu-speaking migrants from central India), and Bengalis in Pakistan's geographically distant eastern wing all practiced radically diverse forms of Islam, from secular to traditional, from Hanbali to Ja'afari schools of Islamic jurisprudence, to practices that had more in common with local variants of Hinduism than they did with each other, and so forth.[14]

In fact, this internal division posed inherently geostrategic challenges, involving not only domestic but also international dimensions. While the populations of ethnic Sindhis and Punjabis were geographically coterminous with the provinces that they inhabited within Pakistan (Sindh and Pakistani Punjab), the same was not true of the Pashtuns or Baluchis in the new state's north and west, respectively. Both populations straddled national borders, with Pashtuns existing on both sides of the Durand Line that divided Pakistan from Afghanistan, and Baluchis occupying the western Baluchistan province of Pakistan, the eastern Sistan and Baluchistan province of Iran, and even the Farah, Helmand, Herat, and Oruzgan provinces of southwestern Afghanistan. Their physical presence and, Pakistani strategists feared, their political allegiances, would straddle these borders as well. Local separatism could find support from governments across the Afghan and Iranian borders, and the Iranian and Afghan governments could use Pakistan's ethnic division against Islamabad. If these geographic and cultural allegiances amounted to threats against the Punjabi-majority Pakistani state, they would amount to an issue of national territorial defense rather than just internal security. For this reason Pakistan, through its history, has in many ways seen Afghanistan as an inherent extension of its own territory, often using Pashtun and Islamic nationalism to garner influence in Afghanistan—and displace Pakistani Pashtun grievances against Islamabad onto Afghan central governments.

This influence in Afghanistan has also been a result of what Pakistani defense planners refer to as "strategic depth." As Aslam Siddiqi of Pakistan's Bureau of National Reconstruction wrote,

---

[13] While the term "domination" may appear a bit strong from the vantage point of history, at the time Hindu-Muslim division was difficult to deny. Recent decades had been rocked by Hindu-Muslim rioting and other violent confrontations from Bengal to Punjab all the way south to Maharashtra and Hyderabad. See, for example, B. R. Ambedkar, *Pakistan or the Partition of India*. Bombay: Thackers Publishers, 1946, Chapter 7.

[14] See Stephen Philip Cohen, *The Idea of Pakistan*. Washington, D.C.: Brookings Institution Press, 2004. For a Pakistani interpretation of Pakistan's national identity crises, see Farzana Shaikh, *Making Sense of Pakistan*. New York: Columbia University Press, 2009.

Pakistan inherited almost all the burden of land defense of United India. This mainly meant the defense of the northwest frontier where was normally [in a united subcontinent,] stationed about eighty percent of the Indian Army. But in December 1947, movements of the Indian armed forces became such a menace to its security that Pakistan withdrew all its forces from the northwest frontier and posted them near the Indo-Pakistan border. So the overall burden of defense [that] Pakistan has got to carry is much heavier than that of United India. . . . Pakistan has to look ahead in the north and watch trends there. . . . The safety of the Indo-Pakistan subcontinent has depended on the degree of influence which its rulers could wield on the areas round about the mountains of the Hindu Kush. . . . *The remedy is a fusion of the two states of Afghanistan and Pakistan in some way or other.*[15]

Afghanistan even served a purpose in Pakistan's defense planning against India. Because India was thousands of miles wide, and most of its economic and military assets were deep into the border, it would be able to absorb military strikes from Pakistan and emerge relatively unscathed. Pakistan, however, was located in a narrow strip of land between the Indus and Durand Line that could easily be traversed, and whose assets lay adjacent to the Indian border and vulnerable to military attack. By extending its influence into and fusing with Afghanistan, Siddiqi reasoned, "Pakistan can have [strategic] depth in defense."[16]

Nonetheless, after independence, a "nation" had to be forged from these disparate ethno-cultural groups, as did the tools of governance to manage it. After partition, Jinnah himself sought to make Pakistan a secular democracy. But within years of independence, there were pressures—from sources like Maulana Mawdudi and his Jamaat-e-Islami (JeI)—to augment the role of specific interpretations of Islam in society. Under these pressures, the country was declared an "Islamic" republic in the country's 1956 constitution, and riots against the Ahmediyya sect, which JeI labeled un-Islamic, broke out in the streets of Lahore and Karachi. Even the democratic nature of the country soon came under threat; in 1958 Gen. Ayub Khan staged a bloodless coup and the military took over the country for the first time.

Because there was little basis for domestic unity, the narrative of "Hindu-domination" that had united the Muslim League constituents before partition was continued; what was once a fear of "Hindu" domination was

---

[15] Aslam Siddiqi, *Pakistan Seeks Security*. Pakistan: Longmans, Green, 1960, pp. 52–3 (Emphasis added).
[16] Ibid.

converted into fears of "Hindu *Indian*" domination that would unite the new nation. As one Pakistani writer put it,

> if it is not anti-Indianism, then in what other terms could we possibly render Pakistani-Muslim nationalism? The "ideology of Pakistan" . . . is nothing except anti-Indianism. In every walk of life in Pakistan . . . a vast majority of people have been inculcated with fantastic anti-Indian notions. . . . Anti-Indianism, in short, runs deep in Pakistani state and society. . . . People have no other alternative frame of reference in which to define Pakistani nationalism.[17]

This frame would have two main effects on Pakistan. The first was that rather than focusing on internal divisions, the new "nation" of Pakistan would be united based on opposition to an outside enemy: India. The second was that, in order to maintain internal unity as well as a credible opposition to India, a strong military had to remain in place—and arguably, in control. Military rulers have ruled for 38 of Pakistan's first 60 years, while exerting considerable influence even when civilian governments were in power. As journalist and former Pakistani Ambassador to the United States Hussain Haqqani writes, "the armed forces rationalize their dominant role by depicting India as an eternal threat to Pakistan's very existence."[18]

The military's domination of Pakistan started with a compelling narrative: to preserve Pakistan's internal unity (including secession attempts by Baluchi and Sindhi movements, and sectarian religious strife) as well as the external integrity of the country (the perennial military threat from India and even Afghanistan), a wholly *Pakistani*, anti-India military force must dominate.

But the power of the military became undergirded not only by a narrative, but also by economics. One of the major, but lesser discussed causes of partition was a divergence of economic views. Nehru, in his quest for a united India, sought a highly centralized, socialist state that would redistribute wealth through policies like land reform and industry nationalization. Others, including both Mohandas Gandhi and a number of Muslim League partisans, opposed this vehemently, seeking instead a more decentralized, market-oriented economic model.[19] The result was that while India quickly instituted

---

[17] Najum Mushtaq, "Ideological Crossroads," *The New International*, 10 June 2001.
[18] Hussain Haqqani, *America's New Alliance with Pakistan: Avoiding the Traps of the Past*, Carnegie Endowment Policy Brief, No. 19, October 2002, available at http://www.carnegieendowment.org/files/Policybrief19.pdf, accessed 16 January 2009.
[19] See, for example, S. V. R. Nasr, "Pakistan: State, Agrarian Reform and Islamization." *International Journal of Politics, Culture, and Society*, 10, 2 (Winter 1996): 249–72.

land reforms such as the abolition of the *zamindari* system to break up much (but certainly not all)[20] of the hold that feudal landowning practices would have on the new country, Pakistan resisted such efforts. This lack of land reforms kept power vested in a number of feudal, land-owning elite families—"landed elites." Even as far into Pakistan's independence as 1968, 43 families of the "landed elite" still controlled 46 percent of manufacturing, 75.6 percent of insurance assets, and 74 percent of all assets of private firms.[21]

In the early years of independence, the military and the landed elite made an unofficial alliance to bring about the quick administrative integration of the new state—a strong nexus that would affect the political and economic development of the country into the next decades.[22] The economic elite came to staff the officer corps (upper echelons) of the Pakistani Army, whose retirees would often head important civilian bureaucracies.[23] Meanwhile, the army, starting from the military government of Ayub Khan in 1958, invested its own capital in ventures controlled by the economic (particularly the industrial) elites, often going so far as to give retired officers extremely favorable entitlements and subsidized prices on real estate throughout the country in order to secure the loyalties of the officers, as well as ensure their political and economic clout even after their military service.[24]

The deficit of internal cohesion and a fear of external threats drove a constant sense of state insecurity, which compelled economic elites to bolster the military to respond to this insecurity, in turn enabling the military to heighten the *perception* of national insecurity.

---

[20] Despite enacting some land reforms, the Nehru Congress regime required institutional economic support for its political efforts. Accordingly, it based itself "on a coalition of urban and rural interests united behind an urban-oriented industrial strategy. Its senior partners were India's small but politically powerful administrative, managerial, and professional English-educated middle classes and private-sector industrialists. Private-sector industrialists welcomed the freedom from foreign competition and dependency that was enabled by the second and third five-year plans' import substitution and industrial self-reliance strategies. . . . The junior partners . . . were rural notables, mostly large landowners who survived intermediary abolition and blocked the implementation of land ceilings legislation." Most of the groups were comprised of Hindu upper castes. Lloyd Rudolph and Susanne Rudolph, *In Pursuit of Lakshmi: The Political Economy of the Indian State*. Chicago: University of Chicago Press, 1987, p. 50.

[21] Lawrence J. White, *Industrial Concentration and Economic Power in Pakistan*. Princeton, NJ: Princeton University Press, 1974; Lawrence J. White, "Pakistan's Industrial Families: The Extent, Causes, and Effects of their Economic Power." *Journal of Development Studies*, 10, 3 and 4 (April 1974): 273–304.

[22] Ayesha Jalal, "Review: Pakistan's Predicament." *Third World Quarterly*, 11, 3 (July 1989): 233–8.

[23] Ayesha Jalal, *The State of Martial Rule: The Origins of Pakistan's Political Economy of Defense*. Cambridge: Cambridge University Press, 1990.

[24] Akmal Hussain, "Pakistan's Economy in Historical Perspective," in Wilson John (ed.), *Pakistan: The Struggle Within*. New Delhi: Pearson-Longman Press, 2009, pp. 34–85.

The lack in domestic identity that lay beneath this cycle of militarization took a major shock in 1971. Through the late 1960s, the West Pakistan-based military apparatus of Ayub Khan and Yahya Khan had sought to impose a highly Islamized form of Pakistani nationalism, as well as West Pakistani administrative dominance onto the whole country. This imposition extended to Bengali East Pakistan, whose population accounted for a near majority of united Pakistan. Yet Bengali nationalists in East Pakistan, led by Mujibur Rahman's Awami League, sought to retain their own cultural identity as well as political autonomy. East Pakistan's ports and plantations, in fact, provided a large percentage of Pakistan's economy and federal budget, but much of their products were rechanneled into development efforts in West Pakistan. Based on its six-point movement for Bengali autonomy, the Awami League won a decisive majority of East Pakistan's votes in the 1970 elections, giving it a full government in the National Assembly, the authority of which included West Pakistan. Fearing the dissolution of the Pakistani state, the (West) Pakistani military intervened and began a massive campaign killing between 50,000 and 300,000 East Pakistanis, particularly Hindus, and sending millions of Bengalis across the border into India.

East Pakistani migrants had long been a source of irritation in India's northeast, and the sudden influx of refugees amounted to a humanitarian crisis within India. Perhaps more consequentially, Indian defense analysts, most prominently K. Subrahmanyam, saw the crisis in East Pakistan as an opportunity to militarily intervene and decisively weaken Pakistan after all the conflict between India and Pakistan in 1948 and 1965.[25] New Delhi continued its training of the Mukti Bahini and other anti-Pakistani Bengali militants, and began a military buildup along the western border, compelling a (West) Pakistani preemptive air strike that marked the commencement of the Indo-Pakistan war of 1971.

In the ensuing hostilities, India supported the separation of East Pakistan from the west, resulting in the independence of Bangladesh. This loss had a number of implications for Pakistan. First, it lost its eastern wing, and with it access to the region's resources and to the Bay of Bengal. Second, the division of Pakistan was a rejection of the "two-nation" theory that was the raison d'etre of the Pakistan state: Islam proved insufficient to bind a nation together. And third, the involvement of India in the "dismemberment" of Pakistan made it abundantly clear to the Pakistani establishment that India had hegemonic designs for the country, and that Pakistan could face further existential threats from its eastern neighbor.

---

[25] Sumit Ganguly, *Conflict Unending: India-Pakistan Tensions since 1947*. New York: Columbia University Press, 2002, pp. 63–5.

# "Strategic Assets"

In the wake of these changes, the nature of Pakistani militancy shifted. The role of Kashmir and its accession to Pakistan increased in the Pakistani national narrative, as an external rallying point that would provide domestic cohesion, to exact revenge (or justice) on India for breaking Pakistan up, and to strip India of its Muslim-majority province in order to disprove India's secular credentials and the "one-nation" theory, India's own national narrative that stated that Hindus and Muslims could in fact coexist as a single nation. General Zia ul-Haq, the military leader who took the reins of Pakistan in a coup in 1977, thought of another method of opposing Indian hegemony: by "Islamizing" Pakistan with influences from Saudi Arabian Hanbali-Wahhabi Islam, Pakistan could be pulled away from South Asia's Hindu-influenced Sufi Islamic culture and toward a more "authentic" West Asian Islam.[26]

Zia began his "Nizam-e-Mustapha" or Order of the Prophet, by using organizations like the Islami Jamiat-e-Talaba, the student wing of the Deobandi JeI, to institutionalize the role of Islam in politics, society, bureaucracy and even the military.[27] The Soviet invasion of Afghanistan in 1979 compelled a greater Pakistani involvement in Afghanistan's internal affairs that strengthened Zia's Islamist system: the use of American money and weapons, and "mujahideen", weapons, religious doctrine, and money from Saudi Arabia and other parts of the Islamic world increased this tie between Pakistani identity and Islam.

From the late 1970s, the Pakistani military and the recently bolstered ISI agency began using a number of Islamist proxies to accomplish its strategic aims vis-à-vis both Afghanistan and India. A militant training infrastructure was established in Pakistan's Northwestern Frontier Province (NWFP, today's Khyber Pakhtunkhwa) that trained Islamist fighters who then went on to fight in Afghanistan.[28] This would, once again, redirect Pashtun nationalism away from Islamabad and against an external enemy, the Soviet Union. It would also give Islamabad influence and extra strategic depth in Afghanistan. The same infrastructure was also used to train Sikh Khalistani and Kashmiri militants that

---

[26] Lawrence Ziring, "A Historical Perspective on Ethnicity, Tribalism, and the Politics of Frontier Policy in Pakistan," in Veena Kukreja and M. P. Singh (eds), *Democracy, Development, and Discontent in South Asia*. New Delhi: Sage Publications, 2008, p. 218; S. Akbar Zaidi, "South Asia? West Asia? Pakistan: Location, Identity." *Economic and Political Weekly*, 44, 10 (7 March 2009): 36–9.

[27] Vali Reza Nasr, *The Vanguard of the Islamic Revolution: The Jama'at-I Islami of Pakistan*. Berkeley, CA: University of California Press, 1994.

[28] Praveen Swami, *India, Pakistan and the Secret Jihad: The Covert War in Kashmir, 1947–2004*. New York: Cambridge University Press/Foundation Books, 2006. According to Swami, similar sub-national state agents had been part of a proxy war by Pakistan that had gone on in lower-intensity in Kashmir since Independence.

would return to Indian Punjab and Indian-administered Kashmir, respectively, to fight the Indian state.[29]

A number of these groups—including the Hizb-ul-Mujahideen, Harakat al-Ansar, and others—were trained in the NWFP and southern Afghanistan with the specific intention of attacking and inciting local uprisings against Indian forces in Indian-administered Kashmir. They received active state patronage from elements of the Pakistani Army as part of the army's efforts to weaken India and its hold over Jammu and Kashmir. "Taken in its totality," wrote Lt. Col. Javed Hassan in *India: A Study in Profile* for the Pakistani Army's Faculty of Research and Doctrinal Studies, "India will be cut to its proper size and dimension, that is, only quasi powerful and very much a manageable military power."[30]

Of course, the Kashmiri uprising against the Indian state had both influences from Pakistan, as well as domestic (local) sources. After a period in which the Union Government in Delhi rigged a number of elections in Kashmir (in 1984, 1986, and 1987), a large-scale insurgency started in 1989, with the Kashmiri gentry taking up arms against the Indian state. Even though the Kashmiris of the Valley initially used informal methods of resistance—including weapons fashioned from "the steering shafts of rickshaws"[31]—Pakistan's own Afghanistan-tested militant infrastructure soon intervened. Sending weapons and militants across the Line of Control into Srinagar, while providing training in Pakistani areas to indigenous Kashmiris, Pakistani citizens, and militants from the wider Islamic world to rebel against India, Pakistan upped the ante in the Kashmir Valley, hoping that once and for all, India would fully be divested of its Muslim-majority province.

The effort quickly moved from one of Pakistan-supported Kashmiri militancy to one that was primarily Pakistani—a type of proxy war between Indian and Pakistani irregular forces, with the Kashmir Valley as the main staging ground. Kashmir-focused groups like the LeT were formed from *Punjabi* cadres from the southern region of Pakistani Punjab. The scale of the conflict quickly aggregated: as militants staged increasingly brazen attacks on both civilians and Indian security forces, the latter responded with an increasingly strong hand against both civilians and militants.[32]

Meanwhile, a larger geostrategic change happened in the subcontinent: the nuclear tests of May 1998, in which India and Pakistan tested five and six

[29] B. Raman, *The Kaoboys of R&AW: Down Memory Lane*. New Delhi: Lancer Publishers, 2008.
[30] Javed Hasan, *India: A Study in Profile*. Rawalpindi: Services Book Club, 1990.
[31] William Dalrymple, "Bhutto's Deadly Legacy," *New York Times*, 4 January 2008.
[32] Praveen Swami, *India, Pakistan, and the Secret Jihad: The Covert War in Kashmir, 1947–2004*. New York: Taylor and Francis, 2007.

nuclear weapons, respectively, to a great deal of international condemnation. Some argued that this development made the region far more volatile, such that an incident as small as a terrorist attack or as large as a conventional war could easily tread into the realm of nuclear war. Others, however, said that it simply *changed* the nature of the military conflict, lowering it from the higher to the lower rungs of the strategic ladder. It was said that the doctrine of "mutually assured destruction" or MAD—the theory that no country with a nuclear weapon will actually use it against another country with a nuclear weapon, because the second country would simply retaliate and in the end, both would be destroyed or irrevocably damaged—would prevail. And given the sensitivity of both India and Pakistan to threats from the other, even nonnuclear, conventional strikes could arguably be deterred, out of the fear that they would escalate to a nuclear confrontation. These deterrence theorists, in turn, felt that nuclear weapons brought stability to South Asia, ruling out any direct conflict.

But less than a year after the nuclear tests, this debate over the effect of nuclear weapons on Indo-Pak conflict was resolved in a "draw" of sorts, with the "stability-instability paradox," the notion that, while nuclear weapons made large-scale war less likely due to the fear of escalation, they created *incentives* for low-intensity warfare, so long as a certain threshold is not crossed.[33]

In February 1999, Pashtun guerrillas entered the Kargil District of Ladakh, in the northern portion of Indian-administered Kashmir. Once they realized that these were, in fact, infiltrations supported by Pakistani irregular troops and the Pakistani military itself, the Indian Army launched a counter strike, mobilizing 200,000 troops to respond, and even the Navy to blockade Karachi port. Despite the mobilization, India restrained itself from escalating the war: unlike previous wars, India did not open up additional fronts of retaliation, delayed its use of airpower, and did not ultimately blockade Pakistan's supplies—even though all these steps would have weakened Islamabad and hastened the end of the war. Diplomatic intervention and admonition from Washington, where Pakistani Prime Minister Nawaz Sharif had flown to unsuccessfully seek diplomatic support, arguably contributed to a resolution of the conflict and the withdrawal of Pakistani troops. Although it cannot be assumed that either belligerent will always behave the same way in future cases, the Kargil War did make it clear that a limited or low-intensity conflict between India and Pakistan was in fact possible, even though both had nuclear weapons.[34]

---

[33] Glenn Snyder, "The Balance of Power and the Balance of Terror," in Paul Seabury (ed.), *The Balance of Power*. San Francisco: Chandler Press, 1965.
[34] Ashley J. Tellis, C. Christine Fair, and Jamison Jo Medby, "Limited Conflicts Under the Nuclear Umbrella: Indian and Pakistani Lessons from the Kargil Crisis," RAND Corporation, 2002.

The lower-intensity conflict in Kashmir was still ongoing, as were Pakistani efforts to retain influence in Afghanistan. After the Soviet Union withdrew from Afghanistan in 1989, local Islamist militias and tribal warlords of the country sought to fill the power vacuum. What resulted was another decade of tumult in which militias such as those headed by the Uzbek Rashid Dostum, the Tajik Ahmed Shah Massoud, and the Pashtun Gulbuddin Hekmatyar fought among one another to retain control of Kabul. By 1994 the Taliban, refugees of the civil war trained in Saudi-funded madrassas along the Afghan-Pakistan border, rallied in the name of Pashtun Nationalism (in the guise of Pan-Islamism) to take control of Afghanistan. Seeking a cohesive force through which it could influence affairs in Afghanistan, Pakistan's ISI—along with Saudi Arabia and a passive United States—supported the Taliban's expansion from the south to the north of Afghanistan through the late 1990s, against a loose federation of militias called the Northern Alliance, who in turn were backed by Iran, India, and Russia.[35]

As a result of decades of ethnic and sectarian strife, as well as the militant infrastructure established in NWFP to train Afghan and other guerrillas, a cocktail of militant groups flourished within Pakistan's borders. They range from the sectarian Sipah-e-Sahaba (founded in 1985) and Lashkar-e-Jhangvi (1996), Sunni extremist outfits that target Shi'a Muslims; their Shi'a counterparts, the Tehreek-e-Jaferia (1993) and Sipah-e-Mohammad (1992); to the ethnic Baluchistan Liberation Front (1960s) and militant cadres tied to political parties such as the Muttahida-Qaumi Party (MQM) and Pakistani People's Party (PPP); and Kashmir-centered Islamist organizations like LeT (1990), HUJI (1989) and al-Badr (1998); to the Islamist Afghan Taliban, which was established by Afghan refugees in 1994 and later supported by the ISI, had established links in Karachi, Baluchistan, and elsewhere, going so far as to see the establishment of the anti-statist "Tehreek-e-Taliban Pakistan" in 2007.[36]

Pakistan's ISI constituted many of these groups to serve a few purposes: as proxies in the domestic civil clashes that often resulted from partisan politics in places like Karachi and to ensure against regional separatism; to extend Pakistan's influence in Afghanistan; and, by circumventing New Delhi's conventional military superiority as well as the balance brought about by nuclear weapons, to attack and weaken India and its control over Kashmir.

A number of these groups, however, soon gained autonomy. Debates remain over how independent groups like LeT and the Tehreek-e-Taliban

---

[35] Ahmed Rashid, *Taliban: Militant Islam, Oil and Fundamentalism in Central Asia*. New Haven: Yale University Press, 2001.

[36] Hussain Haqqani, "The Ideologies of South Asian Jihadi Groups," *Current Trends in Islamist Ideology*, April 2005.

Pakistan are from the ISI and the Pakistani state. Some say that they remain under the direction of the military. Others argue that, due to economic globalization, transnational networks, and divergent political goals, these groups have become financially independent and even operationally autonomous. In fact, there have been a number of incidents in which agents formerly under the patronage of the Pakistani military—most prominently Ilyas Kashmiri, the erstwhile Pakistani Special Services Group (SSG) commando, who, under the instructions of the military, had joined the Harakat-ul Jihad ul-Islami—have planned and carried out attacks on high-ranking military officials, including former Pakistani President Pervez Musharraf[37] and Prime Minister Benazir Bhutto.

To this end, the 2000s have been colored by what many have understood as a low-intensity civil war within Pakistan: movements such as TTP, Baluchi and other separatist rebels, and even independent agents such as Ilyas Kashmiri have all targeted the Pakistani state apparatus, which has responded with its own military campaigns. Meanwhile, that same Pakistani apparatus is alleged to maintain close links with, and utilize other groups such as LeT, the Afghan Taliban, and the Gulbuddin Hekmatyar and Serajuddin Haqqani militant networks of northern Pakistan, among others, in its own strategic practices vis-à-vis Kashmir, Afghanistan, and India. What has resulted is a complex "web" of militant groups that abound in Pakistan.

# External Balancing

Despite the vast militant and military infrastructure that it had established even at the outset of its existence, it seemed that Pakistan still could not keep up with and successfully balance against India on its own. While India tended to spend much smaller percentages of its overall economy (between 2% and 4% of GNP, compared with Pakistan's 5–7%) on the military, in absolute terms this amounted to greater expenditures than those of Pakistan, on account of India's larger overall size and economy. Owing to this reality, the Pakistani establishment decided that internal balancing was not sufficient, and looked to other countries to try to offset India's influence—both to bolster Pakistan's own military efforts and to counter India along with other, like-minded countries.

As early as the 1950s, Pakistan and the PRC established a rapport. One reason was simply geographic. China had—in October 1949 and October 1950,

---

[37] "Musharraf Assassination Plot Foiled," CNN News, 20 September 2002; Salman Masood and Mike Nizza, "Gunmen Fire on Musharraf's Plane," New York Times, 6 July 2007.

respectively—annexed Tibet and Xinjiang (East Turkestan), and needed a way to connect them. The territory of Aksai Chin in Kashmir, over which China and India fought a brief war in 1962, was used to develop a road link between China's two new provinces. When the PRC faced a Western blockade in the Pacific Ocean following the Korean War of the early 1950s, Pakistan opened up an air corridor to give China extra-regional access. After 1962, Pakistan strengthened the Chinese presence in Kashmir by leasing the Shaksgam Valley to the PRC through the Sino-Pak Frontier Agreement of 1963, which remains in effect. Shaksgam is adjacent to the Pakistan-administered "Northern Areas" of Kashmir, through which the Karakoram Highway was built to facilitate direct overland transport between Pakistan and China. Since then, China has been looking to the Karakoram highway and the rest of Pakistan as a means of access to both Central Asia and, more consequentially, the Arabian Sea.

Another major reason for the Sino-Pak connection, especially after Sino-Indian War of 1962, was for China to weaken India. By bolstering Pakistan's military in particular, China has looked to "prevent India from reaching out beyond South Asia, by keeping it focused on the western front, and by using Pakistan as a form of 'proxy deterrent' against India in its

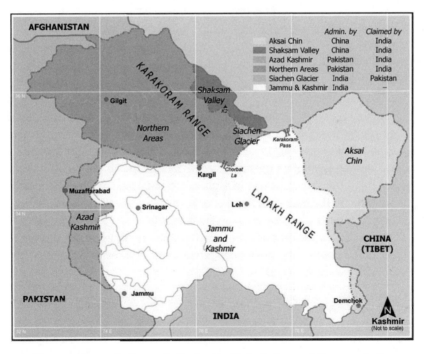

**FIGURE 4.1** *Map of disputed Kashmir—United States Library of Congress, geography and map division, digital ID g7653j.ct000803.*

own backyard."[38] To this end, China has provided Pakistan with military equipment over the years, particularly nuclear and missile technology, to "balance" India.[39]

A second relationship of Pakistan's that has been of lasting consequence is that with the United States. The United States, looking to counter a Soviet threat wherever it could, sought an ally in Pakistan, which was separated from the Soviet Union only by the tiny Wakhan Corridor of eastern Afghanistan. In fact, it has been argued that the British supported the partition of the subcontinent and the creation of Pakistan for the purposes of the Cold War: as a separate country between India and the Soviet Union, Pakistan would serve as an extra buffer between the Arabian Sea and any southward expansion by the Soviets.

Seeking allies in its effort to "balance" India, Pakistan quickly signed on to the Southeast Asia Treaty Organization (SEATO), the Central Treaty Organization (CENTO), and a Mutual Defense Assistance Agreement with the United States, all of which came with economic and military aid that tremendously bolstered Pakistan's military economy. This engagement had its ups and downs—the United States cut military aid to both India and Pakistan following the 1965 war—until 1971, when Pakistan was the facilitator of the Sino-US détente and America brought a warship (the USS *Enterprise*) into the Bay of Bengal to pressure India to ease off of East Pakistan in the 1971 war.[40]

Although Pakistan's efforts to build a nuclear bomb (which came on the tail of India's 1974 "peaceful" nuclear explosion) pushed the United States and Pakistan apart in the mid to late 1970s, the Soviet invasion of Afghanistan in 1979 brought the two together again. During the 1980s, billions of American dollars were funneled into Pakistan to assist the Islamist fighters in Afghanistan in the guerrilla campaign against the Soviet puppet government. While the fall of the Soviet Union in the early 1990s brought about a decline in the Washington-Islamabad military alliance, events in Central Asia—the 9/11 attacks on the United States by the Afghan Taliban-backed Al Qaeda, and other issues related to the geopolitics and energy resources of the region—brought the United States back to Pakistan again after 2001.

The American invasion of Afghanistan in 2001 partly changed the nature of the Pakistani establishment's engagement with the militant groups within

---

[38] Iskander Rehman, "Keeping the Dragon at Bay: India's Counter-Containment of China in Asia." *Asian Security*, 5, 2 (May 2009): 114–43.

[39] Yaacov Vertzberger, *The Enduring Entente: Sino-Pakistani Relations, 1960–1980.* New York: Praeger Press, 1983; Mushahid Hussein, "Pakistan-China Defense Cooperation." *International Defense Review*, 26, 2, (February 1993): 108–11.

[40] James Mann, *About Face: A History of America's Curious Relationship with China, from Nixon to Clinton.* New York: Vintage Press, 2000.

its borders. Under American pressure, Pakistan was compelled to ban organizations like the Sipah-e-Sahaba and Lashkar-e-Jhangvi, and even attempt to de-Islamize its own institutions, for example, through the 2001 removal of then director-general of the ISI, Lt. Gen. Mahmood Ahmad, a well-known Islamist, and most significantly, to militarily oppose groups on its western borders like the Afghan Taliban, with whom it had previously had a strong symbiotic relationship.

# Paired Minorities

The military infrastructure that developed at the outset of Pakistani independence and that has grown and evolved over the decades had one major goal: to resist Indian hegemony. In Pakistani eyes, its own victimhood has been *geographic*, stemming from India's preponderant size and resources; *religious*, in that South Asian Islam is heavily influenced by the Hindu-influenced Sufi culture, which General Zia sought to counteract with his move toward Wahhabism; *military*, in the absolute and relative dominance of Indian forces over Pakistani forces, which has been demonstrated in nearly every conventional conflict between the two states; *political*, in that India has never accepted the very existence of Pakistan and will do anything in its power to end it; and, most poignantly *ideological*, Hindu Indian antagonism was the basis for the Pakistani nation and its subsequent integrity—neither of which India has ever accepted.

The "power" imbalance due to size, economics, and demographics is a natural fact that would be undone only with a great deal of difficulty. (This might mean a radical reshaping of the subcontinent and the de facto fragmentation of India that would appear unacceptable to New Delhi.) Insofar as this imbalance is based in geography, smaller states like Pakistan may always feel some sort of insecurity.

And yet, despite its overwhelmingly larger size and capacities, India, has long seen *itself* as the primary victim in the relationship. *Geographically*, the very creation of Pakistan was thought to have divided the strategic unity of the subcontinent, and removed land that was rightfully Indian; *religiously*, ideologues on the Hindu far-right have long conceptualized the Muslim presence in the subcontinent as an invasion and dilution of the purity of a more morally upstanding Indian, Hindu religion; *militarily*, Indian strategists have admonished Pakistan for its "offensive" nuclear, conventional, and in particular, asymmetric capacities and terrorism, while excusing their own as "merely" defensive; *politically*, Pakistan has invited external powers, from China to the United States, to intervene in the affairs of South Asia, destroying the solidarity that the subcontinent should have had, that is, the Pax India in which India's writ reigns supreme; and *ideologically*, the "two-nation" theory upon which Pakistan is based is in opposition to India's own existence as a multi-religious, pluralistic democracy.

Militarily alone, the two countries are caught in a security dilemma: defensive measures of one were thought to be offensive by the other. And in the case of India, even as India prepared for war with China, Pakistani strategists saw that the same military infrastructure could (and thought it *would*) be used against Pakistan. This was particularly true because many Pakistani strategists did not see India's perception of the Chinese threat as legitimate; they saw China as unwilling or unable to fight any war of significance with India, and in such a case, India would have had enough time to prepare and defend itself sufficiently.[41]

With the Indian test of a "peaceful nuclear device" in 1974, codenamed "Operation Smiling Buddha," said to be in response to the Chinese test at Lop Nur, Xinjiang Province, in 1964, many Pakistanis "believed that the Buddha had smiled in anticipation of Pakistan's death."[42] This was particularly because the nuclear test came on the heels of the 1971 Pakistani defeat and loss of its eastern wing at India's hand.

Retired Pakistani Brig. Gen. Feroz Hassan Khan outlines a number of the other military threats that Pakistan has perceived over the years: a "forward-leaning policy" along the line-of-control in Kashmir; the 1984 seizure of the Siachen glacier; plans for preventive strikes at Kahuta, Pakistan's main nuclear research facility; large-scale military mobilizations such as the 1987 Operation Brasstacks and 2002 Operation Parakram, both seen as disproportional responses to low-intensity conflicts with Pakistani support (the Khalistan movement and the 13 December 2001 bombing of the Indian Parliament, respectively); the fact that "nearly two-thirds of the Indian armed forces [are] organized, structured, and predisposed against" Pakistani vulnerabilities adjacent to the border; the existence of nine (out of 12) Army corps deployed along the Pakistani border; three strike corps that are built around armored divisions, mechanized divisions, and Reinforced Army Plain Infantry Divisions (RAPID) to fight in the Pakistani plains and deserts; that India is capable of moving forces from its Eastern and Southern Commands to the western front within one to 2 weeks; India's naval concentration along its western coast, easily able to blockade Karachi; and the fact that India's air bases are concentrated in the west and northwest.[43]

---

[41] Feroz Hassan Khan, "Pakistan's Evolving Strategic Doctrine," in Wilson John (ed.), *Pakistan: The Struggle Within*. Pearson-Longman, 2009.
[42] William Langewiesche, "The Wrath of Khan," *Atlantic Monthly*, November 2005.
[43] Feroz Hassan Khan, "Pakistan's Evolving Strategic Doctrine," in Wilson John (ed.), *Pakistan: The Struggle Within*. Pearson-Longman, 2009.

Moreover, many Indians have long seen Pakistan as an unviable project, contending that it will collapse, fragment, turn into a failed state, be reabsorbed into India, or another such failed scenario—and that India ought to encourage one of these alternative futures. As early as the 1940s, then Indian Deputy Prime Minister Sardar Vallabhai Patel was among the first to articulate this view.[44] For much of Indian independent history, the common perception was that a strong or successful Pakistan would *prove* the two-nation theory, thus disproving India's own ability to function as a cohesive nation. Many Indian planners, in turn, worked to ensure that Pakistan was not a successful national project.

In fact, the two-nation theory is based on the premise that Muslims "have a distinct way of life" whose rights "could not be preserved in a Hindu-dominated India."[45] The question of the two-nation theory will fundamentally not be answered by events in Pakistan, but by the status and sociopolitical integration of Muslims *within* India.

These identity-based clashes are also intimately linked to Kashmir. As a secular state, India is not inclined to give a Muslim majority region up to its Muslim neighbor *only because* the region is Muslim. But extending that logic, if Kashmir should not go to Pakistan on account of its Muslim majority, then the other Muslim-majority provinces that currently comprise Pakistan also should not have gone to Pakistan either. This strengthens the "Pakistani assertion that Indians have never reconciled themselves to [the very idea of] Pakistan," let alone its existence.[46]

Even as Indian overtures are made to Pakistan—such as Prime Minister Atal Bihari Vajpayee's (BJP) 1999 trip to Pakistan and the Lahore Declaration that India accepts Pakistan—many Pakistanis may not have found such overtures credible. While there have been multiple Pakistani attacks against India, none of them had the effect that a single Indian victory had on Pakistan. In 1962,

the Chinese had inflicted a humiliation on India, felt nationally by leaders and citizens of all shades and stripes. That is how the Pakistanis felt, in 1972, having suffered a comparable defeat at the hands of the Indians. In truth, they felt even worse, for while the Chinese had merely seized

---

[44] See, for example, Sundeep Waslekar, "The Future of Pakistan," *Strategic Foresight Group*, 2002; Surman Guha Mozumder, "India Worried about Disintegration of Pakistan: US Scholar," *Rediff News*, 6 November 2007; Harsh Pant, "Is India Ready for Pakistan's Coming Collapse?," *Rediff News*, 10 March 2009.

[45] Feroz Hassan Khan, "Pakistan's Evolving Strategic Doctrine," in Wilson John (ed.), *Pakistan: The Struggle Within*. New Delhi: Pearson-Longman, 2009.

[46] Stephen Philip Cohen, "India, Pakistan and Kashmir." *Journal of Strategic Studies*, 25, 4 (December 2002): 32–60.

some (mostly useless) territory from India, the Indians had, by assisting in the creation of Bangladesh, blown a hole in the founding ideology of the Pakistani nation. To this there could be only one effective answer—to assist in the separation of Kashmir from India, and thus blow a hole in the founding idea of Indian secularism.[47]

And while issues of identity lie beneath the distrust, there is also a more strategic security dilemma. The strategic goals of each country lie in direct opposition to one another: Pakistan's strategic aim has been to balance against India, by "seeking parity" with and "escaping from" a South Asian Indian identity,[48] balancing internally and externally against India.

India's "strategic aspiration," meanwhile, has traditionally been "to serve as a friendly regional peacekeeper." It has sought a "Pax India to replace the earlier Pax Britannica." To this end, India is offended not only by the expression of autonomy by its smaller neighbors, but also by the invitation by those neighbors of external actors (such as China or the United States) into the region.[49]

In the end, both countries have felt they are the victim of the other: what Stephen Cohen has referred to as a "Paired Minority complex" in which perceptions are "held by important groups on both sides—even those that are not a numerical minority, and which may even be a majority—that they are the threatened, weaker party, under attack from the other side."[50] Accordingly, each has amassed a response mechanism and defense infrastructure to counter the other, feeding a never-ending security dilemma or cycle of inexhaustible distrust about the other.

---

[47] Ramachandra Guha, *India After Gandhi: The History of the World's Largest Democracy*. New York: Harper Collins, 2007, p. 465.

[48] Aparna Pande, *Explaining Pakistan's Foreign Policy: Escaping India*. London: Routledge Press, 2011.

[49] George Tanham, "India's Strategic Culture." *The Washington Quarterly*, 15, 1 (Winter 1992): 129–42.

[50] Stephen Philip Cohen, "India, Pakistan and Kashmir." *Journal of Strategic Studies*, 25, 4 (December 2002): 32–60.

# 5

# Extra-regional Powers: The United States and China

## The United States

Toward the end of World War II, US Presidents Franklin D. Roosevelt and Harry Truman—along with their legions of diplomats both overt and clandestine—made their rounds around the globe, trying to solicit various countries' assistance in the burgeoning Cold War with the Soviet Union. A major prize for President Truman would have been the British colony of India, soon to be the Union of India and the Dominion of Pakistan.

Truman hoped that the United States could maintain an anti-Soviet ally in a peninsular India, whose geostrategic location at the crossroads of the Indian Ocean would be able to facilitate energy trade and support America's global Navy—one that dominated Sea Lines of Communication and would be able to transport battle legions across seas—which was increasingly following Britain's legacy of global naval dominance; and that India's burgeoning democracy would adopt an open economy and serve as a model to counter communism in the third world.

The first few years of Indian independence were amicable enough. In India's domestic political milieu, countering communism was appealing to Nehru's Congress-led government, which in 1959 was challenged and later dismissed by the CPI in Kerala. Understanding the depth of poverty in India and the allure of communist parties in places like West Bengal and Kerala, the United States developed massive food and economic aid programs for India, to demonstrate that there was a viable alternative to communist economic management. This resulted in large American investments in Indian infrastructure, and US Ambassador to India John Kenneth Galbraith developed the largest ever US foreign aid program to any country.

On the strategic front, things were slightly different. US Presidents Eisenhower and Kennedy had hoped that India would counter communist

Chinese aggression on its northeastern flank. But Nehru's conciliatory attitude toward the Chinese in the 1950s demonstrated to Washington that India would not be up to the task. Meanwhile, India did not see eye-to-eye with America's strategic ambitions in the region. In line with its own "Monroe Doctrine," New Delhi was averse to see a large, extra-regional superpower have any influence in South Asia. It saw Washington, with its rising naval capacities, as a successor to British imperial power. Rebuffing the nascent "Washington Consensus," Nehru opted for nonalignment.

Meanwhile, Washington signed CENTO, as well as SEATO, both of which brought Islamabad and Washington together strategically, and even signed a Mutual Defense Assistance Agreement with Pakistan in 1954. Washington's intention in doing so was to keep the Soviet Union (separated from Pakistan by only the Wakhan Corridor of eastern Afghanistan) away from the Arabian Sea and to counter communism where it could. Pakistan, whose diplomats framed its own challenges vis-à-vis the Soviet Union, communism, and American strategy, was happy to sign on to the American military alliance. But to India, this was a direct affront. The terms of America's relationship with Pakistan guaranteed the latter arms, weaponry, and even political support, all of which, from Islamabad and New Delhi's perspectives, had India in the crosshairs.

But these disagreements did not yet mean decidedly negative Indo-American relations. The year 1962 was a watershed year for multiple countries: the US and Soviet Union were trapped in the Cuban Missile Crisis at almost exactly the same time that India and China began their October 1962 border war. The western world's preoccupation in Cuba meant that the United States would do little to intervene in India's favor in its war with Beijing (though it may have hoped to under different circumstances). Moreover, unaware of the emerging split between the Chinese and the Soviets, the United States feared that intervention against Beijing would raise the stakes in its confrontation with the Soviet Union. In the immediate aftermath of 1962, US-India cooperation against China—in the form of weapons sales and covert operations—increased. But this was to be short lived.

The paradox of high expectations of the relationship, coupled with divergent strategic goals—America's aim of having India do Washington's anticommunist bidding in South Asia, and India's hope that Washington would recognize and sanctify New Delhi's dominance of the subcontinent[1]—contributed to unease in the 1960s.

---

[1] A situation that was indicative of this dynamic was when India sought American help in restraining Pakistan's military activities in East Pakistan and "help India push the Pakistanis out" in 1971. In response, US National Security Adviser Henry Kissinger reportedly said, "Those sons-of-bitches (Indians), who never have lifted a finger for us, why should we get involved in the morass of East Pakistan?" See "Nixon's dislike of 'witch' Indira," BBC News, 29 June 2005.

But perhaps more consequential was the Cold War, and America's evolving views of China. By 1964, China had tested nuclear weapons and solidified its strategic partnership with Pakistan through the 1963 Sino-Pak Treaty of Friendship. Most significantly for the United States, signs of a fissure with the Soviet Union were emerging. Indeed, the Soviet Union had (diplomatically) supported India against China in the 1962 war, political tensions between the Communist Party of the Soviet Union (CPSU) and Communist Party of China (CCP) were making themselves more visible, and by 1968, Moscow had amassed troops on its border with China in preparation for a border conflict. The split was so deep that Moscow even sought American assistance in launching a joint attack on China's nuclear facilities.

The offer was laughed off in Washington, primarily because of the larger opportunity it seemed to present. Since the early 1950s, America's National Security Council had hoped for a split between the Soviet and Chinese communists that would divide the communist world and give Washington the upper hand.[2] With an increasingly powerful China facilitating a war against American troops trapped in a Vietnamese quagmire, a détente that could redirect Chinese energies against the Soviet Union seemed ideal.[3]

This Sino-American détente, initiated in the late 1960s and extending into the early 1970s, put a definitive damper on America's relations with India. The administration of US President Richard Nixon used Pakistan as an important intermediary to conduct secret diplomacy with Beijing. Once negotiations were underway, Washington would present its bona fides to China by supporting Pakistan, Beijing's ally, in its 1971 war with India, which had also warmed up to the Soviet Union (certainly vis-à-vis China) since 1962.[4] To make things worse, the US administration at the time was particularly antagonistic toward India, with President Nixon referring to Indian Prime Minister Indira Gandhi as an "old witch," and National Security Adviser Henry Kissinger, in the course of discussions on the 1971 war, referring to "the Indians" as "bastards anyway."[5] Sensing the rising hostility of a US-Sino-Pak entente, India made official its common cause with the Soviet Union with the August 1971 Indo-Soviet Treaty of Peace, Friendship and Cooperation.

---

[2] NSC 34/2, "US Policy toward China," 28 February 1949, in US Department of State, *Foreign Relations of the United States, 1949*, Vol. IX, pp. 491–5. On the State Department's "wedge strategy," see Chen Jian, *China's Road to the Korean War*, pp. 49–50, 114; and Gordon H. Chang, *Friends and Enemies: The United States, China, and the Soviet Union*. Stanford, CA: Stanford University Press, 1990, pp. 16–17.

[3] James Mann, *About Face: A History of America's Curious Relationship with China, from Nixon to Clinton*. New York: Vintage Press, 2000.

[4] James Mann, *About Face: A History of America's Curious Relationship with China, from Nixon to Clinton*. Random House, 1998, pp. 26–53.

[5] "Nixon's dislike of 'witch' Indira," BBC News, 29 June 2005.

In the December 1971 Indo-Pakistani war, not only did the United States support Islamabad politically, but even convinced Iran and Jordan, both US allies at the time, to send their F-86, F-104, and F-5 fighter jets to aid Pakistan.[6] More decisively, when Pakistan's defeat in the eastern theater (East Pakistan) seemed imminent due to India's naval blockade, the United States sent its warship, the USS *Enterprise*'s Task Group-74, from the South China Sea to the Bay of Bengal to ward off a complete Indian onslaught. The Soviet Union's nuclear submarines trailed the USS *Enterprise*, arguably deterring an all-out American intervention.

While India had little difficulty defeating Pakistani military forces, the political and strategic support that the superpowers had lent India and Pakistan during the war unequivocally put India on the side of the Soviet Union, explicitly ending its bout with "nonalignment." This was a direct affront to America's perceived interests. In the fear that India's alliance with Moscow would enable a Soviet naval capacity in the Indian Ocean, Washington hoped to deny India the ability to expand its maritime assets. It increased weapons shipments to Pakistan, in part to keep India tied up on its northwestern border.

From New Delhi's perspective, the experience of a *nuclearized* trilateral US-Sino-Pak alliance threatening Delhi impelled India, which had seriously considered its own nuclear deterrent in the wake of China's first tests, to move forward on the development of its own nuclear device. As India's chief defense strategist, K. Subrahmanyam, wrote, "had India possessed nuclear weapons, the *Enterprise* would not have steamed into the Bay of Bengal. . . in what appeared from New Delhi to constitute atomic gunboat diplomacy."[7] In May 1974, India carried out the "Smiling Buddha" Peaceful Nuclear Explosion at Pokhran, in Rajasthan's Thar Desert.

From an American perspective, this was a bit of a paradox: Jawaharlal Nehru's India was perhaps the most vociferous advocate of a nuclear-free world, and yet the same country was plowing ahead with its own atomic program. From India's perspective, however, there was no contradiction: Delhi sought a *world*—not certain countries—free of nuclear weapons; so long as powerful countries were maintaining and expanding their arsenals, there was no reason other countries should be restricted from doing the same.

Regardless, India's nuclear test ran in direct opposition to America's nonproliferation goals—namely, the Nuclear Nonproliferation Treaty (NPT) that the United States had pioneered in the late 1960s and that India would

---

[6] Lester H. Burne, *Chronological History of U.S. Foreign Relations: 1932–1988*. London: Routledge, 2003.

[7] K. Subrahmanyam, "India: Keeping the Option Open," in Robert M. Lawrence and Joel Larus (eds), *Nuclear Proliferation: Phase II*. Lawrence, KS: University of Kansas Press, 1974, p. 122.

come to call the institutionalization of "nuclear apartheid." By this New Delhi meant that the only nuclear weapons states permitted by the NPT were those that already had nuclear arsenals: the United States, Soviet Union, the United Kingdom, France, and the PRC, countries that were coterminous with the permanent five members of the UN Security Council. With America's nonproliferation agenda hampered, Washington imposed sanctions and tight controls on dual use nuclear equipment—officially through the establishment of the Nuclear Suppliers Group—to restrict the development and expansion of India's nuclear program.

Yet it wasn't only the United States that saw India's Smiling Buddha nuclear test as a grimace: the Pakistani nuclear scientist Abdul Qadeer Khan "believed that the Buddha had smiled in anticipation of Pakistan's death."[8] In tandem with Prime Minister Zulifiqar Ali Bhutto, A. Q. Khan took up the cause of a Pakistani nuclear weapon in earnest,[9] seeking to vindicate a now famous 1965 interview in which then-Foreign Minister Bhutto stated that "Pakistan will eat grass or leaves, even go hungry in order to develop a [nuclear] program of its own."[10] Bhutto initiated Project-706, with Kahuta Research Laboratory (also known as Khan Research Laboratories) as well as the Pakistan Atomic Energy Commission to begin efforts on a nuclear weapons program with assistance from China as well as clandestine theft from A. Q. Khan's employers in Europe. Islamabad's efforts to develop nuclear weapons were also opposed by Washington, which began to curtail economic military aid in the late 1970s in response.

But this decision was quickly reversed. With the loss of its Iranian ally (to the Islamic Revolution that toppled the US-allied Shah) as well as the Soviet Union's invasion of Afghanistan (which had until then remained a buffer between the Soviet- and American-backed worlds), Washington feared that the Soviet Union might soon link with Iran, overrun Pakistan, and perhaps even reach the Arabian Sea and join naval forces with its new Indian ally against the United States. To do what it could to prop its Indian Ocean flank and resist the Soviet Union, Washington not only ended its brief, post-1971 isolation of Islamabad, but also ratcheted up its military support.

---

[8] William Langewiesche, "The Wrath of Khan," *Atlantic Monthly*, November 2005.

[9] Pakistan's flirtation with nuclear weapons began as early as the late 1960s, when Islamabad followed New Delhi's lead in resisting the Nuclear Nonproliferation Treaty. Following the bifurcation of Pakistan in 1971, Bhutto organized a meeting of a number of Pakistani scientists at a meeting in Punjab, initiating a program for a Pakistani nuclear weapons program under the auspices of the Pakistan Atomic Energy Commission, headed by Munir Ahmed Khan. Steve Weissman and Herbert Krosney, *The Islamic Bomb: The Nuclear Threat to Israel and the Middle East*. New York: Times Books, 1981, Chapter 12.

[10] Quoted in "Bhutto was father of Pakistani Bomb," International Institute for Strategic Studies, 3 May 2007, available at http://www.iiss.org/whats-new/iiss-in-the-press/press-coverage-2007/may-2007/bhutto-was-father-of-pakistani-bomb/, accessed 12 January 2011.

The Afghan operation empowered the Pakistani military, and in particular its asymmetric capability. American—and through Washington, Israeli, and Chinese—weaponry and Saudi money and religious doctrine flowed into northern Pakistan and Afghanistan via the newly bolstered ISI of Pakistan. Washington's actions vis-à-vis the Afghanistan-Pakistan region came with great fallout for New Delhi. The new political-military arrangement that Washington had made with Islamabad required that the United States turn a blind eye to Pakistan's development of nuclear weapons capacity. Meanwhile, the same military infrastructure—weapons and training facilities in particular—that was used to train Afghan Mujahideen was also used to train Khalistani insurgents that returned to fight in India's Punjab. Washington's passive support for Pakistani General Zia ul-Haq's campaign of "Islamization" of Pakistan also contributed to the longer-term radicalization of much of Pakistani society, while setting the stage for Islamabad's military support for the insurgency against New Delhi in Indian-administered Kashmir in the 1990s. And perhaps most consequentially, America's support for Pakistan's military dictatorship had the effect of further embedding the military in the country's political fabric—and therefore its role in defining Pakistan as an anti-India entity.

Although New Delhi was not pleased with the Soviet Union's invasion of Afghanistan, it continued to depend on Moscow for strategic cooperation. Particularly after their 1971 Treaty, the Soviet Union became India's main supplier of weaponry and military equipment—including the subsequent upgrades and repairs to that equipment. This also came with strategic alignment against China—and thus against Pakistan and the United States. India and the United States ended the Cold War as adversaries in the great strategic competition of the twentieth century.

# China

To the north, mainland (Han) China and the Indian heartland had minimal contact for centuries. But this came to an end in 1949, when Chinese communist forces invaded the Tibetan plateau, bringing Han Chinese influence up to India's doorstep. Prime Minister Nehru initially tried to forge a positive relationship with the Chinese—a policy dubbed "Hindi-Chini Bhai-Bhai" (Indians and Chinese are brothers)—based on their shared postimperial economic, and presumably nonaligned status. This went so far that Nehru quickly made statements acknowledging the PRC's control over Tibet, even though the legitimacy of its acquisition was questionable, and remains disputed even today.

Tensions quickly arose, however, over Chairman Mao Tsetung and Prime Minister Nehru's perception of their counterpart's positions on Tibet. Despite Nehru's bonhomie toward China, he had hoped to see Tibet remain a neutral buffer between India and mainland (Han) China. To this end, he encouraged Mao to maintain Tibet's autonomy within the People's Republic, while encouraging the Tibetan government of the Dalai Lama to accept this autonomy, even over independence.

Mao, however, suspected that Nehru harbored dastardly plans for China's control of Tibet; he thought of Nehru as a "counter-revolutionary" seeking to reestablish Tibetan independence, or even promote Indian control of the Plateau. This reached a new threshold when, in the wake of a brutal crackdown on uprisings in Tibet in 1959, the Dalai Lama fled Lhasa through the Tawang pass, in India's Arunachal Pradesh (then called the "North Eastern Frontier Agency," NEFA), and was given asylum in India. Mao saw this granting of asylum as an Indian act of provocation.[11]

The boundary between the NEFA and Tibet was indicated by the McMahon Line, which was delineated between British India and Tibet in the Simla Accord of 1914. India considered this the de jure and de facto border between India and Tibet, and anything south of the line (including NEFA) to be Indian Territory. After the occupation of Tibet by Chinese communist forces, however, Beijing articulated its view that the Simla Accord and the McMahon Line that it established were illegitimate because the Accord had been brokered by a colonial power. Beijing argued that, in fact, NEFA lay in "Southern Tibet," and was thus a part of Tibet and China.

Through the late 1950s, there were a number of encroachments by Chinese troops across the McMahon Line, resulting in a few small-scale military standoffs between Indian and Chinese troops. In November 1961, in an effort to ensure against a larger scale Chinese invasion, Nehru adopted a "Forward Policy" along the McMahon Line. This involved setting up 60 small, unsupported military forces in the disputed territories—including 43 that were north of the McMahon Line—that would serve as an alarm or tripwire in case an intervention of larger forces was needed. Coming on the heels of Operation Vijaya in 1961, in which New Delhi successfully—and forcibly—annexed the Portuguese colony of Goa in western India, the Forward Policy was meant as a show of force to deter a war with China.

The policy was not successful. By October 1962, a full-fledged border war broke in both the eastern and western borders with China, in which a horribly

---

[11]John Garver, "China's Decision for War with India in 1962," in Robert S. Ross and Alastair Iain Johnston (eds), *New Approaches to the Study of Chinese Foreign Policy*. Stanford, CA: Stanford University Press, 2005.

unprepared India lost over 3,000 soldiers, most of whom had been trained and equipped to operate in the plains of Punjab rather than the cold mountains of the Himalayas. India officially lost Aksai Chin in Kashmir (though it had been occupied and administered by China long before the beginning of hostilities), and most importantly, lost face domestically and in the world, radically altering India's perceptions of China.[12]

The 1962 war made India tremendously fearful of Chinese intentions thereafter. Motivated by this post-1962 fear, India took the opportunity to enhance its military presence in the region, and raise its guard vis-à-vis China. In fact, in his analysis of the conflict, US Navy Lt. Cdr. James Barnard Calvin argued that India *benefited* from the 1962 War: the material losses were relatively minimal; though somewhat humiliated, the country was politically united; India received 32,000 square miles of disputed territory in the eastern sector (NEFA, later Arunachal Pradesh); India was awakened to the reality that it must accept external military aid; and India recognized the shortcomings of its army and worked to enhance its capacities, including doubling manpower over the next 2 years and resolving many of the earlier logistical problems it had faced.[13]

By 1964 the Chinese tested their first nuclear weapon at Lop Nur, Xinjiang Province, with the technical assistance it had received from the Soviet Union in the 1950s. Though the Chinese nuclear weapons program was largely a reaction to American threats to bomb China during the Korean War of the early 1950s,[14] New Delhi saw itself in the crosshairs of the new Chinese weapon, since it came in the wake of the 1962 Sino-India war (a situation not unlike that faced by Pakistan in 1974). India sought to develop its own means of deterring a Chinese attack and began work on its own nuclear program.

Relations between China and India essentially froze after 1962: diplomatic ties were cut off, trade was nonexistent, and even border skirmishes came to a near halt. In 1967, there was one more incident in which Indian and Chinese troops fired upon one another, at Chola by Nathu La pass, Sikkim, for whose defense India was responsible until its absorption as an Indian state. Until 1987, when the Indian Army initiated a major military buildup at the Sumdorong Chu Valley, very little passed along the border. But underneath this frozen relationship was a minor Cold War that manifested in three areas: proxy and asymmetric warfare, the nuclear realm, and strategic balancing.

---

[12] Neville Maxwell, *India's China War*. New York: Pantheon Books, 1971.

[13] James Barnard Calvin, "The China-India Border War (1962)," Marine Corps Command and Staff College, April 1984, available at http://www.globalsecurity.org/military/library/report/1984/CJB.htm

[14] John Wilson Lewis and Litai Xue, *China Builds the Bomb*. Stanford, CA: Stanford University Press, 1991, Chapter 2.

After the 1962 war, India enhanced its counter-Chinese cooperation with the United States in a few ways. The first was, of course, weapons procurement; the shamefully inadequate Indian forces had been held hostage to Nehru's policy of nonalignment and self-sufficiency during the 1962 war. Seeking to keep India's distance from the United States, Nehru had initially refrained from modernizing the Indian Army with the newest military technology. This changed both during, and especially after the Chinese war, when India made a number of purchases of western defense technology in order to bolster its northern defenses.

Second, India's R&AW, newly formed in 1968, and Intelligence Bureau (IB) stepped up cooperation with the US Central Intelligence Agency (CIA), which had been supporting anti-PRC Tibetan rebels since 1957.[15] It is unclear whether Nehru's government knew the extent of the CIA's initial involvement in Tibet, or whether he knowingly (and passively) chose to condone it. But despite Chairman Mao's claims, there was little to no direct Indian involvement with the CIA operation prior to the 1962 war, except that India refused to expel Tibetans that had been living in and operating from north Indian cities. Nehru did, however, restrict their activities in response to Chinese complaints.[16]

China used the opportunity to initiate long-term engagements with a number of insurgent groups within India. From at least the mid-1960s, the Chinese PLA trained Naga, Mizo, and Manipuri guerrillas from a variety of insurgencies in India's northeast, as well as India's LWE movements,[17] in large part to keep Indian armed forces concentrated in areas other than the northern border.

The nuclear balance was another reason for the mutual distrust.[18] By the early 1970s, China reportedly brought its first nuclear missiles, the CSS-1 medium-range ballistic missiles and CSS-2 intermediate range ballistic missiles, to Tsaidam Basin in Qinghai Province (then northern Amdo of central Tibet).[19] Both were capable of reaching sites in southern Siberia and Central

---

[15] Mikel Dunham, *Buddha's Warriors: The Story of the CIA-backed Tibetan Freedom Fighters, the Chinese Invasion, and the Ultimate Fall of Tibet.* New York: J. P. Tarcher, 2004; Kenneth Conboy and James Morrison, *The CIA's Secret War in Tibet.* Modern War Studies, Lawrence, KS: University Press of Kansas, 2002.

[16] See, for example, John Garver, "China's Decision for War with India in 1962," in Robert S. Ross and Alastair Iain Johnston (eds), *New Approaches to the Study of Chinese Foreign Policy.* Stanford, CA: Stanford University Press, 2005.

[17] "Left-wing Extremism" in the Indian context encompasses the Naxalites, the leftist political and violent movement that was launched against the landed elites of eastern India in the West Bengal town of Naxalbari in 1967, as well as the "Maoists" movements of eastern India.

[18] For an excellent historical overview of Indo-Chinese security perspectives, see Waheguru Pal Singh Sidhu and Jing-dong Yuan, *China and India: Cooperation or Conflict?.* New Delhi: India Research Press, 2003.

[19] John Ackerly, *Nuclear Tibet*, International Campaign for Tibet, June 1993.

Asia (then the Soviet Union), the South China Sea, and northern India.[20] While the number of missile bases in southern and western China *targeting* India remained under debate—it has been argued that most were aimed at the former Soviet Union and at US interests in the South China Sea, and would require remobilization in order to target them toward India—the very fact that they *could* reach India was enough to alarm Indian strategists, prompting an Indian nuclear buildup of its own.[21]

Meanwhile, in the wake of 1962, China strengthened its partnership with Pakistan. There were a number of reasons for this engagement. One was a result of the Sino-Soviet split, in which ideological and geopolitical tensions between the Soviet Union and PRC splintered the worldwide communist movement. In order to counter-contain the Soviet Union on its southern rim and restrict its access to the Arabian Sea, China sought to bolster Pakistan militarily, in a manner reminiscent of the initial British objective to develop Pakistan as a counterweight to Moscow.[22] A second reason for Chinese engagement with Pakistan was economic: China could make a great deal of money in weapons sales (from conventional weapons and later nuclear and missile technology) to Pakistan, and also, via their shared border region in northern Kashmir and Karakoram, gain access to the Arabian Sea for itself.

Finally, China's support for Pakistan was an effort to *counter* Indian influence in Asia and box New Delhi into the subcontinent. Nehru, through the nonaligned movement, had sought to establish India as the political leader of the third world of developing nations; given their postcolonial status, this included most of the countries of Asia that lay in China's East Asian sphere of influence. By militarily supporting Pakistan, India's geographically adjacent enemy, China could keep India occupied with a proxy Pakistani military threat and out of China's way. In 1963, China and Pakistan solidified their relationship with the Sino-Pak Treaty of Friendship, which granted China de facto control over the Shaksgam Valley in Kashmir. By 1986, China completed construction of the Karakoram Highway that connected Kashgar in Xinjiang Province with the Hunza Valley in Gilgit, northern Pakistan. In the 1965 and 1971 wars, China unequivocally stood with Pakistan and, though it fell short of militarily intervening in the 1971 conflict, continued to supply diplomatic cover as well

---

[20] R. R. Subramanian, "Missile Equation in South Asia," *The Pioneer*, 1 October 1997.

[21] S. B. Asthana, "The People's Liberation Army of China: A Critical Analysis." *Combat Journal*, 30, 2 (September 2001): 49.

[22] Indeed, when the USSR collapsed in the late 1980s and early 1990s, Sino-Pakistan relations did not necessarily *weaken*, but they did take on a different bent, having lost their anti-Soviet thrust. Thus China no longer unequivocally supported Pakistan's position vis-à-vis India. John Garver, "Sino-Indian Rapprochement and the Sino-Pakistan Entente." *Political Science Quarterly*, 111, 2 (Summer 1996): 323–47.

as weaponry. By the 1980s, China had transferred a large amount of nuclear and missile technology to Pakistan—from weapons grade uranium to weapons designs, and even an entire production plant of the M-11 (Dongfeng-11) missile, which was the basis of Pakistan's Shaheen series missiles.[23]

As an Indian cliché on Sino-Indian relations put it, though India and China began their modern histories with an attempt to forge a political bond, New Delhi would soon say "bye bye" to Indo-Chinese "bhai-bhai."

---

[23] Waheguru Pal Singh Sidhu and Jing-dong Yuan, *China and India: Cooperation or Conflict?* New Delhi: India Research Press, 2003, p. 53.

# 6

# Geographic Dislocation: The Fallout of Intraregional Conflict

Given the geographic basis of the subcontinent's original "strategic unity," environmental shifts play a central role in regional geopolitical dynamics. The year 2005 alone was a major watershed year for South Asia. In the beginning of the year, the region was still reeling from the tsunami that was initiated by an earthquake with its epicenter off the west coast of Sumatra, Indonesia. The tsunami killed over 220,000 people in South and Southeast Asia, with over 15,000 in India alone.[1]

Toward the end of the year, a 7.5-magnitude earthquake, with its epicenter in Muzaffarabad, Kashmir, killed more than 80,000 people in the region. The fallout also enabled nefarious actors like the Jamaat-ud-dawa, the "charity" wing of the militant group LeT, to raise enough funds to become financially independent of the Pakistani state.[2] The annual visitations of floods, extreme heat, droughts, and storms have caused death, destruction, and disease and generally brought life to a standstill in one region or the other of the subcontinent. Joint water management along the shared river basins—the Indus in the case of India and Pakistan, Ganges in the case of Nepal, India, and Bangladesh, and the Brahmaputra involving China, India, and Bangladesh—have been central elements of bilateral relations. Even a seemingly basic environmental issue like access to clean, potable water has been a daily struggle for many in the region.

---

[1]National Earthquake Information Center, "Magnitude 9.0 – Off the West Coast of Northern Sumatra: 2004 December 26th," US Geological Survey, National Earthquake Information Center, US Geological Survey, 26 December 2004, available at http://earthquake.usgs.gov/earthquakes/eqinthenews/2004/us2004slav/#summary/

[2]Stephen Tankel, "Lashkar-e-Taiba: From 9/11 to Mumbai," *International Centre for the Study of Radicalisation and Political Violence*, April/May 2009.

# Vulnerabilities[3]

But environmental issues like these take on another dimension with *the global climate crisis.* With over 1.5 billion people, South Asia has the greatest population in the tropical, equatorial region in which it is located—far more than West Asia's 211 million, Southeast Asia's 554 million, or even all of Africa's 922 million.[4] India is also home to a third of the world's poor, the population that lives on less than one dollar a day, which constitutes over 40 percent of India's population.[5] The poor are the most vulnerable to the effects of climate change, having the least recourse from the status quo and minimal physical protection from environmental shifts. Most of India's poor live in rural areas that are directly dependent on climate-sensitive resources such as agriculture, forests, and river water. India's diversity of topography—mountains, rivers, forests, deserts, and coastlines—means that climate change would affect different regions in different ways, and single across-the-board responses may not work.

The economic costs of climate change for India will be tremendous. Agriculture, which contributes nearly 30 percent of India's GDP,[6] is dependent on seasonal rains, a fertile and nonsaline coastline, and river-based irrigation—agricultural inputs that could be harmed by rising heat, rising sea levels, or river depletion, respectively. The Indian Agriculture Research Institute estimates that with every one degree Celsius rise in global temperature, India will lose 4–5 million tons in wheat production.[7] "Even a 100 cm sea level rise can lead to coastal welfare loss of US$ 1,259 million."[8] Add to this migration, infrastructure strain, and damage from ecological disasters, and the costs

---

[3] The following section samples from a paper published as Neil Padukone, "Climate Change in India: Forgotten Threats, Forgotten Opportunities." *Economic and Political Weekly,* 45, 22 (29 May 2010): 47–54.

[4] United Nations, "World Population Prospects: The 2008 Revision", Population Division of the Department of Economic and Social Affairs of the United Nations Secretariat, 2009, available at http://esa.un.org/unpp

[5] Shaohua Chen and Martin Ravallion, "*The Developing World is Poorer than We Thought, But No Less Successful in the Fight Against Poverty,*" Development Research Group (DECRG), World Bank, World Bank Policy Research Working Paper No. 4703, 2008.

[6] The Energy and Resources Institute, TERI Energy Data Directory and Yearbook 2001/2002, New Delhi, 2002.

[7] Ashok Sharma, "Climate Change to Impact Indian Agriculture: IARI," *Financial Express,* 28 January 2008.

[8] At an exchange rate of 48 rupees to the dollar, this is equal to 6043.2 crore rupees. Joyashree Roy, Anupa Ghosh, and Gopa Baruah, "The Economics of Climate Change: A Review of Studies in the Context of South Asia with a Special Focus on India," Report Submitted to The Stern Review on the Economics of Climate Change, 2007, available at http://www.hm-treasury.gov.uk./media/5/0/roy.pdf

increase. Currently, India spends over 2.6 percent of its GDP on adapting to environmental events like flooding.[9]

Meanwhile, some of the more consequential effects of climate change will harm human security profoundly. Anomalous weather patterns such as floods, droughts, rising temperatures and heat waves, and river recession are among the environmental scenarios that *already* harm large numbers of Indians.[10] To put this in perspective, India's Ministry of Home Affairs' (MHA) disaster management unit reported a countrywide death toll of 2,404 just from flooding in 2008 alone.[11] Tack on the deaths from droughts and heat waves, their longer-term effects—displacement, disease,[12] human trafficking,[13] and resource-based conflict—and their aggravation due to climate change, and the situation is even more forbidding.

Climate change will cause or amplify events that hasten the reduction of resources. Competition over these diminishing resources would ensue in the form of political or even violent conflict. Resource-based conflicts have rarely been overt and are thus difficult to isolate. Instead they take on veneers that appear more politically palatable. Conflicts over resources like water are often cloaked in the guise of identity or ideology. Environmental, resource and climate issues serve as multipliers, if not igniters, of political conflict.

As Vandana Shiva highlights in *The Violence of the Green Revolution*, insufficient distribution of water and agricultural profit contributed to the grievances that fuelled the Punjab insurgency of the 1980s. While producing more grain and being more weather resilient, the genetically modified seeds

---

[9]Sunjoy Joshi, "Remarks at Inaugural Session, Global Summit on Sustainable Development and Climate Change," Conference organized by the Observer Research Foundation and The Rosa Luxemburg Stiftung, 24 September, 2009.

[10]Jyoti Parikh, "Climate Impact, Risk, Vulnerability and Adaptation," remarks at *The Adaptive Response to Climate Change*, Global Summit on Sustainable Development and Climate Change, Conference organized by the Observer Research Foundation and The Rose-Luxemburg Stiftung, 24 September 2009, available at http://www.orfonline.org/climate-change/J-Parikh.ppt

[11]Harmeet Shah Singh, "Flooding deaths now 2,400 in monsoon-hit India," *CNN*, 24 September 2008.

[12]Temperature-related fatalities related to heat waves, water-borne diseases brought about by floods (i.e. diarrhea, cholera, and biological contaminants), malnutrition and starvation from crop failure, and safety and public health infrastructure damaged by environmental disasters are all potential scenarios induced by climate change. (Joyashree Roy, Anupama Ghosh, A. Majumdar, P. Roy, A. P. Mitra, and C. Sharma, "Socio-Economic and Physical Perspectives of Water-Related Vulnerability to Climate Change: Results of Field Study in India." *Science and Culture*, Special Issue, 71, 7–8 (2005): 239–59; S. Bhattacharya, C. Sharma, R. C. Dhiman, and A. P. Mitra, "Climate Change and Malaria in India." *Current Science*, 90, 3 (2006): 369–75).

[13]"The Kosi floods [of 2008] opened up a huge "market" of children—close to three lakh—to the merchants of misery who have been buying them for sums as low as Rs. 500 from their vulnerable families." (Amitabh Srivastava, "Children for Sale," *India Today*, 20 March 2009.

introduced by the 1960s Green Revolution consumed far more water than did natural seeds, requiring greater irrigation, absorption of aquifers, and river diversion for their upkeep. Moreover, the hyper-efficiency of the seeds drastically and abruptly changed the economy of Punjab: the farmers who relied on agriculture for their employment and income were put out of work with nothing to fill the void. Tacked onto political pressures associated with center-state relations and external material support, the state was aflame with violence within years.[14]

Meanwhile, water is at the core of the Kashmir conflict between India and Pakistan. The Chenab, Sutlej, and Jhelum tributaries of the Indus River System flow from the mountains of the Himalayas, through Kashmir, and continue on to the Punjab provinces of both India and Pakistan. In Pakistan, what is left of the Punjabi river water flows on to Sindh, which has become dependent on this flow as groundwater aquifers have diminished in recent decades.[15]

Water sharing between Pakistani Punjab and Sindh has caused inter-province tension that is deflected onto the source of these rivers, namely Kashmir.[16] Behind closed doors, many in the Pakistani government confess that the struggle over Kashmir is driven by concerns over water more than anything else. Despite the resource-based impetus for conflict over Kashmir, it has become drenched in issues of politics and identity. As the Strategic Foresight Group has written, "It is more convenient to support the Kashmiris for their cause than openly admit . . . that Kashmiri youth are being sacrificed to safeguard Pakistan's lifeline."[17]

These types of issues could only deteriorate in the wake of some anticipated climate change scenarios. To India's east, a change in climate would raise both the temperature of the oceans and the amount of moisture that condenses in the atmosphere, increasing the magnitude and frequency of the typhoons, tropical cyclones and tidal bores to which Bangladesh seems prone. Meanwhile, rising sea levels in Bangladesh will physically reduce the amount of land in the country while salinating agricultural land.

The number of environmental refugees that would be forced—by concerns over food, land, employment, and meteorological disasters—to move further

---

[14]Vandana Shiva, *The Violence of the Green Revolution: Ecological Degradation and Political Conflict in Punjab.* London: Zed Press, 2002.

[15]Abdul Rehman, "Waterlogging and Salinity Management in the Sindh Province," Pakistan National Program, International Irrigation Management Institute, December 1998.

[16]Jack Kalpakian, *Identity, Conflict and Cooperation in International River Systems.* London: Ashgate Publishing, 2004.

[17]Sundeep Waslekar, "Final Settlement: Restructuring India-Pakistan Relations," *Strategic Foresight Group,* 2005.

inland and into India would increase dramatically. Even with the relatively few Bangladeshis who have entered India so far (compared with prospective numbers), conflicts have arisen in India; the mere presence of Bangladeshis in India has become an explosive political issue,[18] while receding insurgencies in India's northeast have resurged in response to migration from the Ganges delta state.[19]

On a larger scale, glaciers in the Tibetan Plateau—which extends as far south as Nepal, Northern India and Northern Pakistan—source most of the rivers in Asia. These include the Indus, Ganges, and Brahmaputra river systems, which are the lifelines of the subcontinent, providing drinking water, irrigation, transportation, electricity, and livelihoods to most of the 1.5 billion people of South Asia.

Global temperatures are anticipated to rise by 2–5 degrees Celsius over the next half century. The Tibetan Plateau, long seen as a barometer of global climate conditions, is no exception. Zheng Guoguang of the China Meteorological Administration (CMA) says that "in Tibet, the [temperature has risen] an average 0.32 degrees Celsius every decade since . . . 1961," compared with the national Chinese average of 0.05–0.08 degrees Celsius rise every 10 years.[20] Even if current warming trends remain constant, the Plateau's glaciers would be reduced by a third in 2050 and by half in 2090, according to a survey conducted by the Remote Sensing Department of the China Aero Geophysical Survey.[21] As these glaciers melt, the rivers they source will experience massive flooding in the short-term and recede in the longer-term.[22]

In Nepal, as the country aims to generate hydroelectricity and irrigation projects, management of the Koshi, Gandaki and Karnali river systems and communication with India about their conditions will become a central issue;

---

[18]Ashok Swain, "Displacing the Conflict: Environmental Destruction in Bangladesh and Ethnic Conflict in India." *Journal of Peace Research*, 33, 2 (May 1996): 189–204.

[19]Mirza Zulfiqur Rahman, "Illegal Bangladeshi Migrants: Agitation and Turmoil in Assam," Institute of Peace and Conflict Studies Analysis, #2652, 19 August 2009; Anand Kumar, "Changing Nature of Insurgency in Northeast and Role of Bangladesh," Paper presented at IDSA Weekly Fellows' Seminar Series, 24 July 2009.

[20]Compare these figures with the global average of 0.2 degrees Celsius increase in temperature per decade. Xinhua News, "Met Chief: Tibet Challenged by Global Warming," Xinhua News Agency, 6 May 2009.

[21]"Global Warming Threatens 'World Barometer'," *China Daily*, 30 December 2006.

[22]These estimates by Chinese government agencies are, in fact, conservative in their discussion of Tibetan glacier retreat. Other sources, such as the Intergovernmental Panel on Climate Change in its "fourth assessment" report in 2007, argued that the glaciers might recede as early as 2035. Given the controversy that emerged in the wake of this claim, the author has used the more conservative—but nonetheless alarming—Chinese statistics.

coordination with Nepal, for example, was vital in the Indian response to the north Indian floods of 2008. To the northeast, the Yarlung Tsangpo (Brahmaputra) River makes its way from southern Tibet, southward into Arunachal Pradesh and Assam, and finally ends in Bangladesh, where it merges with the Ganges. Sudden flooding or drought could complicate Indo-Nepali relations as well as the already tense political situations in the two Indian states, while causing domestic disturbances in the disaster-torn Bangladesh that would cascade into India. Meanwhile, although the Indus Water Treaty between India and Pakistan has kept a relative peace over Kashmiri waters since 1960, a large shock to the Indus River may change the course of political events in India's northwest.

By virtue of demographics, topography, and geopolitics, South Asia is ground zero for environmental crisis. Cross-capital joint water management projects would enable each country to manage their own resource allotment more efficiently—including manage floods, reduce waste, and store monsoon water—as well as share in the hydroelectric, agricultural, and the physical potential of their neighbors' water resources. Yet efforts of this sort remain unimplemented due to a seemingly insurmountable amount of political distrust between the capitals of the region.

# "South Asian" Disunity

This distrust even made its mark on the very words that are used to describe the region. For generations, the geographic region abutting the southern flank of the Eurasian plate was called the "subcontinent." Any unity that could be ascribed to this entity—be it cultural, geographic, historic, or political—became associated with the "subcontinent." To distinguish this subcontinent from the European, West Asian subcontinents, the area south of the Himalayan Mountains was referred to as the "*Indian* Subcontinent." In this context, the term "India" referred not purely to the Republic of India, the largest nation-state to emerge from the British Raj in 1947, but to the geographic and cultural region abutting the Indus or Sindhu River that lies in present day Pakistan.

When India became a separate nation-state, distinct from the other nation-states of the subcontinent—Pakistan, Bangladesh, Sri Lanka, Nepal, Bhutan (and Burma)—it was argued that this nomenclature was no longer valid. The subtext of this word, its critics held, was that the whole geographic mass was "Indian," and therefore belonging to the Republic of "India" and New Delhi. The Pakistani Foreign Office released an official statement arguing that, as India is only one of the countries of South Asia, the term "Indian Subcontinent" is entirely inappropriate as a description for the whole region. Its use betrays India's long-cherished dream of exercising hegemony in the region, a dream that India has failed to realize and it will never succeed in achieving. The Government of Pakistan therefore hopes that the use of the term "Indian Subcontinent" to refer to South Asia will be avoided.[23]

Thus "South Asia" became a more neutral, politically correct term to refer to the region, leaving behind the historical baggage—and cultural, geographic, and economic contiguity from which it extended—of the "Indian Subcontinent."[24]

The term received official sanction in the late 1970s, when President Ziaur Rahman of Bangladesh and King Birendra Bir Bikram Shah of Nepal conceived of a multilateral organization that would work toward the resolution of intraregional problems. The South Asian Association for Regional Cooperation (SAARC) came out with dialogues to act on these goals. SAARC would have as its aims intraregional cooperation on economic development, political trust, investment, and regional security issues. The SAARC declaration placed mutual respect for the sovereignty and territorial integrity, as well as noninterference in the internal matters of all the member states as key principles. Annual meetings between the regions' heads of state were to take place, with foreign secretaries meeting biannually.[25]

One of the key aims of SAARC was to economically reintegrate the region through increasingly free customs and tariff regimes within the subcontinent, toward the goal of a South Asia Free Trade Agreement, which was signed in 2004 and brought into force 2 years later. It was agreed that SAARC would keep bilateral issues such as the Kashmir dispute off the table and only discuss issues of multilateral concern without being implicated by bilateral issues.

Yet these lofty goals have faced major challenges in implementation. T. V. Paul writes that state-to-state cooperation has failed, while human and regional insecurity have prevailed in South Asia owing to two key factors. The first is the presence of *weak states*. The weakness of the states is owed partly to how recently the nation-state paradigm was brought (or imposed) upon the land in each country by their respective capitals. This relatively new relationship between certain geographies and people to each capital makes it difficult for capitals to "provide collective goods such as security, order, and welfare to its citizens in a . . . legitimate manner untrammeled by internal or external actors,"

---

[23]Quoted in Adrian Rehmat, "Subcontinental Semantic," *Himal Southasian*, August 2000.
[24]See, for example, Sugata Bose and Ayesha Jalal, *Modern South Asia: History, Culture, Political Economy*. London: Routledge, 2004, p. 3.
[25]"Charter of the South Asian Association for Regional Cooperation," available at http://www.saarc-sec.org/SAARC-Charter/5/

the key hallmarks of effective statehood.[26] Internal security challenges, such as secessionist movements, are often dealt with ineffectively while being displaced onto neighboring states so that national capitals can strengthen their domestic positions. In other cases, internal security challenges are manipulated by external greater powers—India and Pakistan, as well as China and the United States in the case of the small countries of South Asia.

The second major impediment, according to Paul, is the existence of *weak cooperative interstate norms*. The countries of South Asia are "hyper-sensitive on" the issue of their own "sovereignty, but are unwilling to fully accept the sovereignty norm vis-à-vis their neighbors."[27] This is perhaps the epitome of India's Monroe Doctrine as applied to the subcontinent. Regional cooperation would necessitate a degree of "bandwagoning" or the surrender of some autonomy to a supranational institution, SAARC, for the sake of mutually beneficial economic or strategic goals that would be more palatable to people adjacent to the borders. But this is autonomy, or sovereignty, on which none of the capitals of South Asia has been willing to compromise, in light of the otherwise tense political distrust of the region, much of which is based on India's perceived hegemony.

From a diplomatic angle, SAARC was unacceptable to New Delhi for a number of reasons. First, it felt that the notion of bilateral issues being separate from regional ones was partly a hollow one. The rise of SAARC as a means of managing challenges in the subcontinent was largely a method of multilateralizing what were fundamentally, from India's perspective, bilateral issues. Much as Nepal had sought to offset India's influence with its conversion into a "Zone of Peace" with China as another alternative, it was now seeking to offset Indian influence (or hegemony) in conjunction with a coalition of the smaller countries of South Asia. And throughout its history, India has long preferred bilateral dealings in accomplishing policy-oriented goals rather than publicly engaging in multilateral forums in which it would have to publicize this sovereignty paradox. With SAARC, this tendency was even more pronounced, as New Delhi felt SAARC was a forum with which the smaller nations of South Asia could band together to oppose India.

India's advantage in the subcontinent, the geography of which tends toward strategic unity and economic integration, eroded in the immediate wake of partition. Nearly all of India's neighbors saw New Delhi, driven by its Monroe

---

[26]T. V. Paul, "State Capacity and South Asia's Perennial Insecurity Problems," in T. V. Paul (ed.), *South Asia's Weak States:* Understanding the Regional Insecurity Predicament. Stanford, CA: Stanford University Press, 2010, p. 6.
[27]Ibid., p. 118.

Doctrine to unite and dominate South Asia, as a hegemon whose will was to be resisted. This international skepticism has also translated into rallying cries in the domestic politics of each country: As C. Raja Mohan writes, "huge anti-India constituencies have formed in all of India's neighboring countries," including the Bangladesh Nationalist Party, the Maoist Parties of Nepal, and the Pakistani Military and Islamist militants. "The leaders of these nations have not found it easy to resist the temptation of playing to the galleries by 'standing up' against India. Enlightened self-interest," in the form of economic and strategic cooperation with New Delhi, "has often become the casualty in the charged anti-India politics of [the] neighborhood."[28] Rather than cooperating with India, with whom most of the South Asian countries share topographic features such as river and monsoon systems and the Gangetic plain, the other SAARC countries have sought to spurn New Delhi by inviting Chinese and American assistance in projects like road, dam, and water basin construction—to say nothing of military development for deployment within the region.

The geographic unity of the subcontinent gave way to political disunity, and as a result, strategic and economic unity was sacrificed. Despite the South Asian Free Trade Agreement (SAFTA) of 2004, intraregional trade remains below 6 percent of South Asia's total trade with the world. And the subcontinent's intraregional trade as a percentage of its total trade volume has barely changed from around 2 percent in 1980 to 3 percent in 2004.[29]

Meanwhile, due to insecurity complexes fed by New Delhi's Monroe Doctrine, munitions, militants, and nuclear weapons have abounded in the subcontinent, leading US President Bill Clinton to refer to South Asia as "the world's most dangerous place." With infrastructural links and political unity severed at the time of partition, the subcontinent's full economic and strategic potential appeared consigned to the annals of history.

---

[28]C. Raja Mohan, "Beyond India's Monroe Doctrine," *The Hindu*, 2 January 2003.
[29]R. Newfarmer and M. D. Pierola, "SAFTA: Promise and Pitfalls of Preferential Trade Agreements," *Mimeo*, Washington, D.C.: World Bank, 2006; John S. Wilson and Tsunehiro Otsuki, "Cutting Trade Costs and Improved Business Facilitation in South Asia," in Sadiq Ahmed and Ejaz Ghani (eds), *South Asia Growth and Regional Integration*. New Delhi: Macmillan India Ltd. 2007.

# PART THREE

# Looking Beyond

# 7

# Economic Shift

## Open Markets

The early 1990s brought about major shifts in India's strategic and economic environments. The first was the 1991 collapse of the Soviet Union, India's principle political ally, arms supplier, and trading partner. The second was a major currency crisis caused by an overvalued rupee and fiscal deficits. India had borrowed a great deal of capital, much of it from the Soviet Union, to finance its defense acquisition and other economic programs,[1] while a shock to India's oil supply caused by the 1991 Gulf War catalyzed India's balance-of-payments crisis.[2]

In response to the crisis, India looked to the International Monetary Fund (IMF) for a $1.8 billion loan, the terms of which required that India undertake a program of structural adjustment and liberalization of its economy.[3] Accepting the terms, India initiated a major economic liberalization program in which its previously closed economy was opened up to foreign investment, breaking down one of the pillars of India's traditional autonomy strategy. Likewise, the "License Raj" system that encouraged heavy domestic regulation was slowly dismantled, enhancing the development of the private sector. To address the budget deficit, defense spending was also reduced. From 3.6 percent of GDP in 1987, defense spending came down to 2.1 percent in the late 1990s, the lowest figure in nearly four decades.[4]

---

[1]Anita Inder Singh, "A New Indo-Russian Connection." *International Affairs*, 71, 1 (January 1995): 70.
[2]Valerie Cerra and Sweta Chaman Saxena, "What Caused the 1991 Currency Crisis in India?," IMF Staff Papers, 49, 3 (2002), available at http://www.imf.org/External/Pubs/FT/staffp/2002/03/pdf/cerra.pdf
[3]Rakesh Mohan, "Economic Reforms in India: Where are We and Where do we go?," Lecture at a Public Seminar organized by the Institute of South Asia Studies, Singapore, 10 November 2006.
[4]Jasjit Singh, *India's Defense Spending: Assessing Future Needs.* New Delhi: IDSA and Knowledge World, 2001.

The opening of India's economy came with a far more unexpected turn of events. Before the economic liberalization program, India's economic growth rate averaged 3.5 percent from the 1950s to 1980s, a number derided as a sluggish "Hindu rate of growth."[5] By the early 2000s, that number reached 7 percent, and by the middle of the decade, the number had gone up to nearly 9 percent.[6] While these figures only tell half of the story, the qualitative changes in India's economic environment were tremendous: there was a far greater degree of economic and financial interdependence with the rest of the world; both public and private sector Indian firms started to move beyond the borders of India and South Asia and into economic agreements with countries around the world in a way that had never been seen in Indian history; and market access became India's central need.

## Strategic Interdependence

This opening of markets brought with it a change to India's economic and strategic worldview. No longer would it be New Delhi's objective to keep India—or the subcontinent as a whole—economically self-sufficient, isolated, or insulated from the rest of the world. Instead, the region would benefit from cross-national trade, open borders, foreign direct investment (FDI), and even local comparative advantages in the production of goods rather than centralized economic management.

Even local economic autonomy was encouraged. Regional economic hubs, from cities such as Mumbai, Hyderabad, and Bangalore, to resource-based economies in mineral-rich areas such as Jharkhand and Chhattisgarh—two states that were carved out of Bihar and Madhya Pradesh, respectively, in 1999 in order to ensure more local administration of affairs—and special economic zones that encouraged more liberalized economic policies and investment practices throughout the country, began to sprout.

And when India opened up its markets to foreign investments, it was in a sense opening its economy up to foreign *interventions* in the country. European, American, East and Southeast Asian firms began investing in a multitude of different sectors of India. A deregulated capital market has been

---

[5]Arvind Virmani, "India's economic growth: From socialist rate of growth to Bharatiya rate of growth," Working paper 112, Indian Council for Research on International Economic Relations, February 2004.

[6]These figures, for 1997 and 2006, respectively, are from the CIA World Factbook, "India," 2010, available at https://www.cia.gov/library/publications/the-world-factbook/geos/in.html, accessed 23 February 2010.

bullish for years, leading to higher Foreign Institutional Investor (FII) inflows and FDI—a fivefold increase from 7.2 percent of GDP in 1990/91 to 36.6 percent in 2007/08 in a variety of sectors. Outflows and Indian investments abroad have been equally noteworthy, reaching 10 percent of GDP in 2009.[7] The liberalization of the capital markets alone—not to mention a number of other sectors in need of investment—is not yet complete, leading analysts to anticipate a sustained period of foreign investment and growth for India,[8] with particularly bullish analysts conjecturing that India will be the world's second or third largest economy by 2050.[9]

## Energy Dependence

For decades, India was largely energy independent, producing most of the energy that it consumed domestically, from its own coal reserves in the eastern and northeastern sections of the country, uranium deposits for India's nuclear power plants, and a few oil and natural gas reserves off the western coast of Maharashtra and Gujarat, in Assam, and the Bay of Bengal.

With the massive amount of construction, infrastructure development, consumption, and other economic growth that emerged, India's energy consumption has increased tremendously. Since the economic development trajectory that was established in 1990, India's energy consumption has grown from less than 7.8 quadrillion British Thermal Units (Btu) to over three times that number to 20 quadrillion Btu in 2008,[10] making India the world's fourth largest consumer of energy after the United States, China, and Japan.

As domestic supplies diminish, or are otherwise insufficient to serve India's growing energy needs, India has started to look abroad to ensure its energy security. In fact, as early as 1992, what was once a central energy ministry was broken down into four separate ministries—Coal; Petroleum and Natural Gas; Nonconventional Energy Sources; and Power. To manage this expansion, the Ministry of External Affairs has created an Energy Security Unit with enhanced coordination with the energy ministries and companies

---

[7]Rakesh Mohan, "Capital flows to India," in Bank for International Settlements (ed.), *Financial Globalization and Emerging Market Capital Flows*, 44 (2008): 235–63.

[8]Kenneth M. Kletzer, "Liberalizing Capital Flows in India: Financial Repression, Macroeconomic Policy, and Gradual Reforms," SCCIE Working Paper No. 04-16, Santa Cruz Center for International Economics, 2004.

[9]Goldman Sachs, "Dreaming with BRICs: The Path to 2050," *Global Economics Paper*, No. 99, 2003.

[10]"India: Country Analysis Brief," Energy Information Administration, US Department of Energy, August 2010.

abroad.[11] Meanwhile, the Ministry of Petroleum and Natural Gas (MPNG) has established an International Cooperation division to "devise an international strategy, gather information on 'countries of relevance,' organize India's participation in bilateral and multilateral forums, and liaise with the MEA and Indian embassies and high commission abroad."[12]

---

[11]Indian Ministry of External Affairs (MEA), *Annual Report 2007–08*. New Delhi: Policy Planning and Research Division, 2008, p. xiii.
[12]Tanvi Madan, "India's International Quest for Oil and Natural Gas: Fueling Foreign Policy?" *India Review,* 9, 1 (January–March 2010): 2–37; Ministry of Petroleum and Natural Gas, "International Cooperation Activities," available at http://petroleum.nic.in/ICWorkAllocation.htm

# 8

# Balancing China

With the end of the Cold War, meanwhile, Sino-Indian relations took a different turn. Diplomatic ties were restored in the late 1980s, with Rajiv Gandhi's historic visit to Beijing, only the second by an Indian official in over two decades. Trade increased tremendously, such that in 2010, China was India's largest trading partner. And in the 1990s, a number of military confidence-building measures were established: the Agreement on the Maintenance of Peace and Tranquility and the Agreement on Confidence-Building Measures, which spelled out a number limitations on the use of force, as well as information exchange mechanisms.[1] Even China's previously unequivocal support for Pakistan on the question of Kashmir became muted: whereas in the past, China always came out on the side of Pakistan in any military confrontations; in the 1999 Kargil War, China expressed its desire for a peaceful resolution to the conflict. Not to mention, both India and China had long since abandoned their support for the insurgencies within the other country.

With these developments in mind, two new Indian narratives regarding China emerged, countering the conventional security narrative that had dominated since 1962. The first was liberal institutionalism: that increased trade and economic integration would raise the costs of conflict and make military confrontation less likely. The old joke was extended, from Hindi-Chini "Bhai-Bhai," and then Hindi-Chini "bye-bye," bilateral relations were now defined by Hindi-Chini "buy buy."[2] The second narrative was that China and

---

[1]Waheguru Pal Singh Sidhu and Jing-dong Yuan, *China and India: Cooperation or Conflict?* New Delhi: India Research Press, 2003, Chapter 4.

[2]C. V. Ranganathan, "India-China Relations: Retrospect and Prospects," in Lalit Mansingh et al. (eds), *Indian Foreign Policy: Agenda for the 21st Century*. New Delhi: Foreign Service Institute and Konark Press, 1998; G. P. Deshpande and Alka Acharya (eds), *Crossing a Bridge of Dreams: 50 years of India-China*. New Delhi: Tulika Publishers, 2001.

India will go so far as to *cooperate* in the military-strategic realm toward their shared aim of a multi-polar world.[3]

At the same time, the original discourse of competitive relations has been bolstered further: in 1998, Indian leaders cited Beijing as the primary reason for its Pokhran II nuclear tests,[4] with Minister of Defense George Fernandes later stating that "China is potential threat number one."[5] Proponents of the "China Threat Theory" site a number of factors: while the CBMs provide a framework to ease military tensions, many of them remain unimplemented.[6] Border tensions remain untouched in the diplomatic realm and, in fact, have come to the forefront of bilateral relations once again. As for the argument of liberal institutionalism, rather than diminishing tensions, the enhanced trade ties may *increase* India's vulnerabilities. While bilateral trade was 40 billion USD per annum in 2009, and reached 60 billion USD in 2010, India has a nearly 20 billion USD trade *deficit* with China: in 2009, Indian exports to China were about 11 billion USD, while China's exports to India were greater than 27 billion USD, compounding the power dynamic.[7] Though a handful of joint military exercises have been carried out, they do not speak to any broader military-strategic cooperation against the United States. But perhaps most central to this narrative are two key developments in China: the expansion and strategy of the Chinese military.

# Chinese Geopolitics and Strategy

China's military strategy emanates from the country's main geopolitical imperatives. The 15-inch isohyet is a contour line that runs from Manchuria in the north to Qinghai Province, nearly parallel to the Great Wall of China. The area east of this line receives more than 15 inches of rainfall per year, while the area to the west receives less than that. As a result of the fertility of the

---

[3]T. K. Arun, "India, China should team up for 21st century," *Economic Times*, 20 December 2009; Aqueil Ahmad, "India and China: Conflict, Competition, and Cooperation in the Age of Globalization," *STWR*, 25 February 2008; K. Subrahmanyam, "China's real competition is within, and not outside," *Rediff News*, 12 April 2010.

[4]Jaswant Singh, "Against Nuclear Apartheid," *Foreign Affairs*, September/October 1998.

[5]"China is threat no. 1, says Fernandes," *Hindustan Times*, 3 May 1998; Praveen Swami, "A hawkish line on China." *Frontline*, 15, 11 (23 May–5 June 1998).

[6]Jozef Goldblat, "Confidence-Building Measures in Asia," in Manas Chatterji (ed.), *Eurasia: Contributions to Conflict Management, Peace Economics, and Development, Volume 1*. Emerald Group Publishing Limited, 2005, pp. 133–9.

[7]Amiti Sen, "Growing Trade Deficit: India keeping close watch on China, mulls steps," *Economic Times*, February 2010.

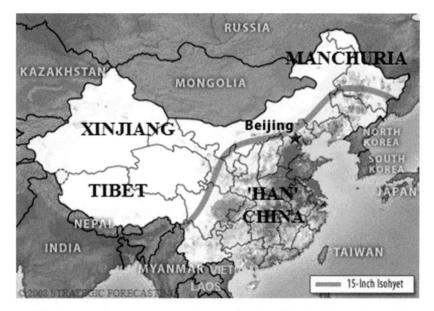

**FIGURE 8.1** *Population density in the People's Republic of China, adapted from George Friedman, "The Geopolitics of China: A Great Power Enclosed," stratfor, June 15th, 2008.*

eastern segment, a majority of the PRC's population—nearly all of the ethnic "Han"—reside east of this line, forming the Chinese "heartland".[8]

This "heartland" is flanked by mountainous regions to its west (Tibet), northwest (East Turkestan or Xinjiang Province), and northeast (Manchuria), and an arid desert to its north (Inner Mongolia), all of which lie within the political bounds of today's People's Republic. Throughout history, Han China suffered repeated land invasions from these outer regions—from the Qin of the north, repeated onslaughts by the Mongols and Turks from the north and west, and the Japanese through Manchuria.

To the south of "Han China", dense, largely impassible forests shape the borders between China and both Laos and Myanmar. The Burma (Stilwell) Road between Assam in British India, which runs through Myanmar and into China's Yunnan province, was so difficult to construct during World War II for this very reason. The Mekong River, with its origins in China's Yunnan Province, extends through Myanmar, Laos, Thailand, and Cambodia, ensuring those countries' economic dependence on southern China, while dense forest makes land invasions and communication difficult.

---

[8]See, for example, Ray Huang, *China: A Macro History*. Armonk, NY: M. E. Sharpe, 1997, Chapter 3.

Vietnam is a slight exception and has the only readily passable land border to China's south, which enabled greater integration of the two regions over history, as well as a brief border war between Beijing and Hanoi in 1979.[9] Securing these vulnerabilities to Han China is a corner stone of Beijing's strategic planning.

For decades, China's sensitive regions have more or less been secured. China's military presence in and "Han-ization" (mass population transfer of Han Chinese to) of Xinjiang have kept the region under Beijing's control, despite occasional protests by Uighur natives. The same applies to the Tibetan plateau, which the PLA invaded and occupied in 1950, and has since administered and "Han-ized."

The mountainous regions to the west and barren region to the north of Xinjiang provide little in the way of external threats to Xinjiang itself.[10] Chinese migrants have also settled much of Mongolia and even Russia's Siberian hinterland adjacent to Manchuria in China's northeast, making the region effectively integrated with and dependent on the Chinese economy.[11] Meanwhile, China has diplomatically resolved all of its border disputes in the favor of the other country—excepting India, with whom borders remain contested.

With these inland buffers more or less secured, the remaining geopolitical threat to Han China is its coast. The South China Sea has been China's main source of economic activity and growth for centuries. Historically, the highly fertile southern sector of China, supplied by the irrigation and transportation lanes of the Pearl and Yangtze Rivers, served as a powerhouse of agricultural growth as well as communication with Southeast Asia and the Indian Ocean.[12] The importance of the coasts was solidified further with the establishment of Hong Kong, Shanghai, and Macau as major destinations for foreign capital in the last few centuries. But particularly since the opening of the Chinese economy to foreign investment in the late 1970s, the coastal provinces have been the main beneficiaries, being the major conduit of raw materials and a host to China's export-based economy. Indeed, as China's economy expands at

---

[9]George Friedman, "The Geopolitics of China: A Great Power Enclosed," *Stratfor*, 15 June 2008, available at http://www.stratfor.com/archived/118032/analysis/geopolitics_china

[10]Graham Fuller and S. Frederick Starr, "The Xinjiang Problem," Central Asia-Caucasus Institute, 2003, available at http://www.cornellcaspian.com/pub2/xinjiang_final.pdf

[11]Josh Kucera, "China is the Destiny of Siberia," *Foreign Policy*, 29 December 2009; Svetlana Soboleva, "Economic Migration to Western Siberia," IISS, *Russian Regional Perspectives*, Vol. 1, No. 2, available at http://www.iiss.org/programmes/russia-and-eurasia/copyof-russian-regional-perspectives-journal/copyof-rrp-volume-1-issue-2/economic-migration-to-western-siberia/

[12]Peter Zeihan, "The Geography of Recession," *Stratfor*, 2 July 2009, available at http://www.stratfor.com/weekly/20090602_geography_recession

a rate of arguably 10 percent per year since the 1970s, infrastructure sprouts, and lifestyles improve, access to oil and energy resources needed to maintain this growth are of particular concern to Beijing.

Since the Chinese economy is so dependent on foreign investment, it is highly vulnerable to an economic blockade of the South China Sea. The means to blockade China are centered on the American-influenced choke-points adjacent to the Chinese Coast: Philippines, Japan, and most seminally, Taiwan, an "unsinkable aircraft carrier" as American General Douglas MacArthur put it,[13] which could serve as a base to interdict naval shipments between the South and East China Seas.

With the western and northern buffer zones controlled, quiescent, and manageable, land borders under Chinese economic, military, or diplomatic control, and a Chinese budget the size of which has no historical precedents, Beijing is more able than any other time in its history to divert capital that would otherwise go to securing its land borders to strengthening its navy.[14] If Taiwan came under de facto Chinese control, its ability to challenge the foreign (namely US) hegemony in its coastal regions and in turn project power further afield would increase tremendously. To this end, the PLA Navy has developed the world's first Anti-Ship Ballistic Missiles (ASBMs) in an effort to deny foreign navies a presence in the region, and is developing its own "unsinkable aircraft carrier" in the form of Sanya Base at Hainan Island.[15]

And as energy sources in the Persian Gulf and Africa and the Sea Lines of Communications (SLOCs) to them increase in importance, many Indian defense planners worry that the Chinese Navy could develop a strong naval presence that infringes on India's traditional strategic space: the Indian Ocean. While most PLA Navy ships have concentrated around the South and East China Seas and the Pacific Ocean, "the PLA Navy's around-the-world cruise in 2002 and its anti-piracy mission off the African coast in 2009 indicate that China is looking to operate more globally."[16]

In what would seem to be stepping stones to the rest of the world, China has developed a number of political-economic and military relationships across Asia that would bolster its energy needs, maritime capabilities, and economic and military strategies. China has sought to warm up to even competitors

[13]Anonymous Statement Regarding Gen. Douglas MacArthur's Statement on Formosa, ca. September 1950. President's Secretary's Files, Truman Papers.

[14]Robert Kaplan, "The Geography of Chinese Power," *Foreign Affairs*, May/June 2010.

[15]Office of Naval Intelligence: *The People's Liberation Army Navy: A Modern Navy with Chinese Characteristics*, Suitland (MD), Office of Naval Intelligence, August 2009, available at http://www.fas.org/irp/agency/oni/pla-navy.pdf; Rajeswari Pillai Rajagopalan, "The Dragon's New Claw," *Deccan Herald*, 20 January 2010.

[16]Drew Thompson, "Think Again: China's Military," *Foreign Policy*, March/April 2010.

such as Taiwan,[17] Japan,[18] and even Vietnam[19] in order to reduce its coastal vulnerabilities.

Meanwhile, in an effort that has been likened to the Silk Road that was at the heart of global trade before the rise, in the seventeenth century, of European-led maritime commerce, China is leading the development of infrastructure to reconnect Central Asia to the rest of the world. In 1996, China established what became, in 2001, the Shanghai Cooperation Organization (SCO), a mutual security and economic engagement organization with Russia, Kazakhstan, Tajikistan, Turkmenistan, Kyrgyzstan, and Uzbekistan.

The organization has facilitated China's extensive involvement in the region's hydrocarbons sector, through energy and resource excavation and pipeline projects. These include some of the only regional energy projects to have actually been given life: a Kazakhstan-China oil pipeline and a natural gas pipeline that extend from Turkmenistan to Uzbekistan, through Kazakhstan, and into China's northwest border in Xinjiang province. In Afghanistan, the Metallurgical Corporation of China and Jiangxi Copper Company have pledged nearly 5 billion USD to explore the Aynak copper mine, the single largest FDI pledge in the country. Beijing also has plans to complete the construction of the Afghan Ring Road, which would traverse Afghanistan and connect China to Iran[20]; has spoken of an Iran-Pakistan-China natural gas pipeline that would extend through northern Kashmir[21]; and even has ambitious plans for a multi-continental railway that would link Beijing to London in 2 days.[22] Despite Russia's extended economic and intelligence connections throughout Eurasia[23], and America's military presence in the region, China, according to

---

[17]Economic and cultural ties have led the way to what many have called a "rapprochement" between the People's Republic of China and Taiwan. See, for example, Michal Roberge and Youkyung Lee, "Backgrounder: China-Taiwan Relations," *Council on Foreign Relations*, 11 August 2009, available at http://www.cfr.org/publication/9223/chinataiwan_relations.html

[18]See, for example, Kayuzo Kato, "China-Japan Rapprochement in Perspective," *Jamestown Foundation,* China Brief, 8, 1 (4 February 2008), available at http://www.jamestown.org/programs/chinabrief/single/?tx_ttnews[tt_news]=4633&tx_ttnews[backPid]=168&no_cache=1

[19]Stein Tonnesson, "Sino-Vietnamese Rapprochement and the South China Sea Irritant." *Security Dialogue*, 34 (March 2003): 55–70.

[20]Philip Smucker, "Afghanistan's Road to Somewhere," *Asia Times*, 20 June 2009.

[21]Wu Jiao and Zhang Jin, "Pipeline pulls region closer," *China Daily*, 15 December 2009; "Pipeline: Iran could ditch India for China," *The Times of India*, 17 September 2009; Pepe Escobar, "Pipelineistan goes Iran-Pak," *Asia Times*, 29 May 2009; "China, Pakistan: The Drivers Behind a Possible Natural Gas Pipeline," *Stratfor*, 11 February 2008, available at http://www.stratfor.com/node/110499/analysis/china_pakistan_drivers_behind_possible_natural_gas_pipeline, accessed on 12 February 2008.

[22]Malcolm Moore, "King's Cross to Beijing in two days on new high-speed rail network," *Telegraph UK*, 8 March 2010.

[23]Frederick Schultz, "Siloviki Syndicalists." *Journal on Terrorism and Security Analysis*, 7 (Spring 2012), 14–33.

Raffaello Pantucci and Alexandros Petersen, "is the power of the future in Central Asia."[24]

There are also a number of Chinese investments in Africa and the Middle East that have raised Indian eyebrows. These include investments in Sudanese oil and infrastructure (as well as a weapons factory outside of Khartoum), in Zimbabwean minerals, crude oil in Angola and Nigeria, and elsewhere.[25] China's relationship with the Middle East—the Arab, Turkic, and Persian worlds—is also based on access to energy resources. China has entered into a number of oil and natural gas exploration deals in Qatar, and has both energy and even political-military cooperation agreements with Saudi Arabia[26] and, to a lesser degree, Iran.[27]

However, China worries that its access to these African and Middle Eastern sources of hydrocarbons will be compromised by geography. Namely, transporting materials to the mainland require a ship journey that passes through either the Strait of Malacca between Malaysia, Singapore, and Indonesia's Sumatra Island, or the Lombok Strait in southern Indonesia. Malacca, which carries about a fourth of the world's traded goods, has been threatened tremendously by piracy for decades,[28] and its relatively small size (25 m deep and 2.8 km wide at its narrowest point) make the Strait of Malacca a vulnerability to some ships and impassable to larger ones.[29] The alternatives, namely the Straits of Sunda and Lombok, the latter of which is much deeper, are

---

[24]Raffaello Pantucci and Alexandros Petersen, "China is the power of the future in Central Asia," *Registan.net*, 22 November 2011.

[25]Princeton Lyman, "China's Rising Role in Africa," Presentation to the US-China Commission, 21 July 2005, available at http://www.cfr.org/publication/8436/chinas_rising_role_in_africa.html; David Shinn, "China's Approach to East, North, and the Horn of Africa," Testimony before the US-China Economic and Security Review Commission, 21 July 2005, available at http://www.uscc.gov/hearings/2005hearings/written_testimonies/05_07_21_22wrts/shinn_david_wrts.pdf

[26]Nawaf Obaid, "The Sino-Saudi Energy Rapprochement: Implications for US National Security," The Gracia Group, Report Prepared for Director, Net Assessment, Washington, DC: Office of the Secretary of Defense, 8 January 2002; Dan Blumenthal, "Providing Arms: China and the Middle East." *Middle East Quarterly*, 12, 2 (Spring 2005): 11–9; Gina Cabrera-Farraj and Sammy Salama, "Report Alleges Saudi Arabia Working on 'Secret Nuclear Program' With Pakistani Assistance," *WMD Insights*, May 2006, available at http://wmdinsights.org/I5/ME2_SaudiArabia.htm; Thomas Woodrow, "The Sino-Saudi Connection," *China Brief*, Jamestown Foundation, 24 October 2002.

[27]John Garver, Flynt Leverett, and Hillary Mann Leverett, "Moving (Slightly) Closer to Iran: China's Shifting Calculus for Managing its 'Persian Gulf Dilemma'," Reischauer Center for East Asian Studies, Asia Pacific Policy Paper Series, October 2009, available at http://www.sais-jhu.edu/bin/y/v/moving_slightly_closer.pdf; John Garver, *China and Iran: Ancient Partners in a Post-imperial World*. Seattle, WA: University of Washington Press, 2006.

[28]Gal Luft and Anne Korin, "Terrorism Goes to Sea," *Foreign Affairs*, November/December 2004.

[29]Donald Freeman, *The Straits of Malacca: Gateway or Gauntlet?* Montreal: McGill-Queen's University Press, 2003; World Oil Transit Chokepoints, Energy Information Administration, Department of Energy, United States Government, January 2008, available at http://www.eia.doe.gov/cabs/World_Oil_Transit_Chokepoints/Full.html

further away and require greater costs and time for transport. Not to mention, Chinese naval analysts like Zhang Ming see India's control of the Andaman and Nicobar Islands in the eastern Bay of Bengal, which "could be used like a 'metal chain' to block the western entrance to the Strait of Malacca," as a threat to their shipping.[30] To this end, the Chinese are looking for alternatives.

In Southeast Asia, China signed an agreement with Cambodia in November 2003 to provide military training and equipment and construct a railway to the South China Sea. In Thailand, the Chinese have begun discussions to develop a canal traversing the Isthmus of Kra to connect the South China Sea with the Bay of Bengal, circumventing the Strait of Malacca.[31] And with Myanmar, China has established a Naval Intelligence "listening post" at Coco Island, plans to lead the development of Sittwe (Akyab) in western Myanmar into a major commercial port, and aims to construct oil and natural gas pipelines that go through Myanmar and into Yunnan province and even a railway or road parallel to the pipeline to facilitate trade.

Of greatest concern to many Indian strategic analysts has been China's "String of Pearls," a set of bases and military-economic relationships with countries along the Indian Ocean and within South Asia—India's traditional area of influence.[32] China's "all-weather" support for Pakistan's military-economic complex is of course the most prominent case of China's presence in South Asia. And while China's support for Pakistan on issues such as Kashmir has thinned, its strategic cooperation remains relatively strong. Largely in response to India's partnership with the United States in the early 2000s, China and Pakistan officially ratified the "China-Pakistan Treaty of Friendship, Cooperation and Good Neighborly Relations" on 4 January 2006, which disallows either country from "joining any alliance or bloc which infringes upon the sovereignty, security and territorial integrity of the other side."[33]

Meanwhile, both China and Pakistan have eagerly developed Gwadar Port, in Pakistan's western Baluchistan province. The port would diversify Pakistan's maritime assets (this necessity became clear to Pakistan after India blockaded

---

[30]Chinese Naval Analyst Zhang Ming, quoted by Robert Kaplan, "Center Stage for the 21st Century: Rivalry in the Indian Ocean," *Foreign Affairs*, 16 March 2009.

[31]Bethany Danyluk, Juli MacDonald, and Ryan Tuggle, *Energy Futures in Asia: Perspectives on India's Energy Security Strategy and Policies*, Report Prepared by Booz Allen Hamilton for Director, Net Assessment, Office of the Secretary of Defense, June 2007; "Energy Futures in Asia," Report Prepared by Booz-Allen-Hamilton for Director, Net Assessment, Office of the Secretary of Defense, 2005.

[32]Christopher Pehrson, "String of Pearls: Meeting the Challenge of China's Rising Power Across the Asian Littoral," US Army War College, July 2006, available at http://www.strategicstudiesinstitute. army.mil/pdffiles/pub721.pdf

[33]D. S. Rajan, "China: Revisiting the 2005 Friendship Treaty with Pakistan," South Asia Analysis Group, Paper No. 2058, 10 December 2006; "China-Pakistan treaty of friendship, cooperation and good-neighborly relations goes into effect," *Xinhua News Agency*, 4 January 2006.

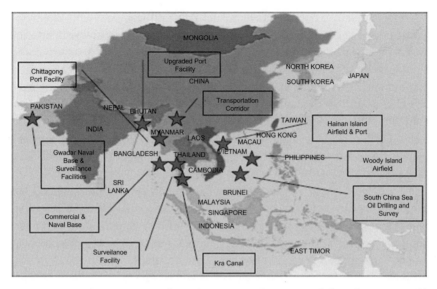

**FIGURE 8.2** *China's String of Pearls From Bethany Danyluk, Juli MacDonald, & Ryan Tuggle, Energy Futures in Asia: Perspectives on India's Energy Security Strategy and Policies, Booz Allen Hamilton for Director, Net Assessment, Office of the Secretary of Defense, June 2007.*

Karachi in the 1971 war); enable the transportation of natural gas from Pakistani and Iranian Baluchistan to both central Pakistan and China via Kashmir (thus circumventing the Strait of Malacca once again); and also give China a solid footprint and listening post in the Arabian Sea. The Karakoram Highway is expected to give way to a railway line extending from China's Xinjiang all the way to Gwadar.

The China-Pakistan equation is, in a sense, old news. What have come to the fore are China's enhanced ties with the other South Asian countries. The Bangladeshi government has looked into Chinese assistance in developing its Chittagong Port, including a container facility. In 2008, Dhaka inaugurated a missile launch pad from which it tested an anti-ship cruise missile C-802A modeled on Chinese designs. The Bangladesh Army, meanwhile, is host to a number of other military technologies from China, from tanks to frigates, and aircraft and artillery.[34] Bangladesh has also proposed a Bangladesh-Myanmar-China highway and railway line, extending from Chittagong to Yunnan Province.[35]

---

[34]Maladdi Rama Rao, "Dynamics of China-Bangladesh Relations," *Policy Research Group*, 10 January 2010, available at http://policyresearchgroup.com/regional_weekly/special_;topics/540.html
[35]Anand Kumar, "Chinese Puzzle in India-Bangladesh Relations," *IDSA Comment*, 19 April 2010, available at http://www.idsa.in/node/5317/261

To India's south, the China Harbor Engineering Company and Sinohydro Corporation are developing Sri Lanka's coastal town of Hambantota into the Port of Hambantota. The deal would mean the construction of an international airport, a highway, a railway, and an oil refinery for Colombo, and a potential mid-Indian Ocean fueling station and military listening post for Beijing.[36] There has also been talk of a weapons factory in Sri Lanka, built by the Chinese company Norinco,[37] while Colombo's 2009 war against the militant group the LTTE, the militant separatist group with whom Colombo had waged a decade-long civil war, was supported both militarily and diplomatically by China.[38]

Although not a maritime asset, Indian strategists fear that the once decisive Himalayan border between Nepal and China is being traversed. As China has recently placed greater economic emphasis on Tibet and Xinjiang (both as a gateway to Central Asia and the Arabian Sea and as a means of solidifying its political control in those provinces), it has developed a high-speed railway from Qinghai Province to Tibet that cuts travel and transport time (previously by road) manifold. The railway line reached Xigatse, on the Nepali border, in 2010, and is set to extend further into Nepal in subsequent years.[39] This is supplemented by a number of roads connecting Nepal to Tibet, and perhaps more consequentially, enhanced political ties. A number of political parties, not least the Communist Party of Nepal (Maoist), have leaned toward Beijing in an effort to balance the country's near-total economic reliance on India. In return, the Nepalis have agreed to limit the activities of its Tibetan diaspora, which has been a major political irritant to the PRC.

## Sino-Indian Conflict?

Particularly as it moves toward the Indian Ocean, the overlap between China's new military strategy and India's traditional strategic sphere could lead the two toward competition. China's presence in the Indian Ocean and subcontinent

[36]B. Raman, "Gwadar, Hambantota, and Sitwe: China's Strategic Triangle," South Asia Analysis, Paper no. 2158, 3 June 2007, available at http://www.southasiaanalysis.org/%5Cpapers22%5Cpaper2158. html; Shirajiv Sirimane, "Hambantota port, gateway to world," The Sunday Observer, 21 February 2010, available at http://www.sundayobserver.lk/2010/02/21/fea20.asp

[37]Vijay Sakhuja, "Sri Lanka: China's Growing Foothold in the Indian Ocean," Jamestown Foundation, China Brief, Bol. 9, No. 12, 12 June 2009, available at http://www.jamestown.org/single/?no_cache=1&tx_ttnews[tt_news]=35119

[38]Peter Popham, "How Beijing Won Sri Lanka's Civil War," The Independent, 23 May 2010; Jeremy Page, "Chinese billions in Sri Lanka fund battle against Tamil Tigers," The Times, 2 May 2009.

[39]Vikram Sood, "Chewing Over China," Hindustan Times, 13 November 2006.

appears to be, in the words of Indian analyst C. Raja Mohan, "tearing up India's 'Monroe Doctrine'."[40]

And though strategic overlap may enhance the existing competition between the two rising economies, many anticipate an increased likelihood of military conflict. This has at its source what Indian analysts term the increasing "aggressiveness" of the Chinese military[41] as a result of its supposedly increased role within the Chinese decision-making elite, which has altered the civil-military balance.[42] Several instances of Chinese cyber warfare and electronic intrusion within India, as well as the January 2007 test of Chinese anti-satellite missile demonstrate Chinese "aggressiveness" and "belligerency."

Of course, China's westward economic and strategic expansion is tied to the securitization of its western buffer regions. By securing its control over Xinjiang and the Tibetan Plateau, Beijing can more easily access resources in Central Asia via the northwestern Horgos border pass in Xinjiang and even the Arabian Sea through the Karakoram Pass through Pakistan. Yet to do so requires stability in the more proximate regions, resulting in a massive military buildup in Tibet.

In an effort to solidify the economic and political integration of Tibet with Han China, Beijing has expanded infrastructure in Tibet, namely the Qinghai-Tibet Railway that was inaugurated in 2006 and connects Han China to Tibet by rail for the first time. Before the introduction of this railway, most communication with Tibet occurred by a roadway that required weeks of travel. The railway, however, takes less than 2 days. Meanwhile, Beijing has increased its military presence in southern and Central Tibet. Medium- and long-range tactical weapons such as Dongfeng-4s, DF-21s and DF-31s have been placed in Delingha, Datong, and Kunming. And southern Tibet has long been the base for missiles that originally targeted the Soviet Union and American bases in the South and East China Seas—but have had the capability to "reach all of India's major cities and military areas."[43] Along its borders with India, Beijing

---

[40]This phrase was used by C. Raja Mohan in "SAARC Reality Check: China just tore up India's Monroe Doctrine," *Indian Express*, 14 November 2005.

[41]Gurmeet Kanwal and Monika Chansoria, "Breathing Fire: China's Aggressive Tactical Posturing," Centre for Land Warfare Studies, Article No. 12, 23 October 2009, available at http://www.claws.in/index.php?action=master&task=422&u_id=7; Bharat Verma, "Unmasking China," *Indian Defence Review*, 24, 3 (July-September 2009).

[42]David Shamhaugh, "Civil-Military Relations in China: Party-Army or National Military?," *Copenhagen Journal of Asian Studies*, 16 (2002): 10–27; Jagannath P. Panda, "Leadership, Factional Politics and China's Civil-Military Dynamics: Post-17th Party Congress Patterns," *Strategic Analysis*, 33, 5 (September 2009): 716–29.

[43]Justin Summers, "The India-China Relationship: What the United States Needs to Know," Asia Society and the Woodrow Wilson International Center for Scholars, Report 30, November 2001, p. 18.

has deployed 13 Border Defense Regiments—nearly 300,000 PLA troops—as well as Su-27 fighter aircraft at six airfields at Huaping, Pangta and Kongka La replete with refueling stations and air defense systems.[44]

It is in this context that the most apparent sign of Sino-Indian tension has arisen: the unresolved border between Tibet and India's Arunachal Pradesh, which China refers to as "Southern Tibet."

The first of a series of hard line Chinese statements on Arunachal Pradesh was articulated at the official level as early as 1986 when Vice-Foreign Minister Liu Shuquing said that "some 90,000 square kilometers of Chinese territory" was under Indian occupation and that unless India "resolves this key to the overall situation" it would be impossible to reach a settlement. This was followed by Chinese incursions into the Sumdorong Chu Valley in Arunachal Pradesh, which overshadowed the 7th round of border talks in July 1986. Twenty years later, on November 20, 2006, this stance was reiterated by China's Ambassador to India Sun Yuxi, when he said that "the whole of the state of Arunachal Pradesh is Chinese territory. And Tawang is only one of the places in it. We are claiming all of that. That is our position."[45]

This diplomatic conflict and the perceived vulnerabilities around it lead many Indians to believe that the border dispute in Arunachal Pradesh would be a major flashpoint for war.

Since 1950, when the PRC took over Tibet, its military control over that region has only had one major geostrategic liability: the handful of mountain passes along the Himalayan border with India and Nepal. Tawang pass, in Indian-administered Arunachal Pradesh and along the border between Bhutan and Tibet, has long served as a point of interaction across the Himalayas. In 1959, for example, the young Dalai Lama Tenzin Gyatso escaped Lhasa and fled into India via Tawang. While Tawang and other passes are not large enough to sustain a large military presence (from either China or India), covert operations to destabilize Tibet can easily be mounted from Tawang in particular. In fact, in addition to passes in Nepal's Mustang region, Tawang may have been one valley used by American (and later Indian) intelligence agencies to facilitate

---

[44]Namrata Goswami, "China's Response to India's Military Upgrade in Arunachal Pradesh: A Classic Case of 'Security Dilemma'," *IDSA Comment*, 18 November 2011, available at www.idsa.in/?q=idsacomments/ChinasResponsetoIndiasMilitaryUpgradeinArunachalPradesh_ngoswami_181111

[45]Jagannath Panda, "China's Designs on Arunachal Pradesh," *IDSA Comment*, 12 March 2008, available at http://idsa.in/idsastrategiccomments/ChinasDesignsonArunachalPradesh_JPPanda_120308

the transfer of counter-communist operatives into Tibet. It is this potential that worries the Chinese today, and a major reason for Beijing's outstanding border disagreement with India.[46]

There are, however, other reasons that China continues to press the issue of Arunachal Pradesh. The first is related to the broader unresolved border dispute: by keeping the Arunachal Pradesh issue alive, Beijing can offer to settle all outstanding border disputes by enshrining the status quo; China would give up its claims to Indian-administered Arunachal Pradesh in exchange for India giving up its claims on Chinese-administered Aksai Chin in India's northwestern sector. Though Beijing officially withdrew its proposal to accept the territorial status quo in October 1985, it has since ramped up its aggressiveness along its southwestern border in an effort to force India's diplomatic hand.[47] But Aksai Chin, which China occupied before and took during the 1962 war, is a highly sensitive political issue within India and the claim is unlikely to be conceded. Largely a legacy of the 1962 War, many Indian analysts believe that giving up Indian claims on Aksai Chin would, all things considered, be an *ineffective* appeasement of China. Even after Delhi relinquished its claims and Beijing undisputedly controlled Aksai Chin, it is argued, Beijing would continue to demand concessions in other Indian territories. The Chinese proposed a swap agreement as early as 1960, before the war, "only to formalize their illegal occupation of Aksai Chin," as one key Indian analyst of China's military strategy puts it.[48]

The second reason is that, in controlling Arunachal Pradesh, the Chinese Army would gain strategic depth. By occupying Arunachal Pradesh, Chinese forces would lose their Tawang vulnerability and be able to access Bhutan and, in the case of a land war with India, extend its forces further into the barrier-free Brahmaputra Valley with greater ease. *Maintaining* such a presence across the Himalayas, however, would be a major difficulty without an alternate supply line. A third, lesser reason includes the limited economic potential of Arunachal Pradesh: timber, mineral resources, and the hydroelectric potential of the Brahmaputra River that, similarly, could be transported back to Tibet only with great difficulty.

But even recently, the land under "dispute" is of so little utility to New Delhi that, rather than thinking of the remaining border as India's own land to be developed, New Delhi treats Arunachal Pradesh as a mere "buffer zone."

---

[46]B. Raman, "The Real Chinese Intrusions," *Outlook*, 15 September 2009.

[47]John Garver, *Protracted Contest: Sino-Indian Rivalry in the Twentieth Century*. Seattle, WA: University of Washington Press, 2001.

[48]Maj. Gen. (ret.) Sheru Thapliyal, "Trigger in the Himalayas: Aksai Chin is a test case of India's resolve," *Force*, 8 August 2010, available at http://www.forceindia.net/guestcolumn7.aspx

Connectivity to and in the region, for purposes of both enabling a military presence as well as local economic development, has been lacking.[49] (This was partly out of fear that Chinese invaders could use any Indian infrastructure to access the Brahmaputra Basin or even the Indian Gangetic heartland).[50] In 2006, New Delhi sanctioned a series of infrastructure development programs along the border. These include 72 roads, three airstrips, and several bridges.[51]

The remaining mountain passes over which a land-based military confrontation might be possible are relatively impenetrable. The People's Liberation Army's attack and occupation of Tawang in 1962 was due to years of preparation for two short-term needs: to counter what China perceived as India's "desire to seize Tibet from China," and to seal the Tibetan border (at Longju) in the wake of the Tibetan uprising of 1959. This brought a massive number of Chinese troops to the Thagla Heights overlooking Tawang in the immediate years before the hostilities of 1962 commenced, at a high monetary cost to Beijing.[52]

In fact, these passes are traversable insofar as an army can penetrate them *during the non-winter months*, but they are not passable insofar as any standing Chinese military presence is sustainable. This unsustainability was arguably the main reason for China's 21 November 1962, unilateral withdrawal from the land it occupied in the eastern sector in the 1962 war; the coming winter would have rendered the Himalayan passes snowbound, cutting off the Chinese supply lines from the north.[53] A relatively small Chinese contingent could enter Tawang and occupy it temporarily. But because it lies adjacent to the Brahmaputra Valley, where there is a greater Indian military presence, this small contingent could be fended off relatively easily. As Ashley Tellis has written,

> India's conventional forces enjoy a comfortable superiority over their Chinese counterparts in the Himalayan theater; the Indian Army has superior firepower, better-trained soldiers, carefully prepared defenses,

[49]Saikat Datta, "On the Wrong Side of Geography?," *Outlook*, 16 November 2009.
[50]John Pike, "Indian Army Eastern Command Order of Battle," GlobalSecurity.org, 22 March 2009, available at http://www.globalsecurity.org/military/world/india/eastcom.htm
[51]Rajeswari Pillai Rajagopalan, *The Dragon's Fire: Chinese Military Strategic and its Implications for Asia.* New Delhi: Observer Research Foundation and Rupa Press, 2009, p. 84.
[52]See John Garver, "China's Decision for War with India in 1962," in Robert S. Ross and Alastair Iain Johnston (eds), *New Approaches to the Study of Chinese Foreign Policy.* Stanford, CA: Stanford University Press, 2005. For a geographic analysis of region and of the sustainability of military forces on either side of Tawang, see, for example, M. L. Sali, *India-China Border Dispute: A Case Study of the Eastern Sector.* New Delhi: APH Publishing, 1998, p. 192.
[53]K. C. Praval, *Indian Army after Independence.* New Delhi: Lancer International, 1990, p. xi.

and more reliable logistics. . . . [T]he Indian Air Force has better aircraft, superior pilots, and excellent infrastructure and would . . . gain tactical superiority . . . in a matter of days if not hours.[54]

Yet many Indian analysts fear that even this Indian military superiority in the region could soon be compromised due to the Qinghai-Tibet Railway that facilitates transport between Mainland China and Tibet. Indian strategists worry that this civilian infrastructure can serve as a conduit for the expansion of Chinese military infrastructures and supplies, and thus that the likelihood for conflict along the Line-of-Actual-Control (LAC, the *de facto* border) is increased. However, the railway was designed primarily for civilian use, and its construction on the permafrost of the Tibetan Plateau was not designed to transport large amounts of military supplies or to withstand military assaults (such as those from even conventional missiles). If Indo-Chinese tensions came to border conflict, and China sent in reinforcements through its western railway, that enabling infrastructure itself could be targeted, and its vulnerabilities exposed.[55]

A border skirmish is essentially the largest military confrontation that Indian planners fear. However, if a larger-scale air or missile battle is feared, then the border issue over Tawang is largely irrelevant; the missiles that could traverse the Himalayas would more likely strike higher-value targets in central India or Indian military installations (including airfields) in the Brahmaputra Valley.

In such a case, India's Agni-II to Agni-V series missiles, which can reach Beijing, would be a strong deterrent. Many Indian hawks question how China's nuclear no-first-use policy would apply to Arunachal Pradesh, which China claims as its own occupied territory. They fear that China may launch a nuclear strike on Arunachal Pradesh and claim it to be a "test" of a nuclear weapon on its own soil.[56] Indeed, "only in the realm of nuclear capabilities does China currently have an overwhelming, uncontestable superiority over India." However, the political issues that divide India and China—namely the location of the border on a patch of land of minimal value—are not significant enough to either country to necessitate nuclear weaponry. Not to mention,

---

[54]Ashley Tellis, "The Changing Political-Military Environment: South Asia," in Zalmay Khalilzad, David Orletsky, Jonathan D. Pollack, Kevin Pollpeter, Angel M. Rabasa, David A. Shlapak, Abram N. Shulsky, and Ashley J. Tellis (eds), *The United States and Asia: Toward a New US Strategy and Force Posture.* Santa Monica, CA: RAND, 2001.

[55]Personal communication with former Indian Air Chief Marshal Srinivasapuram Krishnaswamy, New Delhi, 9 June 2010.

[56]For a representative analysis see, for example, Bhartendu Kumar Singh, "Fearing a Chinese Nuclear Attack in Arunachal Pradesh," IPCS, Article #530, 25 July 2001.

India's own nuclear deterrent would be a means of deterring, as Tellis puts it, "all but the most extreme Chinese threats."[57]

Military deterrence aside, the political fallout from a Chinese nuclear missile strike on India would be enough of a deterrent. China has higher stakes in its Pacific theater, and it is far more likely that Beijing would risk a nuclear exchange with the United States than with India over land that would simply provide a little extra strategic depth.

The 1962 war colored Indian perceptions of Chinese intentions and capabilities. And particularly in the twenty-first century, when China and India are projected to be the two most economically powerful countries in the world's most strategically significant continent, and both countries tend to see their international relations through a realist prism,[58] the legacy of 1962 certainly casts a shadow on India's own perceptions of China. A "repeat of 1962" has been the fear of many Indian defense planners.[59]

Yet the fear of Chinese troops or missiles pouring over the Himalayas and ransacking India is largely overplayed. The border remains largely impermeable without a major, politically unnecessary escalation on China's part. Such an escalation would likely be deterred not only by the Indian conventional and unconventional military presence, but also by politics and diplomacy. At best, the border may serve as a political lever to be drummed up depending on the state of internal affairs in Tibet. As one Indian analyst puts it, "India and China will have to find ways of living with an unsettled border for the foreseeable future."[60]

In the Tibetan theater, the most consequential development is India's nuclear tipped missiles, which are, as Nitin Pai writes, "the New Himalayas that keep [India] secure."[61] Due to China's early start, assistance from the Soviet Union, and greater overall spending power, New Delhi may perhaps never

---

[57]Ashley Tellis, "The Changing Political-Military Environment: South Asia," in Zalmay Khalilzad, David Orletsky, Jonathan D. Pollack, Kevin Pollpeter, Angel M. Rabasa, David A. Shlapak, Abram N. Shulsky, and Ashley J. Tellis (eds), *The United States and Asia: Toward a New US Strategy and Force Posture.* Santa Monica, CA: RAND, 2001.

[58]He, Kai. "Dynamic Balancing—Neoclassical Realism and China's Foreign Policy," *Paper presented at the annual meeting of the International Studies Association, Town & Country Resort and Convention Center,* San Diego, California, USA, 22 March 2006; Yuan-Kang Wang, "Offensive Realism and the Rise of China." *Issues and Studies,* 40, 1 (March 2004): 173–201; Bharat Karnad, *Nuclear Weapons and Indian Security: The Realist Foundations of Strategy.* New Delhi: Macmillan Press, 2002.

[59]See the language in, for example, "Repeat of 1962 can't be ruled out, says Rajnath," *Indian Express,* 4 October 2009; "Unsure of China's Motives, but 1962 repeat not possible: Army Chief," *DNA India,* 7 November 2010.

[60]Pallavi Aiyar, "Realism in India-China Relations," *The Hindu,* 17 September 2008.

[61]Nitin Pai, "Secure Under the New Himalayas," *Pragati: The Indian National Interest,* 6 January 2012.

reach nuclear parity with Beijing, in which the two countries' offensive and defensive systems are approximately equal in overall combat effectiveness. Yet even from India's perspective, parity is largely unnecessary: New Delhi's doctrine has always stressed *minimum* credibility in its nuclear deterrent.[62] The survivability of India's arsenal to a (Chinese) counter-force first strike—one that targets India's nuclear arsenal with the intention of rendering them unusable—is essentially ensured by the fact that India's arsenal is *strategic* rather than tactical: its components are "demated," existing in pieces around the country that require assembly in case the need for their use arises. Their minimum credibility is ensured by the constant evolution of the program itself, from what Tellis has called a "recessed deterrent" to a "force-in-being," a weapon that is not ready for delivery, but which would ensure that an Indian response to a nuclear attack, while delayed, would be certain.[63]

As Pai writes, "as long as the ['New Himalayas'] are high—that's where the *minimum* credible deterrent comes in—it is inconceivable that China or any other power will see merit in mounting a direct military invasion."[64] Indeed, rather than direct military confrontation—whether along the Himalayas or elsewhere—bilateral relations between India and China will likely be defined by strategic competition and geopolitical balancing in other theaters. These include India's "traditional" strategic spaces over which China has been extending its influence in recent years: Central Asia, South Asia, Southeast Asia, and their nexus, the Indian Ocean region.

---

[62]Brajesh Mishra, "Draft Report of National Security Advisory Board on Indian Nuclear Doctrine," National Security Advisory Board, Government of India, 17 August 1999.
[63]Ashley Tellis, *India's Emerging Nuclear Posture: Between Recessed Deterrent and Ready Arsenal.* New Delhi: Oxford University Press and RAND Corporation, 2001.
[64]Nitin Pai, "Secure Under the New Himalayas," *Pragati: The Indian National Interest*, 6 January 2012.

# 9

# Beyond South Asia: A New Strategic Direction

*"India's vision for the future . . . has been to expand India's strategic space. . . . Our engagement with our extended neighborhood—from South East Asia to Southern Africa—has become at once intense and broad ranging. . . ."*

—PRANAB MUKHERJEE, FMR. INDIAN MINISTER OF EXTERNAL AFFAIRS[1]

Since the opening of its markets in the early 1990s, India has moved away from the Monroe Doctrine's foundational tenets as its guiding strategic premise. Having opened its markets to foreign investment, India has found that its *de facto* regional and domestic isolationism was not necessarily an effective way of increasing its economic prowess and security. Moreover, strategic elites have slowly come to the realization that "India's primacy in the region cannot be ensured by fiat or trying to keep the world out."[2]

Driven by a search for (1) markets, (2) energy resources, and (3) methods of countering and balancing against China in the Indian Ocean region, New Delhi is increasingly looking beyond South Asia for its strategic needs.

## "Look East"

In 1994, Indian Prime Minister Narasimha Rao articulated India's official "Look East Policy," in which India would rekindle the trade, cultural, and strategic

---

[1]Pranab Mukherjee, "India and the Global Balance of Power," Address by the minister of external affairs to the Global India Foundation, New Delhi, 16 January 2007.
[2]C. Raja Mohan, "Beyond India's Monroe Doctrine," *The Hindu*, 2 January 2003.

ties it once had with Southeast Asia during and before the British period. With many countries of Southeast Asia, India's new policy was mutually beneficial: such links served India's strategic and economic needs, while "many of these countries found India a deserving candidate to be involved in this balance [against countries like China and the US] because India had no record of an aggressive or expansionist approach towards this region in the past."[3] Although an exact articulation of how exactly India would "look" east was never clearly made, in the years since, substance has been given to these goals.

In 2005, India and Singapore signed the Comprehensive Economic Cooperation Agreement (CECA) in order to facilitate a broader commercial relationship between the two.[4] The city-state has been India's largest trade partner in the region, accounting for 8.72 percent of total FDI inflows into India, while India's direct investments in Singapore, 14 billion USD by 2008–09, have been India's highest.[5] Meanwhile, the Kalaikunda Air Force Base in West Bengal was leased to Singapore for training purposes for a 5-year period.[6]

While Myanmar has strengthened its ties with China, it has long had a history of strategic autonomy that it wishes to preserve. While Yangon[7] was originally driven into Beijing's arms in the wake of international condemnation of its human rights practices in 1988 (including from India), Burma's military leaders have sought to reduce its reliance on China by increasing its ties with India. In 2009, India was Myanmar's largest export market; New Delhi has received contracts to develop infrastructure connecting Myanmar's Kalay-Kalaywa-Kyiga-Tamu Road with the Indian state of Mizoram, including a "friendship bridge" to facilitate cross-border trade and a road link to India's Highway 39; and even has plans to the develop Myanmar's Sittwe and Dawei ports into Indian deep-sea ports.[8] In 2011, Myanmar began to open up its tightly closed political system to outside influence, beginning the

---

[3]S. D. Muni, "India's 'Look East' Policy: The Strategic Dimension," ISAS Working Paper, No. 121, National University of Singapore, 1 February 2011.

[4]"Comprehensive Economic Agreement between the Republic of India and the Republic of Singapore," *Ministry of Commerce*, Government of India, 29 June 2005.

[5]Archana Pandya and David M. Malone, "India's Asia Policy: A Late Look East," Institute for South Asian Studies Special Report, No. 2 (Singapore: Institute of South Asian Studies, 25 August 2010), p. 12.

[6]David Brewster, "India's security partnership with Singapore," *The Pacific Review*, 22, 5 (December 2009): 597–618.

[7]In November 2006, the Burmese Junta changed the capital from Yangon to Naypyidaw in large part to insulate the capital from coastal vulnerabilities such as domestic violence or external regime change.

[8]Pradip Saikia, "Northeast India as a Factor in India's Diplomatic Engagement with Myanmar: Issues and Challenges." *Strategic Analysis*, 33, 6 (November 2009): 877–89; Saurabh, "Dynamics of Indo-Myanmar Economic Ties," *IDSA Comment*, 6 January 2010, available at http://www.idsa.in/idsacomments/DynamicsofIndo-MyanmarEconomicTies_saurabh_060110; Ramnatu Maitra, "The energy ties that bind India, China," *Asia Times*, 12 April 2005.

process of détente with the United States and the west, and allowing its key political dissidents—including democracy activist Aung San Suu Kyi—to begin to participate in the political process. This opening was seen as a major rebuff to Chinese dominance of foreign engagement with Myanmar. But whether these high expectations for Burmese reform pan out remains to be seen.

With one of China's strategic vulnerabilities along its border with Vietnam, Hanoi has remained strategically autonomous despite overtures from China. And as Beijing recently elevated the South China Sea to the status of a "core national interest" along with issues like Taiwan and Tibet,[9] maritime issues also weigh heavily on Sino-Vietnamese bilateral relations. As China develops its Hainan Port, just adjacent to Vietnam's northern coast, into a security-oriented base, and extends its influence into the South China Sea, Sino-Vietnamese tensions have developed into a number of maritime border disputes over the Spratly Islands, Scarborough Shoal, Paracel Islands, and the oil and natural gas resources therein. Seeking to overcome these challenges, Vietnam has even joined the efforts of the United States, with whom it fought a bitter war in the 1960s and 1970s, to develop Vietnam's military capacities and contain China's perceived encroachment in the South China Sea. Vietnam's ties with India, meanwhile, extend from the days of the Cold War, when both were close to the Soviet Union and victims of Chinese military offenses along their respective borders. The China factor remains a uniting theme, and since 2000, India has helped develop Vietnam's military capacities—including with sales of Petya and OSA-11 class missile boats, and even Brahmos Cruise Missiles—in an effort to keep China's South China Sea vulnerability alive. Indian companies have been key investors in Vietnam's offshore oil and natural gas deposits, including areas of the South China Sea that have been contested by both Vietnam and China. When Beijing and Hanoi began to contest the validity of these Indian investments, Indian Navy chief Admiral D. K. Joshi articulated India's willingness and ability to intervene: "Not that we expect to be in those waters very frequently, but when the requirement is there for situations where the country's interests are involved, for example ONGC Videsh, we will be required to go there and we are prepared for that."[10] In addition to naval exercises with Vietnam, India has even sought to turn Cam Ranh Bay, a Soviet-era deep-water port, into a base for the Indian Navy, though the Vietnamese have resisted this for fear of provoking Beijing.[11]

---

[9]Wu Zhong, "A Daring Departure from Deng," *Asia Times*, 6 August 2010.

[10]Zachary Keck, "India's South China Sea Gambit," *The Diplomat*, 5 December 2012.

[11]Iskander Rehman, "Keeping the Dragon at Bay: India's Counter-Containment of China in Asia." *Asian Security*, 5, 2 (May 2009): 114–43.

India's engagement with the other Southeast Asian nations is being facilitated through the development a number of intergovernmental organizations. These include the Association of Southeast Asian Nations, plus China, Japan, South Korea, and India (ASEAN + 4); Bay of Bengal Initiative for Multi-sectoral Scientific, Technological and Economic Cooperation (BIMSTEC), which includes Bangladesh, India, Myanmar, Sri Lanka, Thailand, Bhutan and Nepal; and Indian Ocean Rim Association For Regional Cooperation (IOR-ARC). These institutions have had a mix of successes and failures, largely due to the Southeast Asian countries' needs to balance Indian involvement with Chinese interests, but represent an expansion of India's economic and strategic interests to a new geographic realm.

Further east, India's rapprochement with Japan—after Japanese sanctions on New Delhi following the latter's 1998 nuclear tests—began in 2000, during Japanese Prime Minister Yoshiro Mori's visit to India. Mori announced a resumption of aid and investment in projects like the Delhi Metro and the beginning of an "Indo-Japanese Global Partnership for the 21st century." By 2004, the two countries began conducting joint naval exercises in the Bay of Bengal—where India's fleet is based, through which Japan's energy supplies pass, and where both are concerned about China's naval expansion.[12] Trade expansion has defined another element of Indo-Japanese ties, and by 2007 Japan had announced its financial sponsorship (half of the total costs) of a Delhi-Mumbai Industrial Corridor that would expand rail and road links (including a six-lane highway), ports, airports, and a 4000 MW power plant between India's political and financial capitals.[13]

Another leg of India's eastern Indian Ocean strategy is Australia, with whom—also following Canberry's condemnation of the Pokhran II nuclear tests—New Delhi has conducted a number of joint maritime exercises, mine-clearing operations, and other maritime operations in the southern Indian Ocean.[14] The two countries have signed defense pacts toward military research, development, and training, and have agreed to share intelligence information regarding maritime security. Meanwhile, both public and private Indian companies have invested in Australia's offshore petroleum exploration, while acquiring coal assets in Queensland.[15] Canberry, however, ruled out an

---

[12]K. V. Kesavan, "India and Japan: Changing Dimensions of Partnership in the post-Cold War Period," *ORF Occasional Paper No. 14,* Observer Research Foundation, May 2010.

[13]"Japan to aid India in building new corridor," *Financial Express,* 14 December 2006; "Tokyo Summit to focus on Delhi-Mumbai Industrial Corridor," *Economic Times,* 4 July 2011.

[14]"Australian Navy, Indian Navy to Break Ice at Port Blair Exercise," *India Defence,* 30 December 2005.

[15]Tanvi Madan, "India's International Quest for Oil and Natural Gas: Fueling Foreign Policy?." *India Review,* 9, 1 (January–March 2010): 7; Andrew Fraser, "From Pit to port: India's $10bn coal export plan," *The Australian,* 20 August 2011; Esther Thomas, "India expects Australia to satisfy its coal hunger," *International Business Times,* 6 October 2011.

initiative to unite India, Japan, Australia, and the United States in a "quadripartite alliance"[16] or "Arc of Democracies" to ensure maritime security in the eastern Indian Ocean and southwestern Pacific, citing Chinese threat perceptions.[17]

## Looking West: Middle East and Africa

The countries and waters of the Persian Gulf host nearly 66 percent and 35 percent of the world's proven petroleum and natural gas reserves, respectively. About 40 percent of the world's petroleum products pass through the Strait of Hormuz, while 70 percent pass through the whole Indian Ocean.[18] To the west of the Persian Gulf lies the Suez Canal, the quickest water route to the Mediterranean Sea of Europe, and to its south the Gulf of Aden and the Cape of Good Hope at South Africa, with its southern access to the Atlantic. In light of these natural and geographic resources, and New Delhi's changing strategic needs, India's presence at the center of the Indian Ocean has risen in importance.

The Gulf Cooperation Council (GCC) nations—Saudi Arabia, Bahrain, Kuwait, Qatar, the United Arab Emirates, and Oman—have been a central focus of India's westward economic engagement. Before their independence from Britain in the 1960s, many of the Gulf Arab states used the Gulf Rupiah, a currency issued by the Indian government to offset strains on the Indian Rupee caused by smuggling, in local markets. Thereafter, when independence and a petroleum rush caused a major infrastructure boom in the 1970s, Indian migrants have been a significant source of labor to the GCC countries. Today, the GCC employs over 4 million Indians, who provide India with 24 percent of its total foreign remittances, nearly 11 billion USD.[19] Saudi Arabia is currently India's largest supplier of petroleum, and Indian companies like Oil and Natural Gas Corporation (ONGC), Hindustan Petroleum Corp (HPCL), Bharat Petroleum Corp (BPCL) and Essar Oil have sought to invest in Saudi oil blocks, building off of investment patterns with Qatar, Oman, and the United Arab Emirates.

---

[16]The initial exercises, beginning in 1992, also included Singapore.
[17]"Australia rules out security agreement with U. S., Japan, India," Kyodo News International, 3 April 2007.
[18]Charles Esser, Persian Gulf Oil and Gas Exports Fact Sheet, Energy Information Administration, US Department of Energy, March 2002, available at http://www.eia.doe.gov/cabs/pgulf2.html, accessed 12 March 2009.
[19]"India receives world's largest share of foreign remittances," *Asian Economic News*, 15 September 2007; Reserve Bank of India. "Invisibles in India's Balance of Payments," *RBI Bulletin*, November 2006.

Two-way trade between India and the GCC countries is expected to reach 130 billion USD by 2014, from its 2011 level of 100 billion USD.[20] A great deal of India's economic engagements with the GCC countries are facilitated by the private sector. Beyond energy, food products, pharmaceuticals, textiles, and services are major Indian exports to the Gulf, and an impending Free-Trade Agreement between India and the GCC is expected to boost commercial ties, with a particular emphasis on telecommunications and infrastructure development.[21]

While not quite as extensive as China, India is also establishing a deep economic and strategic presence in Africa. Since late 2002, ONGC-Videsh Limited (OVL) has begun petroleum excavation and infrastructure development projects in Sudan. OVL holds nearly a quarter of the Greater Nile Petroleum Operating Company (GNPOC) conglomerate, and blocks 2, 5A, and 5B of its own. Moreover, OVL has a contract to build a 1.2 billion USD oil refinery, and a 200 million USD multi-product export pipeline from Khartoum refinery to Port Sudan. Bharat Heavy Electricals Ltd. (BHEL), one of India's state-owned manufacturing corporations, has the second largest deal by an Indian company with the Government of Sudan, having signed a contract with the government of Sudan in September 2005 to build, among other things, a power generation plant in the central White Nile state.[22]

Nigeria is another key country in India's relationship with Africa, providing 10–12 percent of India's oil imports.[23] OVL has a 15 percent stake in Nigeria's oil Block 2, as well as 25 percent equity in Blocks OPL 321 and OPL 323. ONGC-Mittal Energy Limited (OMEL), meanwhile, has a stake in Blocks OPL 209 and OPL 212. New Delhi has also agreed to provide training for the Nigerian military. Indian oil companies have also acquired energy assets in other African countries such as Libya (a 3 million USD stake in the Sirte Basin, 10.5% stake in the Libyan National Oil Company, Block 81–1 in the Ghadames Basin, and others); Gabon (IOC-OIL's 90% stake in an oil and gas block); and Côte d'Ivoire.[24]

Two-way trade between the African continent and India passed 50 billion USD in 2011, and New Delhi has set up a 5 billion USD loan package to foster trade and technological development, as well as a 1 billion USD fund for education, railways, and peacekeeping, to which India has long been a major contributor of troops.[25] India's economic engagement has focused on

---

[20]Walid Mazi, "GCC India FTA 'on right track'," *Arab News*, 26 February 2011.
[21]Huma Siddiqui, "India, GCC discuss FTA," *Financial Express*, 16 August 2011.
[22]"Bharat Heavy Gets $457 mln order to build Sudan Plant," *Bloomberg News*, 12 February 2006.
[23]Ruchita Beri, "Oil Factor in India-Nigeria Relations," *IDSA Fellows Seminar*, 12 August 2011.
[24]Tanvi Madan, "India," *Energy Security Series*, Brookings Institution, November 2006.
[25]"India and Africa: Catching up," *The Economist*, 26 May 2011; Teo Kermelliotis, "India woos Africa with $billion loan package," *CNN*, 25 May 2011.

telecommunications and power generation infrastructure, through investments by Bharti Airtel, Tata Power, and Reliance Power, as well as the health and food arenas, where Indian pharmaceutical companies have provided low-cost drugs and also purchased tracts of cheap farming land in Ethiopia, Tanzania, and Uganda to develop agricultural products.[26]

A quietly burgeoning, yet profoundly important relationship that New Delhi has developed in the region is that with Israel. India was initially opposed to the creation of a Jewish state in the Middle East, partly on the grounds that Israel as a homeland for a religious minority followed a similarly "illegitimate" narrative as Pakistan's "two-nation theory"[27]; partly owing to compulsions of India's anti-colonial stance and the sensitivities of India's Muslim population, who were thought to oppose Israel's occupation of the Muslim holy city of Jerusalem and oppression of Muslim Palestinians; and later out of fear of antagonizing the oil-producing Arab states. Throughout the Cold War, India's views of Israel remained lukewarm at best and hostile at worst. New Delhi's unstinting support for the Palestinian cause, compounded by Israel's opposition to Arab client states of the Soviet Union, with whom India became strategically aligned, explains the lack of diplomatic relations throughout most of the two countries' modern histories—yet appears paradoxical considering the intelligence, defense, and technical cooperation New Delhi sought from Israel in the same period.[28] After establishing diplomatic relations in 1992, these small-scale ties came into the open—and skyrocketed. Defense cooperation has defined bilateral ties, based largely around counterintelligence equipment, satellite cooperation, and missile technology. In 2009, Israel reportedly became India's largest supplier of weapons, after Russia.[29]

*Geostrategic* cooperation, however, is limited; Israel has had no compunctions about selling weapons to Pakistan or China (and has only

---

[26]Fantu Cheru and Cyril Obi, "Chinese and Indian Engagement in Africa: Competition or Mutually Reinforcing Strategies?" *Journal of International Affairs*, 64, 2 (Spring 2011): 91–110; Arnab Hazra, "India joins race for land in Africa, China way ahead," *Hindustan Times*, 4 May 2009.

[27]Many in the Hindutva project affiliated with the Rashtriya Swayamsevak Sangh of India, however, did buy into the Two-Nation Theory proponed by Pakistan partisans, agreeing that Hindus and Muslims do in fact constitute two distinct nations. Accordingly, they saw an affinity between Hinduism and Judaism (rooted in their lack of proselytization and alleged opposition to Islam), and between their own "Hindu Rashtra" and the Zionist project. From before the time of independence, Hindutva partisans sought to establish strong relations with Israel.

[28]P. K. Kumaraswamy, *India's Israel Policy*. New York: Columbia University Press, 2010.

[29]In 2009, Israel replaced Russia as India's number one supplier of arms and military technology. See, for example, Yaakov Katz, "Israel now India's top defense supplier," *Jerusalem Post*, 15 February 2009; "End of an era: Israel replaces Russia as India's top military supplier," *World Tribune*, 25 March 2009; See also Harsh V. Pant, "India-Israel Partnership: Convergence and Constraints." *Middle East Review of International Affairs*, 8, 4 (December 2004): 60–73.

refrained from doing so under American pressure), while New Delhi does not share Israel's views of Iran in the "Middle East's New Cold War."[30] After the 1960–80s period in which Israel cultivated ties with Turkey and Iran to balance its hostile Arab neighbors, Jerusalem reversed course. In its post-1993 "New Middle East" doctrine, Israel has warmed up to the geographically proximate Arab regimes while framing Iran as a rising regional threat (while its relations with Turkey have chilled).[31] Today, regional dynamics are bifurcated: Sunni Arabs, most prominently Saudi Arabia, have endorsed the Palestinian and Lebanese factions that are closer to Israel and the United States, while the Shi'ite Iranians influence the anti-Israel Levantine groups: Hamas, Hizbullah, and the Bashar al-Assad regime in Damascus. Even in the wake of the "Arab Awakening" that began in 2011 and toppled many of the status quo Arab regimes and brought greater popular representation to a number of Arab countries, India has endeavored to remain neutral in this conflict, simultaneously engaging with all of the regional parties, all of which seek a "rising India's" economic investments.

# A New Silk Road

The collapse of the Soviet Union and the independence of the Commonwealth of Independent States in Central Asia and the Caucasus opened up the region to massive influxes of external attention. Central Asian markets—energy in particular—have been prized assets for western and eastern companies alike. Turkmenistan has proven oil reserves of between 546 million and 1.7 billion barrels and natural gas reserves of approximately 71 Tcf; Uzbekistan contains 594 million barrels of proven oil reserves and natural gas reserves of 66.2 Tcf; while Kazakhstan has between 9 and 40 billion barrels of oil reserves and 65–100 Tcf of natural gas.[32] The Caucasus and Caspian Sea, meanwhile, are estimated to contain about "250 billion barrels of recoverable oil, boosted by more than 200 billion barrels of potential reserves. That's aside from up to 328 trillion cubic feet of recoverable natural gas."[33]

---

[30]Flynt Leverett and Hillary Mann Leverett, "The United States, Iran and the Middle East's 'New Cold War'." *The International Spectator*, 45, 1 (March 2010): 75–87.

[31]Trita Parsi, *Treacherous Alliance: The Secret Dealings of Israel, Iran, and the United States*. New Haven: Yale University Press, 2007.

[32]Langdon D. Clough, "Energy profile of Central Asia," in Cutler J. Cleveland (ed.), *Encyclopedia of Earth: 2008*, last revised 4 September 2008; available at http://www.eoearth.org/article/Energy_profile_of_Central_Asia

[33]John Daly, "Central Asia's Energy Chessboard," *World Politics Review*, 19 November 2009.

The Ayni Air Force base in Farkhor, Tajikistan, that India had helped develop in 2001 is set to become a *de facto* Indian Air Base, hosting a squadron of MiG-29 fighter jets. The strategic purposes of this military presence—beyond countering Pakistani influence in Afghanistan and Chinese influence in Central Asia—particularly given the high costs of maintaining aircraft out-of-region, and even India's *ability* to utilize this base, however, are questioned along with its likelihood.[34] Indeed in 2013, Russia reportedly began talks to take over (possibly jointly, with India) management of the air base.[35]

India's relations with Kazakhstan are centered largely on energy, and Memoranda of Understanding (MOUs) signed between New Delhi and Astana focus on Natural Gas provision and delivery, including discussions about pipelines and liquefaction infrastructures, and prominently, a nuclear energy deal. India's Mittal Steel (formerly Ispat) has developed a steel mill at Temirtau, outside of Astana.[36] In Uzbekistan, India's Gas Authority of India Ltd (GAIL) has worked with Uzbekneftogas to build Liquefied Petroleum Gas (LPG) facilities, and India has acquired Uzbek-made Ilyushin-78 aircraft from the Chekalov plant.[37] Kazakhstan, as the world's second largest source of uranium deposits, has become a central target for India's energy strategy in the wake of its clearance with the Nuclear Supplier's Group.[38] Turkmenistan, the largest producer of Natural Gas in Central Asia, has been another key focus of India's silk road engagement, and has been the destination of Indian investments in liquefaction facilities, refineries, Liquefied Natural Gas (LNG) ports, city gas distribution, and petro-chemical plants in exchange for discovered fields.[39] These investments are part of an Asian Development Bank-sponsored natural gas pipeline to be developed from Turkmenistan through Afghanistan, Pakistan, to India (TAPI pipeline), contingent on an improved security situation in Afghanistan and Pakistan.

And while India's strategic ties with Russia have waned since the Cold War, two key interests have remained: defense cooperation and the stability of Central Asia. Regarding the former, Moscow remains Delhi's leading supplier of conventional arms. Moscow continues to provide maintenance for India's

---

[34]Joshua Kucera, "Why is Tajikistan's Ayni Air Base Idle?," *Eurasianet*, 9 July 2010.

[35]Joshua Kucera, "Russia Starts Talks On Tajikistan's Ayni Air Base," *Eurasianet*, 7 October 2013.

[36]Marat Yermukanov, "Kazakhstan-India Relations: Partners or Distant Friends?," *Eurasia Daily Monitor*, Jamestown Foundation, 1, 128 (15 November 2004).

[37]Nivedita Das Kundu, "Hamid Ansari's visit to Turkmenistan and Kazakhstan," *IDSA Comment*, 24 April 2008, available at http://www.idsa.in/idsastrategiccomments/HamidAnsarisVisitto TurkmenistanandKazakhstan_NDKundu_240408

[38]Zakir Hussain, "India and Kazakhstan: New Ways Ahead," *IDSA Comment*, 18 February 2009, available at http://www.idsa.in/idsastrategiccomments/IndiaandKazakhstan_ZHussain_180209

[39]Amitav Ranjan, "India, Turkmenistan to sign historic pact on natural fuel today," *Indian Express*, 5 April 2008.

arsenal, which is predominantly of Soviet-Russian origin. Meanwhile, since the early 1990s, both Moscow and New Delhi supported the Northern Alliance against the Taliban factions in Afghanistan, in an effort to clamp down on Islamist extremist and stabilize Central Asia in order to expand its connectivity and to limit Chinese influence in the region. Indian companies like Reliance Industries and ONGC Videsh, meanwhile, have joined with Russian energy firm Gazprom to explore energy assets in the Russian Federation, including the Sakhalin III in northeast Asia, which is estimated to have 1.4 trillion cubic meters in natural gas reserves.[40] Along with Iran, India and Russia aim to reinvigorate regional trade with the North-South Corridor, which would connect Eastern Europe, the Caucasus and Central Asia, with India and Southeast Asia through a mix of road, rail, and sea links.[41]

Russia and the Central Asian Republics themselves have sought to increase India's presence in Central Asia in order to offset what is perceived as China's increasing strategic and economic dominance of the region, particularly in light of America's imminent withdrawal from Afghanistan. To this end, the non-Chinese members of the Shangai Cooperation Organization have lobbied for the inclusion in the body of India, which was granted observer status in 2005.[42]

At the center of India's Central Asia strategy is Afghanistan, which has been the geographic hub of the "New Silk Road" and its historical namesake. In its support for the Northern Alliance against the Taliban, India originally developed, in early 2001, a medical facility at Ayni air base at Farkhor, Tajikistan, along the northern Afghan-Tajikistan border to nurse wounded Northern Alliance fighters. And since the fall of the Taliban regime, India's strategic interests in Afghanistan have been threefold: (i) balancing against China's growing footprint in the region; (ii) curbing Islamist militancy that spreads further southeast into India and specifically, Indian-administered Kashmir, and restricting the Pakistani influence in Afghanistan that abets such militancy, and (iii) developing economic infrastructure that will stabilize the country and enable it to reconnect to the rest of the region. To these ends, New Delhi has been a major economic donor to Afghanistan. It has developed the Zaranj-Delaram highway in Afghanistan's western Herat province, and constructed Afghanistan's parliament building in Kabul. After the 2005 Taliban attack on

---

[40]Rakteem Katakey, "India bags stake in Russia's Sakhalin III," *India Abroad*, 3 May 2008.

[41]"Development of the Trans-Asian Railway: Trans-Asian Railway in the north-south corridor, northern Europe to the Persian Gulf," *United Nations Economic and Social Commission for Asia and the Pacific*, United Nations Publications, 2001, ST/ESCAP/2182.

[42]Erica Marat, "The SCO and Foreign Powers in Central Asia: Sino-Russian Differences," *CACI Analyst*, Central Asia-Caucasus Institute, 28 May 2008, available at http://www.cacianalyst.org/?q=node/4867

Indian aid workers, Afghanistan was the first extra-regional country to which
India sent its own troops outside of UN auspices when it deployed 200 troops
from the Indo-Tibetan Border Police (ITBP) to protect its investment projects.
In 2005, India championed the inclusion of Afghanistan into the SAARC, and
since 2001, has pledged over 2 billion USD in aid, constructing roads and
power plants, developing health and educational infrastructure, and training
the Afghan National Police.[43] And as recently as October 2011, New Delhi and
Kabul signed a Strategic Partnership deal in which India would train and equip
Afghanistan's national army.[44]

Iran, meanwhile, has become a lynchpin in enabling this Indian engagement.
After decades of mistrust—the Shah's Iran originally fell within the US-backed
CENTO, which included and supported Pakistan, while the post-1979 Islamic
Republic of Iran's revolutionary zeal was feared to have negative consequences
for India's hold over Kashmir—by the 1990s, many saw a burgeoning "New
Delhi-Tehran Axis" in India and Iran's enhanced economic and strategic ties.[45]
These included shared opposition to the Taliban and support for the Northern
Alliance. Since 2000, India has sought to develop Iran's first LNG plant, and
even develop an Asian Development Bank-backed Iran-Pakistan-India (IPI)
natural gas pipeline. In the face of American opposition, however, many of
these projects fell by the wayside.[46]

Yet strategic and economic convergence remains between New Delhi and
Tehran. Both seek an alternative to the Pakistan-backed Taliban in Afghanistan,
as well as a new transport corridor to Central Asia. Indian oil imports from Iran
increased by 9.5 percent in 2008–09, accounting for 16.5 percent of India's
crude oil imports and making Iran India's second largest supplier of oil after
Saudi Arabia. By 2008, bilateral trade reached 30 billion USD, considering third-
country intermediaries, while India's ONGC, along with other Indian firms such
as the Hinduja Group, have entered into negotiations to develop the offshore
Farzad B gas field as well as the South Pars gas field, an investment of more
than 11 billion USD over the coming years. Meanwhile, despite being one

[43]"India Extends $450-m Aid to Afghanistan," *Financial Express,* 8 August 2008; James Lamont and
Matthew Green, "India offers to train Afghan police," *Financial Times,* 3 October 2011.
[44]"Afghan Leader signs deal to Deepen Ties with India," *Reuters,* 4 October 2011.
[45]Christine Fair in "Headlines over the Horizon," *The Atlantic Monthly,* July/August 2003.
[46]In fact, New Delhi's engagement with Washington, and Washington's enmity with Iran, has
stymied Indo-Iranian, and Indo-American relations writ large. Under American pressure, India
repeatedly voted to condemn Iran in the International Atomic Energy Agency over its alleged
nuclear weapons program, and the Reserve Bank of India decided in 2010 to prohibit companies
from using the Asian Currency Union to pay for Iranian oil, effectively sanctioning imports of
Iranian petroleum. Largely in retaliation, Tehran has raised the Kashmir issue in forums such as the
Organization of the Islamic Conference (OIC), to New Delhi's ire, and raised the price on natural
gas and petroleum that India has sought to purchase from Iran.

of the world's largest petroleum producers, Iran lacks a significant refinery infrastructure of its own, forcing it to rely on imports for over 40 percent its own consumption. By some accounts, 40 percent of the oil imported by Iran has come from refineries in India.[47] At the beginning of 2012, India surpassed China as the largest importer of Iranian crude oil, circumventing western sanctions on Iran by creating new corporate entities that are independent of Western financial institutions, purchasing Iranian oil with gold rather than dollars (reverting to a barter system that requires Iran to buy Indian goods), and sending currency through institutions such as Turkey's Halkbank, which remains outside the purview of Western sanctions.[48]

And because Pakistan long delayed open transit trade between Afghanistan and India, New Delhi was forced to look further afield. In September 2008, New Delhi constructed Iran's "Eastern Corridor," a road that passes from Chabahar Port on the Arabian Sea, through Iran's eastern Sistan and Baluchistan and South Khorasan provinces, and onward to the town of Milak on the Afghan border. From there it connects with the Indian-built Zaranj-Delaram highway in western Afghanistan's Nimruz Province, which subsequently links to the Afghan Ring Road. New Delhi, Tehran, and Kabul have planned a railway line along the entire route to facilitate trade—particularly of Afghanistan's estimated 1 trillion USD in minerals—to and from Central Asia.[49]

At 135 miles, the Chabahar road to the Afghan border is far shorter than the nearly 1100-mile trip from Karachi to the Torkham border in northeastern Pakistan (via Peshawar), and even the nearly 500 miles from Karachi to the Chaman border in the northwest (through Quetta). Thomas Barfield, author of the comprehensive *Afghanistan: A Cultural and Political History,* puts it simply: the Indian-constructed transport corridor through Chabahar "ends Pakistan's monopoly on seaborne transit trade to Afghanistan . . . [making] Iran the most efficient route into Central Asia."

Though the link is primarily aimed at accessing Afghan and Central Asian natural resources, Barfield argues that "India now has the capacity to dispatch troops and supplies directly to Afghanistan via Iran if it chooses to do so.

---

[47]For an overview of India-Iran relations, particularly in light of American involvement therein, see Neil Padukone, "Can India Facilitate a US-Iran Rapprochement?," Issue Brief No. 15, *Centre for Land Warfare Studies,* March 2010.

[48]See, for example, Neil Padukone, "Between Washington and Tehran," *Pragati: The Indian National Interest,* April 2012; Amitav Ranjan, "To Engage Iran, India looks to beat US, UN sanctions by being 'creative'," Express India, 3 August 2010. In 2013, however, India reduced its dependence on Iranian petroleum owing to the broader sanctions regime. European insurance companies refused to insure ships that would trade with Iran, prohibitively increasing India's risk in transactions with Tehran.

[49]Jayanth Jacob and Saubhadra Chatterji, "India's Track Three: Afghan-Iran rail link," *Hindustan Times,* 1 November 2011.

Should the United States decide to withdraw from Afghanistan, India may well be tempted to step in to preempt the possibility of a Taliban takeover" or increased Chinese presence. The new Indian-constructed link "may change regional power dynamics" in Central Asia.[50]

# Naval Expansion

In 2005, former Indian Chief of Naval Staff Arun Prakash argued that "it is essential that we take adequate security measures to safeguard our assets and interests,"[51] including those in the Gulf, Central Asia, Southeast Asia, and Africa. With its current arsenal of 155 naval vessels operating from major naval bases at Visakhapatnam, Mumbai, Goa, and Port Blair, India is expanding its navy to one with blue water capabilities, including the development of submarines and aircraft carriers for out-of-area operations.[52] While the other naval bases had been active for decades, in the wake of recommendations by the Kargil Review Committee of 1999, an integrated command was raised at Port Blair in the Andaman and Nicobar Islands in 2001.

The focus of India's naval force projection capacities thus far has been intelligence gathering, escorting merchant ships of India and friendly states, joint exercises with the navies of allied countries, and anti-piracy missions. In November 2008, Indian Naval vessel INS *Tabar* played a seminal role in countering Somali pirates that had threatened oil shipments in the Gulf of Aden.[53] Rescue and evacuation missions—notably following the 2004 earthquake in Indonesia and the 2006 Lebanon War—have also been central aims of the Indian Navy, requiring maritime cooperation with other navies of the region, including the United States.

India's ties with the small island nations of the southern Indian Ocean have also been central to its expansion strategy, creating its own burgeoning "chain of pearls." Since 2005, the Indian Navy has gifted a fast attack craft, the INS *Tarmugli*, helicopters, and other military equipment to The Republic of Seychelles, in an effort to preempt China's presence there.[54] With Mauritius,

---

[50]Thomas Barfield, *Afghanistan: A Cultural and Political History*. Princeton, NJ: *Princeton University Press*, 2010, pp. 344–5.
[51]Arun Prakash, "Security and Foreign Policy Imperatives of an Emerging India," 11 November 2005, in Arun Prakash, *From the Crow's Nest: A Compendium of Speeches and Writings on Maritime and Other Issues*. New Delhi: Lancer Publishers, 2007, p. 6.
[52]Balaji Reddy, "Indian Navy to add 125 more ultra modern warships and many submarines in the next ten years," *India Daily*, 30 July 2009.
[53]"India sinks Somali Pirate ship," *BBC News*, 19 November 2008.
[54]Adm. Sureesh Mehta, "The Major Powers and Asian Security: Cooperation or Conflict?," Second Plenary Session, Shangri-La Dialogue in Singapore, 8th IISS Asia Security Summit, 30 May 2009.

India has established an agreement to patrol the Mauritius Exclusive Economic Zone, assisted the establishment of the Mauritian Coast Guard, and has provided equipment, aircraft, and hydrographic surveys to, and even leased land for development from Port Louis.[55] New Delhi also has patrolling agreements with the African Littoral states, having constructed a monitoring station in Madagascar and coastal surveillance programs in Mozambique.[56]

The military dimension of India's naval expansion also has Beijing in mind. China's maritime presence in the Indian Ocean is structurally restricted by geography, a restriction that is in many ways to India's advantage. The narrow Straits of Malacca and Lombok are China's only two naval thoroughfares to the region; that too, only after the PLA-Navy has circumvented the American military barriers of the South China Sea. India, however, has offshore naval assets at Port Blair, in India's own Nicobar and Andaman Islands, close to the head of the Malacca Strait. As early as 1945, Indian statesman and strategist K. M. Panikkar argued, "the Gulf of Malacca is like the mouth of a crocodile, the peninsula of Malaya being the upper and the jutting end of Sumatra being the lower jaw. Entry to the gulf can be controlled by the Nicobars,"[57] foretelling Chinese Naval Analyst Zhang Ming's fears of Indian control.

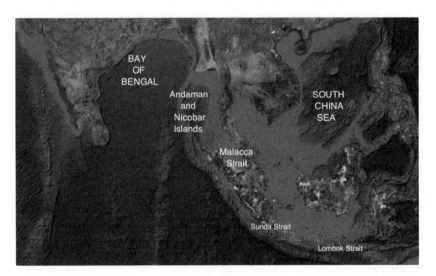

**FIGURE 9.1** *South-Southeast Asia maritime geography—adapted from Google Maps.*

---

[55]Sidhartha, "India eyes an island in the Sun," *Times of India*, 26 November 2006.

[56]C. Raja Mohan, "Sino-Indian Rivalry in the Western Indian Ocean," *ISAS Insights*, National University of Singapore, No. 52, 24 February 2009.

[57]K. M. Panikkar, *India and the Indian Ocean: An Essay on the Influence of Sea Power on Indian History*. London: George Allen and Unwin, 1945, p. 21.

In anticipation of a larger Chinese footprint, India's naval presence in the Bay of Bengal is being enhanced by the expansion of its eastern naval command, headquartered at Andhra Pradesh's Visakhapatnam, which hosts the Indian Navy's submarine fleet. In 2011, nearly a third of the Indian navy's entire fleet, 50 warships, was based at its eastern command. Moreover, India's aircraft carrier, the INS *Viraat*, five Rajput-class guided-missile destroyers, will be shifted from the western to the eastern command. They are to be followed by the INS *Jalashwa* and stealth fighters *INS Shivalik, INS Satpura,* and *INS Sahyadri*, the fleet tanker *INS Shakti*, and even the INS *Arihant*, India's nuclear submarine. According to Sudha Ramachandran, the eastern command has an additional base at Kolkata as well as a new "forward base at Thoothukudi," southern Tamil Nadu, "and an operational turnaround base at Paradee" in Orissa. "In addition to naval air stations at Dega and Rajali, the eastern command has got a new one, *INS Parundu* at Uchipuli, where unmanned aerial vehicles are being deployed."[58]

Moreover, both of these Indian Ocean access points (Malacca and Lombok) and all of China's "pearls" within the Indian Ocean are closer to naval, air, and land bases on the Indian peninsula. Because the Indian peninsula is itself an "unsinkable aircraft carrier," India is likely to maintain military supremacy in the Indian Ocean—certainly over China, with its multiple geographic barriers and island chokepoints.

In the unlikely event of a military confrontation, even in the northern sector, India would be able to blockade Chinese economic or military shipments through the Malacca Strait,[59] Bay of Bengal (via Myanmar and Bangladesh), or even the Arabian Sea (at Gwadar). In fact, the more dependent China is on this South Asian infrastructure, the more vulnerable to a naval blockade or even a direct naval attack China would be in the event of a military face-off with India.[60]

---

[58]Sudha Ramachandran, "Indian Navy pumps up eastern muscle," *Asia Times*, 20 August 2011.

[59]The political/economic problem with such a scenario would be that the blockade would also harm the interests of Indian allies in the Pacific, whether Singapore, Japan, Vietnam, or others.

[60]This idea is also explored in Iskander Rehman, "China's String of Pearls and India's Enduring Tactical Advantage," *IDSA Comment*, 8 June 2010, available at http://www.idsa.in/idsacomments/ChinasStringofPearlsandIndiasEnduringTacticalAdvantage_irehman_080610

# 10

# "Natural Allies"?

# The United States and India in the Twenty-First Century

The collapse of the Soviet Union and the end of the Cold War rewrote much of America's playbook in South Asia. The Soviet Union's withdrawal from Afghanistan prompted a subsequent American withdrawal from Pakistan. India, meanwhile, had lost in the Soviet Union its primary benefactor and strategic partner, causing New Delhi to reassess its own strategic environment. The opening of New Delhi's markets to foreign investment and the structural adjustment programs initiated by the IMF bailout, meanwhile, changed the American view of India's potential as a ripe market.

This economic optimism of the early 1990s, however, was tempered by strategic wariness. Both American and Indian government bureaucracies and media were attuned to resist and even demonize the other. Moreover, it was another rising Asian power that dominated American strategic interest in the immediate post–Cold War period: the PRC. By 1992, a US Department of Defense Planning Guide articulated that a rising China could be America's main contender in the post–Cold War world. But these strategic military concerns were temporarily put on the back burner due to America's interest in trade relations. Despite concerns over human rights in China in the wake of the 1989 Tiananmen Square massacre, US President Bill Clinton began a concerted trade outreach effort, culminating in the extension of *Most-Favored Nation* (MFN) status to Beijing. This rise in trade with Beijing also began to increase America's trade deficit with China, entangling the two countries in a complex, symbiotic trade relationship.

Having its own concerns over China's economic expansion, a wary India trudged on. In May 1998, the Indian government, headed by the National

Democratic Alliance, conducted a nuclear test. The then-Foreign Minister Jaswant Singh argued, in a subsequent Foreign Affairs article, that "the rise of China led to new security strains" that required India to ensure that its nuclear arsenal was credible enough to deter Beijing.[1] The Indian test broke decades of nuclear ambiguity, in which India did not publicly acknowledge or declare the existence of a nuclear weapons capacity, and was immediately followed by a Pakistani test of six nuclear bombs in the Chagai Hills of Baluchistan. Both tests were immediately followed by international censure and sanctions by Japan, Australia, and the United States, as mandated by the 1977 Glenn Amendment to the US Foreign Assistance Act of 1961 that restricts financial ties to countries that acquire, transfer, or explode nuclear materials. Particularly in the wake of strenuous efforts by the Clinton Administration to tighten the nonproliferation regime after the Soviet Union's demise—including Cooperative Threat Reduction Programs in Eurasia, an indefinite extension of the Nuclear Non-Proliferation Treaty that would include a Comprehensive Test Ban Treaty (CTBT), and a push for a Fissile Material Cutoff Treaty (FMCT)—India's reputation as a threat to the nonproliferation regime was renewed by these tests, in a throwback to the US-India antagonism of the Cold War.

Through the 1990s, however, a major development *within* the United States contributed to a change in tone in US-India relations. The Indian diaspora, which had begun to settle in the United States in large numbers in the 1970s, had established itself as an economic heavyweight within the country, and was beginning to organize politically as well. Political lobbying by Indian-Americans began to change perceptions as well as the public discourse on India.[2]

Thus far, there had been two main narratives of India that dominated the halls of Washington. The first was that India was just another third world socialist basket case, replete with poverty, disease, and corruption. The second, solidified under the Nixon-Indira years, was that India was an international irritant, with its Soviet-leaning nonalignment, nuclear proliferation, and destabilizing hegemony over South Asia. As Secretary of State Henry Kissinger reportedly told the US Ambassador to New Delhi in the mid-1970s, "The less I hear about India, the happier I will be."[3]

But by the 1990s, a third narrative was emerging: that India's large 1.1 billion-strong population could be an important market for American goods and services, and a prime example of the emerging "Washington Consensus," the economic doctrine that would drive American strategy in the immediate post–Cold War era. The overt nuclearization of South Asia, meanwhile, convinced

---

[1] Jaswant Singh, "Against Nuclear Apartheid," *Foreign Affairs*, September/October 1998.
[2] Amit Gupta, "The Indian Diaspora's Political Efforts in the United States," ORF Occasional Paper, *Observer Research Foundation*, September 2004.
[3] William B. Saxbe with Peter D. Franklin, *I've Seen the Elephant: An Autobiography*. Washington, D.C.: National Defense University Press, 1992.

American strategists that the region was owed greater attention. At first this attention was negative: raising the specter of conflict in the subcontinent, the detonation of nuclear weapons by India and Pakistan appeared to increase instability between the two countries. But it also spoke to India's potential military might and great power ambitions, particularly vis-à-vis China. President Clinton's trip to India in 2000 began to put India on the Pentagon's map.

The foundation upon which the US-India relationship was built had a number of other points of convergence. The rhetorical bedrock of the "natural alliance" described by the then Prime Minister A. B. Vajpayee was, of course, democracy.[4] As the world's oldest and largest democracies, respectively, the United States and India supposedly shared the goal of ensuring a just and democratic world order, even though this shared democratic tradition had been insufficient to bring the countries together during the Cold War.

The 11 September terrorist attacks of 2001 added another military-strategic dimension to this narrative. To date, Washington had little sympathy for New Delhi's position on Kashmir and the insurgency therein. As far back as the 1950s, American officials had publicly embraced Kashmiri leaders as democratic revolutionaries seeking self-determination. The common American narrative on Kashmir viewed New Delhi as oppressors and the Kashmiris as freedom fighters. But 11 September placed Islamist terrorism at the forefront of American strategic concerns, certainly in the South Asian region. In its search to find Al Qaeda and understand the various linkages between Islamist militant groups in South Asia, the United States began to see organizations like LeT, Hizbul-Mujahideen, and other Islamist groups that had been operating in Kashmir within the purview of its broader "Global War on Terrorism." Thus the issue of terrorism began to bring the United States and India closer strategically: restricting Islamist terrorism and stabilizing the Afghanistan-Pakistan region became another shared interest. And to this end, the intelligence communities of both countries increased counterterrorism cooperation and information sharing.

Most importantly, the crux of the strategic relationship was the larger issue of containing China and policing the Indian Ocean. America's strategic calculations over China began to change, seeing Beijing's naval expansion as a threat to the American-backed order of the South China Sea. Many scholars and American officials began to emphasize the convergence of Indian and American strategic interests over China; that is, both sought to contain Beijing as it rose economically and militarily. This included ensuring that Beijing does not dominate the strategic chokepoints of global trade—energy resources in

---

[4]Atal Bihari Vajpayee, "Address by Atal Bihari Vajpayee, Prime Minister of India," Asia Society Annual Gala, 7 September 2000, available at http://asiasociety.org/policy/address-shri-atal-bihari-vajpayee

the Persian Gulf as well as Central Asia, as well as the major corridors and SLOCs that traverse the Indian Ocean, in particular the Strait of Malacca, the Gulf of Aden, the Gulf of Oman, and southern rim of the Indian Ocean. In fact, the articulation of China's "string of pearls" strategy that has been at the crux of India's perceptions of its own strategic environment had its origins in a publication for the US Army War College.[5]

To this end the US Military and the Indian Armed Forces have conducted a number of training exercises in the Indian Ocean; perhaps more than any bureaucracy, the armed forces—and particularly the navies—of the two countries have become more coordinated since the reversal of ties in the late 1990s. India has conducted more joint naval exercises with the United States than with any other country.[6]

To solidify this ostensible convergence of interest, the administration of US President George W. Bush initiated discussions with India over a civilian nuclear deal that would exempt India from nonproliferation restrictions on the types of technology to which it would have access. The deal, signed in 2005 and ratified by the US Senate in 2008, opens up India's access to nuclear technology and nuclear fuel from the Nuclear Suppliers Group, contingent on India keeping its civilian and nuclear reactors separate (in the past, fissile material for energy-producing nuclear power plants had been used in defense research), allowing the International Atomic Energy Agency to inspect its civilian facilities, continuing its moratorium on weapons testing, and strengthening its nuclear security, including movement toward a FMCT that bans the spread of fissile material.[7]

The deal was to have a number of ancillary benefits, including bringing India into American efforts to, as the document put it, "dissuade, isolate, and, if necessary, sanction and contain Iran's" nuclear program: having unfettered access to nuclear fuel for domestic energy production, the logic went, would obviate the need for India to go pursue plans to tap and import Iranian oil and natural gas.[8] Yet from the beginning, it was assumed that Indian nuclear markets would essentially be ceded to French and Russian companies, since

---

[5]Christopher J. Pehrson, "String of Pearls: Meeting the Challenge of China's Rising Power Across the Asian Littoral," Strategic Studies Institute, US Army War College, July 2006.

[6]"India as a great power: Know your own strength," *The Economist*, 30 March 2013.

[7]US- India Civil Nuclear Cooperation Initiative – Bilateral Agreement on Peaceful Nuclear Cooperation (123 Agreement), US Department of State, 27 July 2007.

[8]At the time of the deal, the United States was facing a major standoff with the Islamic Republic of Iran over its alleged nuclear weapons program. The United States had even hoped to open up an economic sanctions campaign against Iran—a campaign that faced challenges from New Delhi in large part because of India's thirst for energy and Iran's natural gas in particular. Indeed, from 2005 to 2009, India voted on multiple occasions to condemn Iran's nuclear program in the International Atomic Energy Agency, a decision largely seen as coming under American political pressure.

the American nuclear industry had been in decline since the 1978 Three Mile Island nuclear disaster in Pennsylvania. The deal would also remove nonproliferation from the list of irritants that plagued the US-India relationship by bringing India into the nonproliferation mainstream. The "real reason for the agreement on the American side," as Leonard S. Spector put it,

> is to shore up relations with India and to establish our close relationship for the future. The agreement carries considerable symbolism and . . . that's even more important than any business that may be obtained by American vendors. From the Indian standpoint . . . it's again more of the symbolism of the agreement—having a document that demonstrates the United States is ready to build an enduring and deep relationship.[9]

Yet the sale of conventional weapons sales is seen as another means of shoring up strategic ties, and analysts have referred to "fighter diplomacy" as a central backbone of US-India relations.[10] Historically, Soviet, Israeli, and European weapons suppliers provided weaponry to India with few technological or political strings attached. Yet the United States often placed end-user agreements on weapons purchasers, as well as limits on dual-use technology and export controls in order to curtail the potential proliferation of classified technology and nonconventional weaponry—the distribution of which would give away the American producers' technological and competitive edge. Many American weapons sales would also come with caveats for expected political behavior, as many of the ancillary terms of the nuclear deal imply. Indeed, despite the expectations of a strong bilateral relationship, there are a number of irritants and points of strategic divergence.

## Hitches: Pakistan

For its part, one of America's primary medium-term goals in South Asia is the stabilization of the Afghanistan-Pakistan region. The way Pakistani diplomats and military officials to the United States have traditionally, and often very effectively, framed the issue—and subsequently the way many in the United States have taken to seeing the issue as well—is that Islamabad is unable

---

9 "Symbolism Tops Substance in U.S.-India Nuclear Agreement: An Interview with Leonard Spector," *Council on Foreign Relations*, 15 July 2008, available at http://www.cfr.org/india/symbolism-tops-substance-us-india-nuclear-agreement/p16803

10 Manohar Thyagaraj, "Fighter Diplomacy: A 'Passage to India'?." *Air and Space Power Journal*, 20, 1 (Spring 2006): 97–106.

to devote sufficient attention and military resources to the fight against Taliban insurgents in Pakistan's northern areas (Waziristan, Baluchistan, and Khyber Pakhtunkhwa, the former "Northwestern Frontier Province") if it must simultaneously be concerned with securing its eastern border against India.[11] Thus Washington has encouraged India to lower its standing forces along the border with Pakistan to enable the latter to do the same. At the most extreme extension of this logic, many in Washington even hope to pressure New Delhi to make concessions to Pakistan vis-à-vis Kashmir, and perhaps to even intervene in the dispute to open it up to trilateral intervention.[12] India might then be able to concentrate on other strategic issues, including its conflict with China, internal security, and naval strategy.

The fly in this ointment, however, is the view that Pakistan-based elements—allegedly non-state militant groups as well as factions of the military establishment—use this demilitarization (or "diversion") as an opportunity to infiltrate the Line of Control in Kashmir, mount terrorist attacks on mainland India, such as the November 26 attacks on Mumbai in 2008, and even increase Pakistan's nuclear weapons arsenal in the absence of larger-scale conventional conflict with India. Pakistan's nuclear arsenal reportedly doubled from 2006 to 2012, reaching parity with or even overtaking those of India and the United Kingdom—a development that passed with little in the way of protest from Washington.[13]

Indeed, one of India's key hopes with regard to American policy in South Asia has been a "de-hyphenation" of India and Pakistan. "Hyphenation" was the dominant Cold War American policy of seeing India through the lens of Pakistan and how Indian policy might implicate Pakistan, and vice versa—never seeing either in isolation or for its own contributions. The US-India nuclear deal was said to finally *de-hyphenate* the two. Instead of assessing India based on how its actions would affect affairs in Pakistan, Washington would see India on its own merits: as an open market for investment, as well as a strategic partner on the Indian Ocean, particularly vis-à-vis China.

Yet, somewhat paradoxically, as part of thinking of New Delhi and Islamabad on disconnected terms, India hopes to influence American policy regarding Islamabad: namely, India has hoped that Washington will diminish support for—and even be critical of—the Pakistani military establishment. On this

---

[11] Teresita Schaffer and Howard Schaffer, *How Pakistan Negotiates with the United States: Riding the Roller Coaster.* Washington, D.C.: *United States Institute of Peace*, 2011.
[12] An Indian perspective on this American activism is detailed in C. Raja Mohan, "Barack Obama's Kashmir Thesis," *Indian Express*, 3 November 2008; C. Raja Mohan, "The United States and Kashmir: When Less is More," *Asia Policy*, No. 10, July 2010.
[13] David Sanger and Eric Schmitt, "Pakistani Nuclear Arms Pose Challenge to US Policy," *New York Times*, 31 January 2011.

issue, New Delhi has three particular intentions: (i) that Washington be more critical of Pakistani military support for militants in Afghanistan, Kashmir, and within its own borders, including those groups that target India and Kashmir (such as LeT and Jaish-e-Mohammad), rather than simply those that target the west, like Al Qaeda; (ii) that Washington limit or even terminate the sale of arms to Pakistan, which, according to New Delhi, Rawalpindi uses against India; and (iii) that Washington be more critical of Pakistan's record on nuclear proliferation. In fact, in the wake of the 2004 disclosure of Pakistani nuclear scientist Abdul Qadeer (A. Q.) Khan's global nuclear smuggling circuit, the United States reportedly came to a deal with Pakistan in which Khan would be spared international public condemnation and legal action in exchange for military support in Afghanistan.

Indeed, Washington's inability or unwillingness to take Islamabad or Rawalpindi "to task" on these issues lies in its dependence on Pakistan, both for geographic access to Central Asia and for fears of what would happen *in* Pakistan should the United States disengage from the region: the security of Pakistan's nuclear weapons and a hypothetical takeover of the government (and of the nuclear arsenal) by Islamist militants in its borders.

For decades, Pakistan has been the west's only link between the Arabian Sea and Central Asia. The main reason for this sole reliance on Pakistan for access to Central Asia is that, rather than encouraging the cheaper, more stable alternate route from Chabahar to Milak-Zaranj in eastern Iran, constructed with assistance from New Delhi, Washington hopes to censure Tehran. But this aim is largely self-defeating, as Tehran continues to extend its reach into Central Asia in spite of the American isolation.[14] Accordingly, India hopes that the United States will open up and use Iranian routes to Central Asia, circumventing and diminishing its reliance on Pakistan. This would also enable India to engage, unhindered, in trade with Iran, including in petroleum and natural gas.[15]

India would also like the United States to be more critical of the Pakistani military in a more general sense. The military's support for militants in Afghanistan, Kashmir, and even domestically—in Pakistani Punjab, NWFP, and Karachi in particular—as strategic tools eventually come back around to harm India, the United States, and even Pakistanis themselves. In large part for this reason, New Delhi hopes that the United States will limit or terminate arms sales and military aid to Pakistan. From New Delhi's perspective, Islamabad

---

[14]See for example Dario Cristiani, "Iran's Growing Interests and Influence in Central Asia," *World Politics Review,* 10 September 2010; and Suzanne Maloney, *Iran's Long Reach: Iran as a Pivotal State in the Muslim World.* Washington, D.C.: United States Institute of Peace Press, 2008.
[15]Neil Padukone, "Can India Facilitate a US-Iranian Rapprochement?," *Centre for Land Warfare Studies,* Issue Brief, No. 15, March 2010.

invests this military aid in conventional and unconventional weaponry—including an expansion of its nuclear arsenal—to target India, rather than fighting the militant groups for which the aid is intended. Thus India sees America as an inadvertent and often unwitting supporter of Pakistan's war against India.

And yet, American intervention in the other countries of South Asia, even if it goes against India's short-term interests, is unlikely to be opposed by New Delhi with the vehemence of the past. In fact, as Stephen Cohen says, "since the Kargil conflict in 1999," when Washington diplomatically intervened in New Delhi's favor, "India has turned to America to straighten out Pakistan, whereas before that, they did not want [America] in South Asia at all. But they realized that [Washington has] leverage in Pakistan."[16] Moreover, Washington has in fact "come around" to India's thinking on Pakistani support for militants. After the May 2011 raid on Abbottabad, in which US Navy Seals crossed the Afghan-Pakistan border and killed Osama bin laden, Pakistani support for militant groups has become more evident in the US discourse. Consequently, American strategic planners and analysts have looked at Pakistan with a far more critical eye.

# Hitches: Global Governance

Further afield, the United States sees India, as a fellow democracy, as a partner in establishing a liberal and democratic order throughout the world. In particular, this has led the United States to seek Indian interventions against the military junta in Myanmar; assistance in condemning Iran, particularly on its nuclear program; military cooperation in the Iraq war in 2003; and in 2011, an Indian vote in the United Nations Security Council (UNSC) condemning the human rights record of Muammar Qadhafi, thus authorizing a NATO intervention in Libya. However, this globally activist role runs counter to India's skepticism of interventionism in global affairs, particularly those outside of its traditional geographic ambit and based primarily on principles such as human rights or liberalism. India reflexively opposes interventionism due to its own sensitivity on third-party interventions in the Kashmir issue; if India were to intervene in domestic issues like Burmese governance, the argument goes, the international community would thus feel entitled to do the same in Indian-administered Jammu and Kashmir.

---

[16]International Affairs Forum, "IA Forum Interview: Stephen Cohen," *Center for International Relations*, May 2009, available at http://www.ia-forum.org/Content/ViewInternalDocument. cfm?ContentID=6959

Moreover, these types of interventions often run counter to India's strategic or economic interests. In the case of Iran, India has economic interests in the Islamic Republic's natural gas and petroleum reserves, and shares strategic interests with Iran in Central Asia—including a stable Afghanistan that is not dominated by the Taliban. In Myanmar, India had attempted to isolate the regime on the basis of human rights violations in the 1990s. But when it realized that this isolation simply opened the strategic space for Beijing to engage with Yangon economically and strategically, New Delhi realized its folly and sought to reengage with the Junta. In fact, New Delhi often sees America's efforts to isolate or economically sanction countries like Burma and Iran as being not only disagreeable, but also ultimately ineffective, a sentiment that is strengthened by the fact that *India* had been on the receiving end of, but ultimately overcame, such isolation attempts—notably nuclear sanctions and limits on weapons sales—through much of the Cold War.

Nonetheless, the United States hopes that India will take a greater lead in global governance, as the United States *National Security Strategy* of 2006 put it, to "shoulder global obligations in cooperation with the United States."[17] For decades, the chattering class of New Delhi has sought veto power and a permanent seat on the UNSC, in large part as a vindication of India's central global role. And in recent years, American officials have expressed rhetorical support for an ultimate expansion of the UNSC to include India.[18]

Yet many argue that, in fact, India's views on global governance—from climate change to nonproliferation to humanitarian intervention—would run counter to American interests.[19] For its part, though India aspires to a greater global role, when it comes to specific diplomatic endeavors, India's relative backseat at global diplomatic forums has in fact been a vital tool: abstention from UN votes on globally controversial issues so that it can remain ambivalent and not upset one or another potential strategic partner around the world, has allowed it to keep its political options open. India's historical diplomatic strategy has been fairly consistent in this regard: it has often favored unilateral intervention (namely, its own) in South Asia, while condemning it elsewhere.

Additionally, New Delhi often finds these types of "liberal" or humanitarian interventions contradictory; while the United States has opposed dictators on the basis of human rights violations in some places, it has sacrificed

---

[17]United States National Security Strategy, *White House*, January 2006.

[18]In his November 2010 visit to New Delhi, US President Barack Obama became the first American president to publicly articulate support for a permanent seat for India on the UN body. See for example, Scott Wilson and Emily Wax, "Obama endorses India for UN Security Council Seat," *Washington Post*, 8 November 2010.

[19]Personal Interview with US Embassy in New Delhi political affairs staffer, in New Delhi, 20 April 2009.

democracy by supporting dictators in countries where it has vested strategic interests in the status quo, like Pakistan, Saudi Arabia, and China. In 2011, Indian National Security Advisor Shiv Shankar Menon explained his country's policy in a thinly veiled criticism of US policy:

> Do we not have a responsibility to spread democracy and fight for our values abroad? Yes and no. Yes, if we have the means to actually ensure that we are able to spread them. And yes if having democrats as our neighbors contributes to the peaceful periphery that we need. . . . [But] we have seen how high sounding phrases like the "right to protect" are selectively invoked and brutally applied in the pursuit of self-interest, giving humanitarian and international intervention a bad name.[20]

On larger, controversial issues, New Delhi has preferred bilateral agreements in which its concerns are addressed in a relatively closed forum rather than one in which it must openly compromise its more specific individual bilateral interests with multiple countries.[21] This applies to treaties such as the CTBT, the FMCT—nonproliferation efforts outside of which India has remained for decades—and even climate change mitigation efforts such as the United Nations Climate Change Conference.

From India's perspective, the existing nonproliferation regime that has its origins in the NPT of the 1960s and for years enshrined "nuclear apartheid," has become obsolete. India endorses a *global* ban on nuclear weapons, in which every single country—from China to Russia and particularly the United States—eschews them, in which case India would have no need for them and would willingly relinquish its arsenal. But if even one country has them, it is inevitable that others will feel the need to follow suit: after the nuclearization of the United States, Moscow felt compelled to get its own weapon to deter the United States; because Moscow had them, Beijing felt compelled to deter Russia; India felt compelled to deter China (and America after 1971); Pakistan felt compelled to deter India; and so forth.[22]

In the past decade, former and current American statesmen—including former Secretaries of State Henry Kissinger and George Shultz, former Secretary of Defense William Perry, former Senator Sam Nunn, and even serving

---

[20]Shivshankar Menon, "India and the Global Scene," Prem Bhatia Memorial Lecture, No. 16, New Delhi, 2011, available at http://www.maritimeindia.org/article/india-and-global-scene.html
[21]Author's communication with M. K. Rasgotra, former foreign secretary of India, New Delhi, 24 September 2009.
[22]Author's communication with Arundhati Ghose, former Indian representative to the UN Conference on Disarmament, New Delhi, March 2010.

President Barack Obama—have advocated a world without nuclear weapons.[23] This appeared in contradiction to the US Nuclear Posture Review of 2002 that, while occurring at the same time as large bilateral weapons reductions with Russia, explored "bunker-buster" and other smaller weapons that emphasized the tactical, rather than strategic importance of nuclear weapons.[24]

Yet many Indians feel that even if a nuclear-free world were in fact official American policy, it would simply ensure that other countries would no longer have (relatively cheap) nuclear deterrents and that America's conventional superiority would reign supreme.[25] Regardless, it is highly unlikely that the United States would willingly relinquish its nuclear weapons unilaterally. The American academic Charles Glaser and former National Security Adviser Brent Scowcroft argue that "we cannot disinvent nuclear weapons": as long as *the knowledge* to build them exists, countries will want them and we will live in the nuclear age.[26]

Regarding climate change, India views the notion of "differentiated responsibility" as paramount. Because western countries began their process of industrialization earlier than others, they have historically contributed the vast majority of the greenhouse gases that are threatening the earth today. Developing countries like India, however, have only recently begun industrializing, and have contributed relatively little to the aggregate level of carbon emissions. Accordingly, countries like India should not have to sacrifice their present development for the global commons. Given differentiated responsibilities, any legitimate climate mitigation initiative should be just, equitable, and secure developing countries' growth patterns. To that end, India has held out on any international compromises on emissions caps until a just agreement is met.[27] Washington, however, does not view as legitimate any

---

[23]George P. Shultz, William J. Perry, Henry A. Kissinger, Sam Nunn, "A World Free of Nuclear Weapons," *Wall Street Journal*, 4 January 2007; George P. Shultz, William J. Perry, Henry A. Kissinger, Sam Nunn, "Toward a Nuclear-Free World," *Wall Street Journal,* 15 January 2008; Barack Obama, "Remarks by President Barack Obama: Hradcany Square, Prague, Czech Republic," *White House*, 5 April 2009, available at http://www.whitehouse.gov/the_press_office/Remarks-By-President-Barack-Obama-In-Prague-As-Delivered

[24]"Nuclear Posture Review Report," US Department of Defense, 8 January 2002.

[25]This argument has also been explored by Andrew Futter and Benjamin Zala, "Advanced US Conventional Weapons And Nuclear Disarmament." *The Nonproliferation Review*, 20, 1 (2013): 107–22.

[26]Charles Glaser, "The Flawed Case for Nuclear Disarmament." *Survival*, 40, 1 (Spring 1998): 112–28.

[27]Ministry of External Affairs, Public Diplomacy Division, Government of India, "The Road to Copenhagen: India's Position on Climate Change Issues," 2009, available at http://pmindia.nic.in/Climate%20Change_16.03.09.pdf; Uttam Kumar Sinha: "Geopolitics of Climate Change and India's Position." *Indian Foreign Affairs Journal*, 4, 2 (April–June 2009): 104–7; For a critique of this position see Neil Padukone, "Climate Change: Forgotten Threats, Forgotten Opportunities." *Economic and Political Weekly*, 45, 22 (29 May 2010): 47–54.

climate agreement that does not restrict emissions from India and China—
the latter of which has eclipsed that of the United States—and which would
compel the United States to shoulder the majority of the economic burden.

## Hitches: Dealing with the Dragon

Although the Indian and American militaries appear to have the containment of
China as a shared strategic objective, New Delhi often hopes that the United
States will do more to counter China on the political front. China's revisionism
on its borders with India in Arunachal Pradesh and Kashmir are a constant
source of irritation for New Delhi. On this issue, India seeks American political
support and assistance that are not always forthcoming. Yet the United States
has never made its position on Arunachal Pradesh clear, that is, whether
Washington would side with India or intervene on its behalf in the case of
a confrontation. Perspectives diverge on whether it would be in America's
interest to do so and involve itself in another major conflict in which it has little
at stake. Some argue that the United States ought to bolster India's Air Force
because, as Rajeswari Rajagopalan writes,

> a strong Indian Air Force would likely prompt China to focus at least part of
> its air power away from the Pacific and on the Tibet region. In addition, the
> Indian Air Force could also tip the scales in the Indo-Pacific by reducing the
> burden on the U.S. Air Force and providing security in the global commons.
> For instance, with a single air refueling, India's SU-30MKI's combat radius
> can include either the Straits of Malacca or the Persian Gulf.[28]

To this end, many in India's defense establishment think it natural that America
would open up its defense base to India, curtailing the current restrictions on
dual use technology that are in place, and allow India to build up a defense
capability that would enable it to deter and counter China more effectively.
But American perspectives on this prospect vary: some, primarily "offensive
realists," are unrepentant supporters of a strong Indian military bulwark
against China; others fear that bolstering India's defense capacities will simply
antagonize China and Pakistan, both of which are needed in America's global
governance objectives, notably in the global economy, and counterterrorism
in Central Asia, respectively; meanwhile, still others are skeptical that India

---

[28]Rajeswari Pillai Rajagopalan, "Why US Needs India's Air Force," *The Diplomat*, 29 November
2011.

is even up to the task of serving as an effective bulwark and strategically in this realm, conceding that "it's an open question whether India is *willing* [or able] to take such proactive steps."[29] Yet India's strategic nuclear weapons are perhaps the most fundamental instruments that ensure stability along the India-China border. By recognizing and legitimizing India's nuclear program, the US-India Civil Nuclear Deal tacitly bolsters India's nuclear arsenal, ensuring that it will remain sufficiently credible to deter Beijing.

## Hitches: Legacy Systems

Perhaps most profoundly in the medium-term, both countries have governance systems that have been institutionally predisposed against the other. In the United States, this has meant "non-proliferation Ayatollahs," who have written India off due to its noncompliance with the NPT, and "hyphenators" who view India and South Asia through the lens of Pakistan. As Nicholas Gvosdev, Professor of National Security Studies at the US Naval War College, writes:

> Bureaucracies are locked into policies that have become standard operating procedures; presidents and their advisors discover that making significant policy changes disturbs important stakeholders. . . . One of the defining characteristics of US national security policy is the extent to which Cold War institutions and policies remain in place. So while there might be continued active resistance to the vision of a US-India special relationship mounted by a rear guard in the bureaucracy, an even bigger obstacle is the lack of bureaucratic frameworks to nurture ties. . . . The US national security apparatus has never been able to define and operationalize the concept of a "partner" as a mid-way point between a traditional Cold War-era "ally" (not a feasible status for an India whose geopolitical and economic interests are not fully in alignment with Washington's) and being a friendly, non-hostile state.[30]

The Indian political system has been similarly predisposed against engagement with the United States. Vestiges of the IAS's bureaucracies that were extremely skeptical of American capitalism, the importance to coalition politics of leftist

---

[29]Ibid. (Emphasis added)
[30]Nikolas Gvosdev, "Partnerships are made by bureaucracies: The Unfinished Job of Transforming US-India Relations," *Pragati: The Indian National Interest*, July 2010.

parties that reflexively oppose the United States and any affiliation with it largely on ideological grounds, those who canonize "strategic autonomy" and thus resist any attempt to decisively align with the United States on any set of issues, and a strategic legacy that opposes external actors in the region, all continue to exert influence on Indian views of the United States.

Yet, while the United States and India have a number of issues that come between them, there are two main structural differences from the past. The first is that, given India's own economic liberalization and political rise since the end of the Cold War, as well as the evolution of America's own strategic doctrine that places greater emphasis on containing China, the United States can little afford to ignore or alienate India at the expense of shorter-term objectives elsewhere. The process of "de-hyphenation" has resulted in a strange paradox for Washington, in which it hopes to maintain both India and Pakistan as close strategic partners, without having its partnerships with one country antagonize the other. Yet even as the United States provides Pakistan with weaponry and engages in economic and diplomatic agreements with China, Washington keeps India in high regard, ensuring that its bilateral ties with New Delhi are not sacrificed. And indeed, its geostrategic virtues—its presence astride the Indian Ocean, its Chabahar access to Central Asia, and naval presence at Port Blair adjacent to the Strait of Malacca—add to India's indispensability.[31]

The second is that, even as sectors of New Delhi's bureaucracy remain skeptical of America's commitment, these days India has few alternatives. During the Cold War, when the United States irked India, it was able to seek assistance in the Soviet Union, and vice versa. Today, America's primary competitor in the region is China, with whom India is loath to engage on similar terms. In the end, what unites India and the United States—and at the very least keeps their relationship on neutral, yet expanding grounds— outweighs whatever might contribute to its weakening.

India and America may never attain a formal "alliance" in which points of divergence are overlooked and bilateral relations amount to mutual defense pacts. But perhaps more relevant is the notion of a deep *strategic partnership*,

> a system of diplomatic engagement that is . . . halfway between maintaining friendly relations . . . and that contributes to furthering mutually beneficial ties. These ties or contracts might not always be cost free,

---

[31]Neil Padukone, "The Elephant and the Dragon," *The National Interest*, 3 May 2012.

[and may contain negotiated give-and-take transactions,] but are created keeping the partners [often divergent] national and sovereign strategic objectives in mind.[32]

For a United States coming out of the post–Cold War era, and an India hoping to retain its "strategic autonomy"[33] while expanding its economic and strategic trajectory, this may be the best of both worlds.

---

[32]Rudra Chaudhuri, "Strategic Partnerships," *Seminar Magazine: National Security.* No. 599. July 2009.

[33]Sunil Khilnani, Rajiv Kumar, Pratap Bhanu Mehta, Lt. Gen. (Retd.) Prakash Menon, Nandan Nilekani, Srinath Raghavan, Shyam Saran, Siddharth Varadarajan, "Nonalignment 2.0: A Foreign and Strategic Policy for India in the Twenty First Century," *Center for Policy Research*, 2012.

# PART FOUR

# South Asian Threat Perceptions and Regional Integration

# 11

# Small Neighbors

*"Our relations with our neighbors . . . are poised for a positive transformation."*

—PRANAB MUKHERJEE, FMR. MINISTER OF EXTERNAL AFFAIRS[1]

India's engagement with the world—including South Asia—has shifted as a result of its preeminent goal: to continue and expand the trajectory of its economic growth and development. To do so, it feels it must (a) connect with markets that lie beyond South Asia, (b) minimize China's role in the region and its ability to limit India's expansion and connectivity, and (c) maintain peace and stability in the subcontinent, if possible by extending the benefits of its own economic growth to the rest of the region. Regarding the latter, N. Krishnakumar, president of MindTree, an outsourcing firm based in Bangalore has said that, "while not trying to meddle in foreign affairs, we explained to our government, through the Confederation of Indian Industry, that providing a stable, predictable operating environment" that encourages secure foreign investment "is now the key to India's development."[2] To these ends, New Delhi requires the enhanced cooperation, and not the isolation or coercion, of the other SAARC capitals.

New Delhi is moving from a position of domineering confrontation in South Asia to one of greater conciliation and accommodation. This is not due to any newfound benevolence on the part of Indian political elites, but pragmatic

---

[1]Pranab Mukherjee, "India and the Global Balance of Power," Address by the minister of external affairs to the Global India Foundation, New Delhi, 16 January 2007.

[2]Likewise, Vivek Kulkarni, the information technology secretary of Government of Karnataka said that, "we did bring to the government's attention the problems the Indian IT industry might face if there were a war." Quoted in Thomas L. Friedman, *The World is Flat: A Brief History of the Twenty-First Century*. New York: Farrar, Straus and Giroux, 2005, p. 592.

needs. To develop the infrastructures—roads, rail links, energy pipelines, power grids, and water management mechanisms—that would enable New Delhi to access markets and resources in Central Asia, the Middle East, and Southeast Asia, India requires stability in, access to the geography of, and collaboration with, its smaller neighbors.

Other factors have contributed to New Delhi's reluctance to pursue violent confrontation within the subcontinent. The first is the legacy of the Indian IPKF deployed to Sri Lanka in 1987, a period often compared to America's experience in the Vietnam War or the Soviet Union's in Afghanistan. The abject failure of the force and the loss of over 1,000 soldiers and a prime minister as a consequence made New Delhi cognizant of the prohibitively high costs of military intervention and its blowback.

The second factor was that the nuclearization of the subcontinent "minimized the possibility of India being forced to give up territory" to both Pakistan and China "by military means. Security vis-à-vis other states [was] largely guaranteed by the development of a strategic deterrent." Not unrelated, the failure of Operation Parakram—which followed the terrorist attacks on the Indian Parliament in December 2001 and involved an amassing of troops along the Line-of-Control in Kashmir, with ultimately no military engagement—demonstrated the "limited utility of military force in attaining national objectives" in South Asia, particularly under a nuclear umbrella.[3] After Operation Parakram, the Indian Army created a "Cold Start Doctrine" that would enable the Army to swiftly retaliate against Pakistani militant assets in the wake of a terrorist attack, without having a long drawn-out and costly military mobilization.[4] Yet India's civilian defense leaders have been unwilling to operationalize the doctrine, preferring diplomatic channels to deal with Pakistan-based terrorism.[5]

Moreover, India's smaller neighbors are now able to "shop" at what Parag Khanna has called a "geopolitical marketplace."[6] If they find New Delhi to be too uncompromising, Kathmandu, Dhaka, Colombo, Thimpu, Male, or Islamabad can simply engage with Beijing or Washington as an alternative. There are, of course, limits to this strategy, as China's presence in the subcontinent is

---

[3]Dhruva Jaishankar, "The Vajpayee-Manmohan Doctrine: The Moorings of Contemporary Indian Foreign Policy," Pragati: The Indian National Interest Review, No. 19, October 2008.
[4]Gurmeet Kanwal, "India's Cold Start Doctrine and Strategic Stability," IDSA Comment, 1 June 2010.
[5]Shashank Joshi, "India and the Four Day War," RUSI Analysis, 7 April 2010; Dhruva Jaishankar, "Cold Stop," Polaris: The Indian National Interest, 8 April 2010, available at http://polaris.nationalinterest.in/2010/04/08/cold-stop/
[6]Parag Khanna, Second World: Empires and Influence in the New Global Order. New York: Random House, 2008.

restricted by the Himalayan Mountains to South Asia's north, by the Straits of Lombok and Malacca to its east, and arguably the Pamir and Karakoram ranges in the northwest. But the need to balance China has led India to temper its engagement with its neighbors.

# Climate Dynamic

Another leg of the power dynamic with China that has made its mark on the subcontinent, however, is climate change. In China, control over Tibet and the glaciers and waters therein gives Beijing the power to use, divert, or dam the rivers as they see fit—whether to increase supply to their eastern provinces, to generate more electricity, or even as a punitive measure against South Asia. Even if Beijing simply fails to communicate incidents of concern— such as the bursting of dams that create artificial lakes in Tibet—Delhi may be caught off-guard when the incidents strike India.[7] These actions could cause abrupt flooding or drought, ravaging the water supplies on which the subcontinent depends, and implicating South Asian geopolitics in the process. Given the inextricability of water with politics and the already tense disputes over its supply throughout the subcontinent, this is no insignificant matter. Climate change strengthens China's hand in South Asia. Any conflicts between China, India, and other South Asian nations in this realm could make tensions over Arunachal Pradesh pale in comparison.

There are important differences in how climate change affects even countries like China, whose diplomatic position on development-versus-emission-reduction is otherwise similar to India's. The majority of the Chinese mainland is above the equator; despite the environmental damage of China's hyper-industrialization, it is not quite as vulnerable to rising temperatures as are countries in the tropical belt. Moreover, with the Tibetan Plateau under its control, China has far more autonomy over the way that climate change affects its populated eastern provinces than South Asia does. This adds a power dynamic to India's existing vulnerabilities: with Chinese control over the water sources in Tibet, South Asia may be beholden to Chinese actions.

If the Chinese divert Tibetan waters from South Asia without informing Delhi, India would not be able to manage the effects within its own borders or in coordination with Nepal, Pakistan, or Bangladesh in a timely manner. India and China have signed two MOUs and established a "Joint Expert

---

[7]Shripad Dharmadhikary, "Mountains of Concrete: Dam Building in the Himalayas," International Rivers, December 2008, available at http://www.internationalrivers.org/files/IR_Himalayas_rev.pdf

level Mechanism"—in 2002, 2005, and 2006, respectively—to exchange hydrological information regarding the Brahmaputra and Kashmiri Sutlej rivers during annual flood seasons.[8]

But given the scale of the emerging challenges, such ad hoc, case-by-case mechanisms may not be sufficient. A broader, effectual regional communication mechanism with China, complete with formal, protracted and institutionalized information-sharing and coordinated management institutions, may be required to preemptively address any management issues. Such a treaty could have the ancillary benefit of enhancing trade relations that mitigate geopolitical tensions.

Any Chinese reluctance to create a formal institution to manage the issue can be counteracted by a bloc of India, Pakistan, Nepal, Bangladesh, and Bhutan, all of which will be harmed tremendously by China's environmental weapon. Water is an issue on which the estranged South Asian neighbors can and must come together for common survival, reinvigorating an otherwise factious SAARC. United behind the cause of water flow, the South Asian countries can in turn resolve the water disputes that plague their own bilateral relations.

A number of factors now drive New Delhi's engagement with South Asia. These include the need for stability in South Asia in order to expand India's economic growth; India's reluctance to pursue violent means within South Asia; New Delhi's aim of accessing markets in and beyond South Asia; the compulsion to balance China's influence in the region; and the pressure to join forces with its South Asian neighbors to manage the effects of climate change. These changes in worldview are already producing tangible results.

# Nepal

The recent political situation in Nepal has not lent itself to an easy détente with India. Between the Maoist toppling of the monarchy in 2008 and the establishment of the Federal Democratic Republic of Nepal in 2012, Nepal had more than five prime ministers of different political parties and has been unable to establish a new constitution. In the wake of the Maoist Revolution, a number of Nepali political parties have sought to abrogate and renegotiate the Indo-Nepal Peace and Friendship Treaty of 1950, a prospect that worries Indian strategists in light of China's ostensibly rising influence in the Himalayan nation.

---

[8]Government of India, "International Cooperation," website of the Government of India, National Portal Content Management Team, 31 March 2009, available at http://india.gov.in/sectors/water_resources/international_corp.php

Yet T. V. Paul suggests that, because it is weak and illegitimate state institutions in South Asia that account for instability within and between the states of the subcontinent, "the emergence of strong democratic states (that are both internally secure and legitimate) can change the dynamics of the region considerably."[9] India's support for a monarchy in Kathmandu that was perceived to be illegitimate was one of the key sources of antagonism between India and the Nepali people. The popular toppling of the monarchy and slow development of a more representative democratic government in Nepal may increase Kathmandu's legitimacy in the eyes of Nepal's citizens. Though the new Maoist governments have been inclined against New Delhi, the state's very internal legitimacy may, in the medium term, provide for increased stability that enables greater political cooperation with India.

Moreover, despite the altered political dynamic, geography, migration, and economics will ensure that many of the fundamentals remain the same. The open border between the two countries has ensured close economic integration, underwritten by free migration. Indeed, in October 2011, Prime Minister Baburam Bhattarai of the Unified Communist Party of Nepal (Maoist) traveled to New Delhi and inked a Bilateral Investment Promotion and Protection Agreement and sought a 1 billion USD soft loan.[10]

Nepal's rivers have a hydro-electricity generation capacity of 42 GW, of which only 680 MW are currently tapped. Even if its whole population were to receive electricity, the demand would only be about 2 GW (and by 2030, demand would be 11 GW at the most, given a 10 percent annual growth rate). This huge discrepancy gives Kathmandu the potential to export surplus power to India and even Bangladesh and China. India has begun investing in hydroelectric plants—far more seriously than it had in the past given its own energy and water management needs and the competition from Chinese developers.[11] Meanwhile, in 2010, India signed agreements to develop Bhutan's hydropower capacity, which it would export back to India, possibly through a power facility linked to that provided by Nepal.

Perhaps most profoundly, though New Delhi continues to overtly express displeasure with Kathmandu's efforts to enhance ties with China, these are largely expressed through diplomatic and political channels. This is in stark

[9]T. V. Paul, "State Capacity and South Asia's Perennial Insecurity Problems," in T. V. Paul (ed.), *South Asia's Weak States: Understanding the Regional Insecurity Predicament.* Stanford, CA: Stanford University Press, 2010, p. 305.

[10]"Nepal PM under fire in Parliament over India Pact," *Times of India*, 24 October 2011; Dipanjan Roy Chaudhury, "Nepal PM Baburam Bhattarai begins India trip to weed out trust deficit," *India Today*, 21 October 2011.

[11]Ilmas Futehally, "Himalayan Solutions: Cooperation and Security in River Basins," *Strategic Foresight Group*, 2011.

contrast with a similar situation in 1988, when an agreement between Kathmandu and Beijing brought about an Indian decision to blockade Nepal and starve it of access to goods and markets. Enhanced competition has compelled India to temper its own behavior toward Kathmandu.

# Bangladesh

In 2010, New Delhi and Dhaka signed agreements that stabilized the border while making it more porous. The small enclaves along the border—whose residents are legally stateless[12]—are to be resolved with land swaps, often in Bangladesh's favor, as well as an agreement on the use of nonlethal weapons by the Border Security Force.[13] A 10 billion USD development deal will fund the development of road and rail connections that traverse Bangladesh and reach Myanmar, both for economic purposes and to secure India's northeastern "Seven Sister" states from local insurgents and potential Chinese offenses. Notably, overland access to its northeastern states via Bangladeshi territory would enable New Delhi to circumnavigate the Siliguru Corridor—the thin slice or "chicken's neck" of Indian land between Nepal and Bangladesh—to access the northeast, and return the region to its pre-partition natural economic geography in which the Brahmaputra–Ganges delta was more integrated with the subcontinent's northeast.

Also included in the deal were electricity imports from India, commercial concessions that would legalize the exchange of goods that are already smuggled across the border, and the opening of seven trading posts along the border.[14] And the integrated jute industry—in which the produce of eastern Bengal was manufactured into consumer goods factories in western Bengal—that was severed after the 1965 war with Pakistan is coming back in a new way. According to Indian Commerce Secretary Rahul Khullar, yarn mills in Ludhiana will be opening shops in Bangladesh, exporting cotton to Dhaka, and establishing haats or trading posts along the border with Tripura, Meghalaya, and Assam. Different components of industry will complement one another from across the borders.[15]

---

[12]Willem Van Schendel, "Stateless in South Asia: The Making of the India-Bangladesh Enclaves." *Journal of Asian Studies*, 61, 1 (February 2002): 115–47.
[13]Pushpita Das, "The India-Bangladesh Border: A New Beginning," *IDSA Comment*, 10 October 2011.
[14]"India, Bangladesh sign historic boundary agreement, Teesta treaty on hold," *NDTV*, 6 September 2011; R. Vasudevan, "India, Bangladesh sign three agreements," *Asian Tribune*, 7 September 2011.
[15]Summary record of India-Bangladesh commerce secretary level discussions held at New Delhi, Government of India, Ministry of Commerce, 28 March–29 March 2012, transcript available at commerce.nic.in/trade/IndiaBangladeshTalk.pdf

Though progress on the Teesta Treaty, which would develop a dam and water barrage on the Teesta River between Bangladesh and Tripura, was stalled in 2011 due to resistance from West Bengal, a province in eastern India, Dhaka sent a delegation to Bhutan and Nepal to explore water sharing and hydropower generation and sales. This multinational cooperation and trade would require India to be a geographic intermediary. Skepticism about the feasibility of a multi-country power generation grid of this nature certainly remains.[16] But management and maintenance of at least the existing and diminishing resources will require coordination between the capitals and communication at the borders—including a potential Himalayan Rivers Commission of the sort proposed by the Strategic Foresight Group.[17] Moreover, managing the imminent influx of thousands of additional Bangladeshi environmental refugees into the Indian territory may even necessitate a broader-scale approach, such as the opening or softening of the Indo-Bangladesh border, akin to what exists between India and Nepal.[18]

# Sri Lanka

For better or worse, New Delhi has, since the days it was ejected from Jaffna, followed a more laissez faire policy in Sri Lanka. Perhaps the most pronounced example of this was during the 2009 war between Colombo and the LTTE in Jaffna, when New Delhi remained silent—a tacit endorsement of Colombo's autonomy. According to some reports, India even provided naval intelligence to Colombo during the operation.[19] Following the 2009 LTTE war, New Delhi and Colombo enhanced defense ties in 2010, even beginning joint naval exercises off of the Palk Strait in exercises like the six-day SLINEX-11.[20] The countries have also enhanced cooperation in maritime issues like coastal security and fisheries cooperation.

Postconflict development aid has been another major leg of India-Sri Lanka engagement. Bilateral trade between India and Sri Lanka increased from

---

[16]Bishal Thapa, "Powering the Darkening Crisis," *Republica*, 11 October 2011.

[17]Ilmas Futehally, "Himalayan Solutions: Cooperation and Security in River Basins," *Strategic Foresight Group*, 2011.

[18]"Bangladesh, India open border land ports to boost trade," *Deccan Herald*, 23 January 2011; Jayshree Sengupta, "Time to boost India-Bangladesh Trade and Economic Relations," ORF Issue Brief, No. 10, August 2007; Sanjoy Hazarika, "Illegal Migration from Bangladesh: Problem and Long-term Perspective," in B. B. Kumar (ed.), *Illegal Migration from Bangladesh*. New Delhi: DK Publishers, 2006, pp. 25–35.

[19]Nitin Gokhale, *Sri Lanka: From War to Peace*. New Delhi: Har-Anand Publications, 2009.

[20]Vivek Raghuvanshi, "India, Sri Lanka Begin Sea Exercises," *Defense News*, 21 September 2011.

658 million USD in 2000 to 3.2 billion USD in 2008, and India remains one of the top four foreign investors in Sri Lanka, following the United States and members of the European Union.[21] New Delhi has opened up lines of credit for food and petroleum products, as well as a 100 million USD line of credit for the development of the Colombo-Matara railway.[22] Meanwhile, Colombo has terminated arms sales and limited other strategic cooperation with both China and Pakistan.[23]

# Maldives

To the west, India's engagement with the Maldives has also undergone change. The democratic revolution that brought President Mohammad Nasheed to power in 2008 received a major setback in 2012. In January of that year, a coup forced Nasheed to resign against his will and his former vice president, Mohamed Waheed Hassan, seen to be close to Maumoon Abdul Gayoom, Nasheed's more autocratic predecessor, took control of the presidency. Yet throughout the ordeal, India publicly remained neutral. This nonintervention aligns with India's effort to seek conciliation with its neighborhood, but has led many western analysts to worry about both India's commitment to democracy in the region and China's ability to add Male to its "string of pearls."[24]

Yet geography, and the relationship that was established between India and the Maldives under Gayoom in 1988, ensures that India will continue to exert influence in Male. In addition to having built up the Maldivian security forces since 1988, the islands were integrated into India's Coast Guard and coastal radar systems by 2009. For better or worse, that engagement goes deeper than the head of state.

Moreover, India has been supportive in one of Maldives' central existential dilemmas. Rising sea levels threaten to destroy the coral reefs that source a majority of Maldives' food sources (fish), and also threaten to reduce the amount of habitable land in the long term. In response to the latter, Maldivian

---

[21]CIA World Factbook: Sri Lanka, accessed 13 September 2010, available at https://www.cia.gov/library/publications/the-world-factbook/geos/ce.html; "Investments and Development Cooperation between India and Sri Lanka," High Commission of India, Colombo, 29 August 2010, available at http://www.hcicolombo.org/ecserv_indian_investment.cfm

[22]"India extends $416.399 mn as line of credit for Sri Lankan projects," *The Hindu*, 26 November 2010; "Sri Lanka Army to benefit from Indian line of credit," *Press Trust of India,* 13 April 2011.

[23]Hemantha Dayaratne, "A New Phase in India-Sri Lanka Relations," *IDSA Comment*, 3 January 2011.

[24]Nilanthi Samaranayake, "Maldives: Why the US and India Should Remain Calm," *Center for Strategic and International Studies*, PacNet No. 13, 1 March 2012.

politicians led by Nasheed announced a "Global Warming Relocation Fund" to purchase land from other countries—notably India, Sri Lanka, and Australia— to resettle the 300,000 citizens of the Maldives.[25] Though New Delhi has not yet taken an official position on this move, Indian think tanks and media have largely endorsed India's support for Male's climate woes.

---

[25]Arpana Pandey and Arathi Rao, "A New Maldives," *Himal Southasian*, January 2009.

# 12

# Pakistan: Mutually Assured Construction

**P**erhaps the greatest potential for change lies in India's relationship with Pakistan, which nearly defines political enmity in the modern world. As of 2010, bilateral trade remained a paltry 2.1 billion USD per year, most of it through informal avenues such as smuggling and third-country intermediaries. By some economic models, trade potential is as much as fifty times that figure,[1] but has been restricted by politically driven "sensitive lists" that prohibit bilateral imports of thousands of items as harmless as tea and tractor parts; requirements that ships touch a third country before importing goods; restrictions on transit trade to third countries like Afghanistan; and other direct obstacles to bilateral trade and FDI. Meanwhile, Pakistan's unique situation—a national identity crisis that affects both its sociopolitical structure and international relations—adds another dimension to its reluctance to integrate with India, which has resulted in over four wars, massive nuclear weapons buildups, and mutual allegations of support for terrorism against the other.

Indeed, in recent years, various parts of India—Punjab, Kashmir, and urban centers like Mumbai, Delhi, and Jaipur—have fallen victim to terrorist attacks with alleged links to Pakistan. This is nothing new; from before the time of the 1980s Khalistan insurgency—arguably since the first Kashmir war in 1948[2]—militants have received weapons, training, and support from beyond the Pakistani border and been sent back to attack Indian civilians and military personnel. And New Delhi often responded in kind: India's R&AW opened

---

[1]Mohsin Khan, "Improving India-Pakistan Relations Through Trade," *Peterson Institute*, 19 April 2010.
[2]Praveen Swami, *India, Pakistan and the Secret Jihad: The Covert War in Kashmir, 1947–2004.* New York: Routledge Publications, 2006.

the CIT-X and CIT-J desks to carry out terrorist attacks in Karachi and support anti-Islamabad insurgents in Baluchistan in the 1980s,[3] while the Indian Army launched the largest post–World War II military mobilization in the world, Operation Brasstacks, which involved the amassing of over 400,000 troops along the Rajasthan-Sindh border over 5 months in 1986–87. In 1988, India also began the construction of a double-layered fence along the border with Pakistan, which reportedly curtailed the influx of small arms into Indian Punjab.[4] (The infiltration, however, was not entirely stymied. Arms smugglers found alternative routes, including across the India-Pakistan-China triborder area in Kashmir, as well as through sea-based smuggling routes in Gujarat and Mumbai.)[5]

What is novel about the more recent attacks is that they have been met with little in the way of military responses or retaliations. Following the terrorist attacks on the Indian Parliament in December 2001 and conducted under the post-1998 nuclear umbrella, Operation Parakram of 2002 involved an amassing of troops along the Line-of-Control in Kashmir, cost months and millions of rupees to sustain, and compelled an in-kind buildup along the Pakistan-controlled side of the border. Yet Operation Parakram came with few political or military benefits—and ended with no military engagement. Since then, even in the wake of upwards of eight terrorist attacks in urban areas and far more in Indian-administered Kashmir, the Indian Government has hardly even entertained the notion of military retaliation.

Voicing a common Indian frustration, Nitin Pai writes that India's unilateral nonconfrontation "has been largely counterproductive. The Pakistani military establishment perceives Indian moves as arising from weakness, an assessment that emboldens it to instigate [further] acts of terrorism against India. Pakistan's nuclear weapons now serve the effective purpose of protecting its terrorists from punishment."[6]

Whether "punishment" would effectively curb Pakistan-based terrorism, however, is questionable. India's counterintelligence responses of the 1980s—retaliatory R&AW operations—did indeed diminish Pakistan's role in the Khalistan insurgency. Yet this occurred not purely with increased punitive

---

[3]B. Raman, *The Kaoboys of R&AW: Down Memory Lane*. New Delhi: Lancer Publishers, 2008.
[4]Iftikhar Gilani, "Harsh weather likely to damage LoC fencing," *Daily Times*, 4 March 2005.
[5]Ryan Clarke, *Crime-Terror Nexus in South Asia: States, Security, and Non-state Actors*. New York: Taylor and Francis, 2011, p. 56; Paul Wallace, "Counterterrorism in India: Khalistan and Kashmir," in Robert Art and Louise Richardson (eds), *Democracy and Counterterrorism: Lessons from the Past*. Washington, D.C.: US Institute of Peace, 2007, pp. 425–82.
[6]Nitin Pai, "The Paradox of Proximity: India's Approach to Fragility in the Neighborhood," *Center on International Cooperation*, New York University, April 2011.

damages, but through a gentleman's agreement between the two countries' intelligence agencies that was negotiated by then Jordanian Crown Prince Hassan bin-Talal: "It was agreed that Pakistan would not carry out activities in [Indian] Punjab as long as R&AW refrained from creating mayhem and violence inside Pakistan."[7] But more to the point, India's counterintelligence operations and the ensuing agreements did not end Pakistan-based terrorism. Just years later, the same campaign was replicated in Indian-administered Kashmir, and the expansion of terrorism has continued through the rest of mainland India, through cocktails of groups over whom it appears Islamabad and Rawalpindi have increasingly less influence. Retaliation would not necessarily be the panacea it is seen to be.

Military buildups and retaliatory strikes, moreover, would do little to address terrorism itself. "Lashkar-e-Taiba (LeT) and its militant affiliates [could use] the resulting diversion of the Pakistani military to the eastern Line-of-Control to strengthen their holds in western Pakistan and Afghanistan." Targeted strikes on militant camps within Pakistani territory, meanwhile, may

> achieve short-term goals like setting back terrorist capacities. . . . [But] groups like LeT are so distributed throughout Pakistan that eliminating a few camps in the northern areas would be futile; the leadership may be holed up in a cell in Karachi, Lahore, or Peshawar, an attack on which would come with legal, and unforeseeable diplomatic and military consequences, and ultimately have minimal effect on the group's easily adaptable capacities. Even targeted strikes in places like Pakistani-administered Kashmir would likely provoke the Pakistani Army due to sovereignty issues, causing similar military escalation, and even encourage pan-Islamist groups to rally against India's "imperialist" designs.[8]

And if these groups are not beholden to, and even have a confrontational relationship with the Pakistani establishment—as the TTP and HuJI ostensibly do—an Indian retaliation would simply weaken the Pakistani state, further empowering militants that are outside its purview. In fact, to a large extent, the threat many Indian security analysts fear is not that Pakistan will be so strong that it will pose any existential threat to India, but that Pakistan will become so weak that the country may disintegrate and India would have to

---

[7] Ayesha Siddiqa, "The 'Jihad' Against India," Newsline Pakistan, 2 July 2007.
[8] Neil Padukone, "India's September 12th," *ORF Analysis,* 10 December 2008; See also Neil Padukone, "The Next Al Qaeda? Lashkar-e-Taiba and the Future of Terrorism in South Asia," *World Affairs Journal,* November/December 2011.

deal with the fallout: refugee crises, loose nuclear materials and weapons caches, and militants unrestrained by the nation-state system.[9]

Moreover, shows of military strength may not counter any perceptions of "weakness," primarily because such perceptions may not even exist. In fact, the main reason that Pakistan has nurtured and enabled militants is the country's *insecurity* over its unbalanced relationship with India, over a notion of Indian strength and hegemony historically vindicated by the loss of Bangladesh at India's hand, and India's historical military disposition against Pakistani assets along the border and coast.[10]

The Pakistani military's national narrative has at its foundation the notion that India is an existential threat, an idea that legitimizes military rule, massive defense expenditures, the quashing of domestic dissent, and the lionization of militant Islamists and their use as strategic weapons. The latter are tactics that can circumvent New Delhi's conventional military superiority as well as the strategic balance brought about by nuclear weapons.[11]

What would go the farthest in achieving the aim of terror-free Indo-Pak relations and remove the foundational legitimacy of military-mosque control is to reduce Pakistan's insecurity, or *increase Pakistan's security*. This can only happen by the refutation of this India threat theory through a lessening of tensions and relative normalization between India and Pakistan. Under normal bilateral circumstances, peace before reconciliation would appear to be putting the cart before the horse. But because Pakistani insecurity lies at the heart of bilateral relations, the circumstances are changed.

And India is increasingly in a position to increase Pakistan's security by being conciliatory. On the issue of trade, the entire GDP of Pakistan is less than a quarter of the market capitalization value of the Bombay Stock Exchange; if India can even consider withstanding the competition from a global behemoth like Walmart, surely a handful of Pakistani textile manufacturers can be accommodated through unilaterally reduced tariffs. And this economic disparity demonstrates why, even when Pakistan devotes over 7 percent of its economy (and over a fifth of its national budget) to defense while India spends less than half that percentage, the size of Pakistan's military remains dwarfed

---

[9]See, for example, Bharat Karnad, "Rethinking Indian Policies Towards Pakistan," Lecture at Atlantic Council of the United States, Washington, D.C., 14 November 2011, transcript available at http://www.ndu.edu/inss/docUploaded/Bharat%20Karnad%20Transcript.pdf

[10]Feroz Hassan Khan, "Pakistan's Evolving Strategic Doctrine," in Wilson John (ed.), *Pakistan: The Struggle Within*. New Delhi: Pearson-Longman, 2009; Feroz Hassan Khan, "Comparative Strategic Culture: The Case of Pakistan." *Strategic Insights*, IV, 10 (October 2005): 4–5.

[11]Neil Padukone, "Undoing Partition: Pakistan's Military-Economy and the Reintegration of South Asia." *Journal of International Affairs*, 2 November 2011, available at http://jia.sipa.columbia.edu/undoing-partition-pakistan%E2%80%99s-military-economy-and-reintegration-south-asia-0.

by the Indian Armed Forces. Even geographically, Pakistan's population and economic centers lie along the Indus River, nearly adjacent to the border with India and vulnerable to attack. India, with nearly four times as much land that is geologically diverse and spatially distributed, can more easily absorb any *attempt* Pakistan makes to attack it—which accounts for the fact that Pakistan has not won a single offensive of the many it has launched since 1947. There is little Pakistan can do to substantially harm or threaten India; yet there is a great deal India can do to help Pakistan.

In fact, such conciliation is already underway, stemming from India's own evolving strategic aims. A defense reorientation away from Pakistan and toward China at the northern borders and southern Indian Ocean is ending what Indian defense analyst Bharat Karnad calls the Indian Army's traditional "Pakistan fixation."[12] This has been aided by events along the Durand Line that have kept Pakistani forces preoccupied on their own northwestern border and away from the Line-of-Control with India. India has been able to focus on its Agni series missile—intended to deter China—while de-emphasizing its Prithvi series, realizing that Pakistan does not require further military deterrence. New Delhi is beginning to decommission (and reorient) the nearly two-thirds of the Indian armed forces that are predisposed against Pakistan. Even India's naval expansion is shifting away from Pakistan and toward its eastern naval command. Were it not for bureaucratic inertia and institutional turf and budget squabbles, this defense reorientation away from Pakistan might happen even faster.[13] And the objective of keeping the region stable in order to provide a secure business climate and perhaps, in the long term, to access Central Asian markets via Pakistani geography, is changing New Delhi's reflexive stance from the interventionism of its "Monroe Doctrine" days to soft-spoken conciliation, brinking on laissez-faire.

These shifts are already having tangible benefits. India's relative conciliation to Pakistan, which would have the ultimate result of refuting the military's "India Threat" narrative, has opened a space for a national discourse on Pakistan's identity. Such a conversation may shift, if not displace the dominant anti-India discourse, and empower those that seek to provide alternatives. Murtaza Rizvi, editor of Pakistan's *Dawn*, for example, has written that "the problem with our military's thinking . . . [is] that it went about securing the western border because it wanted to" acquire strategic depth in Afghanistan in order to "bring India to its heels. . . . Its emphasis should have been on securing the eastern border first and foremost by building confidence and

---

[12]Bharat Karnad, "Rethinking Pakistan," *The Asian Age,* 31 March 2011.
[13]Bharat Karnad, *India's Nuclear Policy. Praeger Security International.* Westport, CN: London, 2008, p. 58.

trust with New Delhi. Doing so would [result] in acquiring strategic depth in India with many dividends to reap from it."[14]

# Making Sense of Pakistan[15]

The lack of a sufficiently convincing and cohesive Pakistani national narrative has been a central factor in the country's strategic decisions. The national predicament in which the newly established state of Pakistan found itself in 1947—a largely migrant society in which previous borders were abruptly severed and new ones created—brought about profound questions of national identity within a new geographic and political framework: that of a geographically divided nation-state.

As the sociologist Robert Putnam has argued, "in the short run . . . ethnic diversity tends to reduce social solidarity. . . . In ethnically diverse [areas], residents of all races tend to 'hunker down': Trust, even of one's own race, is lower, altruism and community cooperation rarer, friends fewer."[16] Indeed, in 1947, when Sindhis, migrant Punjabis and Muhajirs, Bengalis, Baluchis, and Pashtuns were forced together by the new context of partition, migration, and nation-building, they were faced with questions of identity and how they ought to relate with those in proximity: "who am I? How am I different from those around me? What do I, as a Barelvi from Lucknow, have in common with a Shi'a Sindhi? How do I interact with those around me?"

The Pakistani government, erstwhile Muslim League, and later JeI and the Pakistani military endeavored to forge a common identity between Sindhis, Baluchis, Muhajirs, Punjabis, and geographically separated Bengalis based solely on certain interpretations of Islam. But identity is an organic, emergent process based on context, rather than a forged consensus or controlled process. Contexts can be shaped, but identity cannot be controlled.[17]

---

[14]Murtaza Rizvi, "Look East for Strategic Depth," *Dawn*, 15 June 2011.
[15]This section title is a reference to a book that explores the evolution of Pakistani identity—including its more contemporary articulations, namely Farzana Shaikh, *Making Sense of Pakistan*. New York: Columbia University Press, 2009.
[16]Robert Putnam, "*E Pluribus Unum:* Diversity and Community in the Twenty-First Century." *Scandinavian Political Studies*, 30, 2 (2007): 137. Putnam's statistical analysis refers specifically to data on the state of ethnic relations in the United States, but its concepts are broadly applicable.
[17]See, for example, Ernest Gellner, *Nations and Nationalism*. Ithaca: Cornell University Press, 1983; John L. Comaroff, "Of Totemism and Ethnicity: Consciousness, Practice, and the Signs of Inequality," in John and Jean Comaroff (eds), *Ethnography and the Historical Imagination*. Boulder: Westview Press, 1992, pp. 49–67.

This fallacy accounts for the failure of the military-mosque attempt to forge an Islamic Pakistani identity.

But, Putnam continues, "in the long run, successful [diverse] societies have overcome such fragmentation by creating new, cross-cutting forms of social solidarity and *more encompassing identities*."[18] Indeed, Pakistani identity is a far different issue today than it was immediately after independence; it *was* at question more than it *is*. Day-to-day issues, contexts, and experiences influence how people view the world, those around them, and those they have to relate to. The aggregation of these components forms common identity. In the decades since 1947, those daily questions of identity and sociality have become less relevant, and have been subsumed by new questions associated with day-to-day living; new, more encompassing identities *emerge* from the environment in which Pakistani people have found themselves for over 60 years.

Though regional languages remain, most Pakistanis understand Urdu, for example. Sindhis, Punjabis, Pashtuns, Baluchis, and Muhajirs all deal with the same political, economic, and bureaucratic frustrations, consume many of the same cultural artifacts, and rely on the same institutions.[19] For better or worse, there have been mass migrations of Pashtuns into areas as different as Baluchistani Quetta and Sindhi Karachi, which has the world's largest concentration of Pashtuns.[20] Overlapping economic networks raise the stakes that once-regional ethnicities have in other parts of the country, such that, as Pakistani journalist Syed Talat Hussein writes, Karachi alone, which "provides more than 60 percent of countrywide employment opportunities for the Pashtuns . . . has diluted their demand for separation from Pakistan proper," and has significantly lessened "their resolve to join forces with the Pashtun in Afghanistan for a greater homeland."[21]

Meanwhile, globalization has decentralized the levers of influence away from the hands of a few. In 1959, the Martial Law Ordinance enabled the Pakistani government to take over media sources that it deemed inimical to

---

[18]Robert Putnam, "*E Pluribus Unum*: Diversity and Community in the Twenty-First Century." *Scandinavian Political Studies*, 30, 2 (2007): 137.

[19]Pervez Hoodbhoy, "Why Pakistan is Not a Nation: And how it could become one," *Himal Southasian*, June 2010.

[20]That being said, the particular urban organization of much of Karachi is not always conducive to multi-ethnic intermingling. The ghettoization of ethnicities within slums, their control by rival ethno-linguistic political parties backed by militant gangs, and the control by those parties of public service institutions like hospitals certainly does not contribute to the development of more "encompassing" identities. See for example, Steve Inskeep, *Instant City: Life and Death in Karachi*. New York: Penguin, 2011.

[21]Syed Talat Hussain, "Fire and the Federation," *Himal Southasian*, June 2010.

national security, a "right" that was enshrined with the government by the establishment of the National Press Trust.[22] Yet in 2000, then-President Pervez Musharraf liberalized the Pakistani press and media tremendously. In that year, there was a single television news channel. Eight years later, there were "26 news channels, half of which broadcast 24 hours a day."[23] A multitude of FM radio channels, more than 60 private satellite and cable television networks, a plethora of print media primarily in Urdu, English, and Sindhi, as well as internet-based media, have blossomed. The television media in particular heavily influenced national and international perceptions of Pakistani politics in the wake of the dismissal by President Pervez Musharraf of Chief Justice of the Supreme Court of Pakistan Iftikhar Muhammad Chaudhury in 2007. The dismissal and ensuing media coverage brought about massive popular demonstrations throughout urban and rural Pakistan that hastened, if not brought about the end of Musharraf's rule in 2008.[24]

In addition to tempering domestic politics, the media and citizens themselves are playing an increasing role in redefining Pakistani domestic identity, its internal negotiation of Islam, as well as Pakistan's relationship with India. New media outlets are able to brandish alternative narratives of the Pakistani state and society, to create a "Pakistaniyat" defined in new terms. What this new identity will ultimately mean remains unanswered, yet a process is undoubtedly underway.[25]

This negotiation of national identity is also extending to those Pakistanis along the border with Afghanistan. Khyber Pakhtunkhwa (the erstwhile NWFP) and the Federally Administered Tribal Areas have, since independence from the British, remained under the same administrative terms under which the British Raj governed them. The Pakistani constitution governed FATA through the 1901 Frontier Crimes Regulations, established by the British, which restricted the region from the jurisdiction of the Supreme and High Courts of Pakistan. Through patronage networks that only factored in the electoral franchise and political participation of traditional maliks, or tribal leaders, these two provinces remained largely outside of the Pakistani mainstream that was otherwise being forged. In the 1990s, however, universal adult franchise

[22]Omar Noman, *The Political Economy of Pakistan, 1947–85*. London: Routledge, 1988, p. 29; See also Akmal Hussein, "Institutions, Economic Structure, and Poverty in Pakistan." *South Asia Economic Journal*, 5, 1 (January–June 2004): 69–102.
[23]Adam Ellick, "Pakistan's Opinionated Media Landscape," *New York Times*, 26 May 2010.
[24]Shahan Mufti, "Musharraf's Monster: In Pakistan, Independent TV is young, powerful, and biting the hand that fed it." *Columbia Journalism Review*, 46, 4 (September/October 2007): 46–51
[25]Farzana Shaikh, *Making Sense of Pakistan*. New York: Columbia University Press, 2009; Javed Jabbar, *Pakistan: Unique Origins; Unique Destiny?* Islamabad: National Book Foundation, 2011.

was extended to citizens of Khyber Pakhtunkhwa, enabling their political participation in the Pakistani state.[26]

Moreover, there is a growing recognition within Pakistan that war against India, both conventional and proxy, has not ensured Pakistan's security. The aim of weakening India shows no signs of being reached: Pakistan has fought over four wars with India, and been victorious in none of them, owing to India's preponderant—and arguably insurmountable—conventional military superiority.

The militant infrastructure that was developed to counter India in places like Afghanistan and Kashmir has had massive fallout within Pakistan itself. The 2007 siege of Lal Masjid (Red Mosque) in Islamabad represented a major turning point in this dynamic. In early July of that year, militants allied with the Taliban who opposed the Pakistani government's support for the United States "War on Terror" in Afghanistan, seized the mosque. When negotiations failed, the SSG, the Pakistani Army's special operations team, stormed the mosque, resulting in the capture of 50 militants and 154 deaths. The Taliban saw this assault, particularly coming after Rawalpindi's about-face after 9/11, as a slap in the face after years of support. In retaliation, pro-Taliban rebels in North Waziristan annulled a peace agreement with the Pakistani government and triggered another low-intensity war in the region. Thirteen groups of Taliban-allied militants, which had previously focused on fighting NATO troops in Afghanistan, merged under the leadership of Baitullah Mehsud to form the TTP (or Pakistani Taliban Movement), which had the express purpose of militarily opposing the Pakistani state, and allegedly of enforcing their interpretation of Sharia Islamic law.[27]

Groups like the TTP and agents like Ilyas Kashmiri, a former SSG officer who was on deputation to HuJI and later became the latter's link to Al Qaeda, have increasingly targeted major symbols of even elite Pakistani society, resulting in a sudden upshot of suicide attacks throughout Pakistan, including southern and even urban areas, from one in 2002 to 86 in 2009.[28]

---

[26]Shaheen Sardar Ali, "The Rights of Ethnic Minorities in Pakistan: A Legal Analysis (with particular reference to the Federally Administered Tribal Areas," in Stephen Tierney (ed.), *Accommodating National Identity: New Approaches in International and Domestic Law*. The Hague: Martinus Nijhoff Publishers, 2000, pp. 190–1.

[27]See, for example, Syed Saleem Shahzad, *Inside Al Qaeda and the Taliban: Beyond Bin Laden and 9/11*. London: Palgrave Macmillan Press, 2011; Stephen P. Cohen, "Pakistan: Arrival and Departure," in Stephen P. Cohen (ed.), *The Future of Pakistan*. Washington, D.C.: Brookings Institution Press, 2011, p. 6.

[28]See, for example, Khuram Iqbal, "Understanding Suicide Terrorism: A Case Study of Pakistan." *Journal on Terrorism and Security Analysis*, 7 (Spring 2012): 52–65.

## Chronology of suicide attacks in Pakistan

| Year | Number of suicide attacks in Pakistan |
|------|---------------------------------------|
| 1995 | 1 |
| 2002 | 1 |
| 2003 | 1 |
| 2004 | 5 |
| 2005 | 2 |
| 2006 | 6 |
| 2007 | 60 |
| 2008 | 63 |
| 2009 | 86 |
| 2010 | 68 |

From Khuram Iqbal, "Understanding Suicide Terrorism: A Case Study of
Pakistan," *Journal on Terrorism and Security Analysis*, Vol. 7, Spring 2012.

The violent political fallout, on the streets of Pakistan, of what was long
Islamabad's policy of "bleeding India with a thousand cuts," is compelling
many Pakistanis to reassess both these tactics as well as their broader
strategic relationship with India. The religious leader and head of the Jamiat
Ulema-e-Islam political party, Maulana Fazal-ur-Rehman, reportedly said, of
Pakistan's relationship with India and Kashmir, that "things have changed
so much. Now the concept of winning Kashmir has taken a back seat to
the urgency of saving Pakistan."[29] The columnist Yaqoob Khan Bangash,
meanwhile, wrote that

> despite being practically a war zone since 1989, Indian Kashmir has
> managed a higher literacy, economic growth and per capita income rate
> than most of Pakistan. Thus, why would the Kashmiris want to join Pakistan
> now? What do we have to offer them any longer? It is ludicrous to hope to
> incorporate a large territory, with a different development trajectory over
> the last six decades, when parts of our own country are not under the
> government's control, and when most people in Pakistan are worrying
> about its dire economic and security situation.[30]

---

[29]Quoted in Shashi Tharoor, "Peace in Kashmir?," *Project Syndicate*, 20 February 2012.
[30]Yaqoob Khan Bangash, "Time to Forget Kashmir," *The Express Tribune*, 4 July 2011.

Indeed, there is a growing tide against militarism writ large. General Ahmad Pasha, director of the ISI, reportedly told Der Spiegel, "We are distancing ourselves from conflict with India, both now and in general." He added, "We may be crazy in Pakistan, but not completely out of our minds. We know full well that [domestic] terror is our enemy, not India."[31]

# Reducing Insecurity, Enhancing Security

Admittedly, the perceptions of change within Pakistani strategic thinking are far from pervasive and, particularly among the military-intelligence institutions, their credibility is questionable. And whether they amount to a long-term strategic shift within the Pakistani Army and its ISI agency, the preeminent decision-making institutions of Pakistani strategic and national security practice, remains to be seen. Yet political breathing space between the capitals has allowed a growing Pakistani civil society to begin to question the assumptions at the heart of its national identity crisis. It is also allowing India to focus on its own domestic developments and its geostrategic expansion beyond South Asia. India-Pakistan talks and other confidence-building measures have produced a number of symbolic breakthroughs that portend better days to come: the granting of MFN status and specific discussions on enhanced trade, as well as the parameters of a Kashmir peace based on economic integration. While these efforts all had the backing of the military establishment, expectations of their immediate fruition and payoff should not be raised. Their realization will require more space, and time, between the two countries.

But beyond sociological questions relating to identity and subjective strategic perceptions, there are a number of structural dynamics that contribute to this reconfiguration of Indo-Pakistan relations. The first is the role of events on Pakistan's western border. Washington's relationship with Pakistan has long been based on strategic aims along its border with Afghanistan: the containment and rollback of Soviet influence in Afghanistan, and, since the 11 September 2001 terrorist attacks on the United States and the subsequent invasion of Afghanistan, the curtailment of Islamist terrorism. Both of these goals have required Pakistani assistance.

Since 11 September in particular, Washington has continually pressured both India and Pakistan to refrain from conflict—first following the 13 December 2001,

---

[31]Susanne Koelbl, "Terror is our Enemy, Not India," *Der Spiegel*, 6 January 2009.

attacks on the Indian Parliament and the subsequent buildup of nearly 500,000 Indian and Pakistani troops on each side of the Line of Control, and then in the wake of the November 2008 terrorist attacks in Mumbai, India. Washington had the stability of South Asia in mind (including fears of a nuclearization of any war) as well as the aim of keeping the Pakistani Army focused on its military campaign against militants along Pakistan's western border with Afghanistan. According to many analysts, this increased American focus on the Durand Line has accounted for the decline in Pakistani support for militant groups and infiltrations along its eastern border in Kashmir.[32]

This increased global focus on Pakistan's western border and the broader Central Asian region is part of what has been called a "New Great Game" focusing on regional trade, energy resources, and geostrategic competition. China, the United States, Iran, Russia, and India are among the key actors that have driven this competition. In addition to Soviet and Chinese-constructed infrastructure in the region, Turkey, Iran, and Pakistan have developed a multi-country railway bridging Europe and Southwest Asia,[33] while India, Iran, and Russia are developing the North-South Corridor, a mix of road, rail, and sea links connecting eastern Europe, the Caucasus, and Central Asia, with India and Southeast Asia. All of these strategic and commercial considerations are increasing international presence in what geostrategist Alfred Mackinder called the "pivot area" of the world's geopolitical "Heartland."[34]

And despite the projected drawdown of American forces from Afghanistan by 2014, strategic and economic interests in Central Asia will keep American interests in the region for years to come.[35] These interests include the presence of global Islamist militants along the Afghanistan-Pakistan border, the planned Turkmenistan-Afghanistan-Pakistan-India (TAPI) natural gas pipeline, mineral deposits in Afghanistan and other resources in Central Asia, and efforts to contain China. In fact, since August 2011, the United States has been in negotiations with the Afghan government in Kabul to keep upwards of 10,000 American troops in Afghan bases beyond 2024—to say nothing of a lasting CIA presence in the country.[36]

---

[32]See, for example, Praveen Swami, *India, Pakistan and the Secret Jihad: The Covert War in Kashmir, 1947–2004*. New York: Routledge Publications, 2006.

[33]Zaheer Mahmood Siddiqui, "Pak, Iran and Turkey to launch freight train," *Dawn*, 1 August 2010.

[34]Halford Mackinder, "The Geographical Pivot of History," in Halford Mickinder (ed.), *Democratic Ideals and Reality*. Washington, D.C.: National Defense University Press, 1996, pp. 175–94.

[35]Personal Conversation with Col. Lawrence Wilkerson, former Chief of Staff to Secretary of State Colin Powell, 27 October 2010, Washington, D.C.

[36]Ben Farmer, "US Troops may stay in Afghanistan until 2024," *The Telegraph*, 19 August 2011; Matthew Rosenberg, "US Softens Deadline for Deal to Keep Troops in Afghanistan," *New York Times*, 23 December 2013.

Importantly, India's own aims vis-à-vis Pakistan have changed dramatically. While Pakistan was once at the center of India's strategic and military objectives, today, India's long-term goals center on continuing and expanding its economic growth. To this end, New Delhi has three main aims vis-à-vis Pakistan. The first is to access Central Asian markets and energy resources via Pakistani geography. With a planned 11 billion USD investment in Afghanistan's Hajigak iron mine along with an adjacent 6 million-ton steel plant, New Delhi hopes to transport iron ore through Pakistani territory; any other routes (including India's own Chabahar road through Iran, which comes with a mix of road, rail, and sea transport) would raise costs tremendously.[37]

Major energy projects may provide the structural foundations that turn the bilateral tide. In Pakistan today, power shortages cripple businesses and lead to circular debt, where costs of electricity subsidies are constantly displaced onto suppliers, while the country faces a 350 percent increase in energy demand by 2030, but lacks the finances to undertake major energy projects alone.[38] Two projects to fill the gaps are the IPI natural gas pipeline and TAPI natural gas pipeline, the latter of which is being planned by the Asian Development Bank. Importantly, in contrast to the IPI project, the United States endorses the TAPI route. This support is essential, as any natural gas pipelines would require American-made parts that are restricted under the Iran Sanctions Act (ISA), which limits annual investments in Iran's energy sector exceeding 20 million USD.

While improving India's energy access and earning Pakistan over 200 million USD a year in transit fees alone, this trade would also come with a strategic dimension. These pipelines, as well as other Central Asian trade that would traverse Pakistan and enter India, would flow from the northwest of the region, putting Pakistan "upstream" of India, much as the Khyber Pass was India's "door to the outside world" prior to partition. This trade would give Islamabad strategic leverage in transnational economic projects, increasing Islamabad's confidence in its relationship with Delhi—a far less volatile way to do so than increasing Pakistan's weapons arsenal, Washington's traditional strategy of choice. Even if the resulting trade comes under the control of the armed forces due to the military's dominant economic role within Pakistan, enhanced commercial ties could reorient Islamabad's (and Rawalpindi's) engagement with the region.

---

[37]Sanjeev Miglani, "India eyes Pakistan for access to Afghan mine bonanza," *Reuters*, 21 March 2012.
[38]Medha Bisht, "Energy Crises and Riots in Pakistan," *IDSA Comment*, 11 October 2011.

Yet India's own commitment to a transnational pipeline has waxed and waned. The original plans for the IPI pipeline were thwarted primarily due to pressure from Washington and the resulting disputes with Tehran over pricing. There is increasing skepticism about the utility of a pipeline, which, as a fixed piece of infrastructure, would keep recipient countries (such as India) dependent on single countries. This not only puts excessive power in the hands of monopoly suppliers and transit providers, but also limits the number of sources of energy to the "upper riparian" of the pipeline. An alternative proposal to accessing Iranian—and Turkmen, Russian, and Qatari, and other—natural gas is liquefied natural gas plants, gasification and liquefaction terminals that would keep gas imports fungible and reduce dependence on any one country. Meanwhile, even the fruition of the TAPI pipeline is contingent on stability in Afghanistan and Pakistan, which, at the moment, appears a long-term prospect at best. Yet transnational trade across conventional modes of transmission—roads and rail—remains a goal for New Delhi, given the reduced costs of that overland transit.

Second, India hopes to minimize China's role in the region, including its sway in Central Asia. To this end, India developed the Ayni Air Base in Tajikistan to be able to project power into that region. The Chabahar Port and Road, more consequentially, have a key objective of providing a naval counterweight to *China's* presence at Gwadar Port—not of encircling Pakistan. Closer to home, India has diverted a great deal of its military budget from its western border with Pakistan to enhance its responsive capacities along India's northern and northeastern borders with China. New Delhi is improving the efficiency of military transport from Central India to its northern border with China at Himachal Pradesh and Kashmir through the Pir Panjal mountains, by constructing a tunnel through Rohtang Pass, currently the only route to the northwestern border with China, though it is largely impassable at present.[39]

Indian strategist Bharat Karnad has even suggested that the three strike corps currently facing Pakistan—the primary military threat from India that concerns the Pakistani Army—be consolidated into a single corps, and that the remainder be shifted to the Demchock Triangle, adjacent to the LAC with China, south of Aksai Chin. This presence would "cut off the Chinese life-line to Xinjiang, the Lhasa-Xinjiang Highway. . . . There is no other way to neutralize the inherent ground advantage the [PLA] holds in any potential confrontation with India."[40] The primary reason this realignment of Pakistan-adjacent forces

---

[39]Lydia Polgreen, "India Digs under top of the world to match rival," New York Times, 31 July 2010.
[40]Bharat Karnad "India's Future Plans and Defence Requirements," in N. S. Sisodia and C. Uday Bhaskar (eds), *Emerging India: Security and Foreign Policy Perspectives*. New Delhi: Institute for Defence Studies and Analyses, 2005, p. 69.

has not yet occurred, however, is not for strategic reasons, but because the existing strike corps are

> a bureaucratic and political investment by the military in the armor and mechanized forces. . . . After the last pay commission and the hike in ranks, at every turn in Delhi in the defense industry, you run into . . . so many flag-rank officers . . . that they will not allow a diminution of their position and the kind of power and clout they wield within the military. That's bureaucratic politics.[41]

India is also shifting many of its Arabian Sea naval assets from its Pakistan-focused western command to its eastern command to interdict a potential People's Liberation Army Naval onslaught. And even when Pakistan, in response to India's May 1998 nuclear tests, tested its own Ghauri class missile, India did not "announce a retaliatory series of Prithvi missile tests, which is considered to be a Pakistan-specific weapon. Instead, it reaffirmed its decision to upgrade the Agni missile, which is regarded as a crucial component of any future missile-based deterrent system to counter *China*."[42]

And finally, New Delhi hopes to maintain stability in the Indian subcontinent, including limiting the expansion and influence of militant groups that threaten both India *and* Pakistan. Conflict or even tension with Pakistan would limit India in these global aims by geographically restricting the potential for economic engagement with Central Asia, diverting Indian attention and resources from China, and increasing the likelihood of violent catastrophe (from a terrorist attack to, more remotely, a nuclear exchange) that would harm Indians, divert finances, and otherwise impede economic growth. To these ends, India has refrained from military retaliations, buildups, and attacks against Pakistan.

## Terrorism in the India-Pakistan Dynamic

In the medium to long term, Indian conciliation would realign the strategic dynamic between India and Pakistan. In the interim, is New Delhi to lie supine regarding Pakistan-based terrorism and passively await it, should it happen? Certainly not: in addition to the direct casualties and damage, both physical and psychological, a single Mumbai-scale terrorist attack in India based from

---

[41]Bharat Karnad, "Rethinking Indian Policies Towards Pakistan," Lecture at Atlantic Council of the United States, Washington, D.C., 14 November 2011, transcript available at http://www.ndu.edu/inss/docUploaded/Bharat%20Karnad%20Transcript.pdf

[42]Waheguru Pal Singh Sidhu and Jing-dong Yuan, *China and India: Cooperation or Conflict?*. New Delhi: India Research Press, 2003, p. 55, emphasis added.

Pakistan, even one that had no links to the Pakistani establishment, could easily cease any bilateral détente.

South Block, the government building that houses the Indian Prime Minister's Office and Ministries of Defense and External Affairs, would be under pressure from Parliament, the media, and voters to answer questions of why New Delhi is wasting time legitimizing a culpable Pakistani government with talks and not conducting retaliatory strikes against training camps in Pakistan instead.

That said, even the Mumbai attacks of 2008 did not *derail* the burgeoning rapprochement—the proverbial train simply stopped, resuming after the political air had cleared. And the process toward normalization would nonetheless recommence because it is India's long-term *strategic interest and objective* to pursue and attain détente. Still, in the event of an attack, today's fragile calm would degenerate into further animosity and everything else that once gave the Line-of-Control the moniker of "the most dangerous place on earth." The end of Pakistan-based terrorism (in India) is an utmost priority for India.

A response that *would* prevent that from happening, and would more effectively stave off terrorism from both Pakistani and domestic sources, lies within India's own counterterrorism and governance capacities. India's history is replete with large-scale security lapses and "intelligence failures." In fact, it has become so easy to carry out terrorist attacks in India that even third and fourth countries have purportedly brought their proxy wars to Indian soil; in February 2012, for example, Iran was alleged to have carried out attacks against Israeli embassy assets in New Delhi using networks of Shi'a Indians that the Islamic Republic of Iran had cultivated.[43]

Perhaps not surprisingly, a central dimension of even "Pakistan-based" terrorism is its indigenization in India. On the one hand, many of the terrorist attacks in urban India that were initially attributed to Pakistani and Islamist militants ultimately turned out to be carried out by Hindu fundamentalist groups within India aiming to frame Islamist groups and discredit Muslim communities. These include the 2006 bomb blasts in Malegaon, Maharashtra, the 2007 Samjhauta Express bombing, and the 2007 attack at the Ajmer Dargah in Rajasthan, among others.[44]

---

[43]See, for example, Bharat Karnad, "US Wrong on India's Iran Policy," *The Diplomat*, 19 March 2012.
[44]Mateen Hafeez, "NIA to nail Hindu radicals in Malegaon chargesheet," *Times of India*, 13 May 2013; Mustafa Plumber and Anubhuti Vishnoi, "Purohit supplied RDX for Samjhauta bomb: ATS," *Indian Express*, 16 November 2008; Smruti Loppikar, Debarshi Dasgupta, Snigdha Hasan, "The Mirror Explodes: Hindu Terror is a Reality, yet India refuses to utter its name," *Outlook India*, 19 July 2010.

On the other hand, it has become the modus operandi of LeT, for one, to contract much of its bombing campaign in mainland India to local groups like the Students Islamic Movement of India (SIMI), Indian Mujahideen (IM), and their affiliates. These Indian organizations were originally militant defectors from the Deobandi Jel-e-Hind that have since been coopted by Salafi and Ahl-e-Hadith groups like LeT.

Their strength lies in the fact that these militant groups are veritable extensions of the organized crime syndicates of Mafiosi such as Dawood Ibrahim. Ibrahim was notorious for having organized and carried out the 1993 bombings in Bombay, which followed the anti-Muslim riots associated with the Hindu chauvinist-led demolition of the Babri Masjid in Ayodhya, Uttar Pradesh. The events splintered Bombay's organized crime, which had previously been primarily profit-driven, along religious lines. Subsequently, Ibrahim relocated the base of operations of his segments of the industry—known as "D-Company"—to Dubai and later Karachi. His extradition from Pakistan has since been a major diplomatic quarrel between New Delhi and Islamabad.

Yet Ibrahim's logistics networks within India have remained largely intact, providing much of the operational capacities of India's Islamist militant movements. Recruitment, weapons and personnel smuggling, and coastal reconnaissance networks between northern Pakistan, Sindh, Gujarat, Mumbai, and extending through north India to Bangladesh, have long been smuggling assets of the D-Company network, and have been shared with organizations like LeT. Indeed the operational capacities of South Asian Islamist militancy are largely coterminous with those of South Asian organized crime, much of which is based in India.[45] It has been argued, for example, that the boats used by the 26 November attackers were merchant vessels gifted to LeT by D-Company.[46]

D-Company and IM recruits are motivated by both profit and ideology. The latter is arguably tied to a sense of incompatible justice related to the status of Muslims within India, particularly the repeated riots and pogroms that result in massive Muslim casualties and slow, if any justice. The former is associated with the fact that the lines between the licit and illicit economies in India are so blurred. Organized crime has become such an accepted and even intrinsic element of much economic activity in India. Prior to the economic reforms of 1990, a number of foreign products were highly taxed and even forbidden; this provided a large space for organized crime syndicates to fill the demand

---

[45]Ryan Clarke, *Crime-Terror Nexus in South Asia: States, Security, and Non-state Actors.* New York: Taylor and Francis, 2011.

[46]"Captured Mumbai Terrorist Reveals Plot to Slaughter 5000," Herald Sun, 1 December 2008.

through the black market. The 1975 emergency imposed by Prime Minister Indira Gandhi that illegalized and hyper-regulated other goods enabled a massive expansion of this criminal-controlled black market, much of it based out of the port city of Bombay.

After India's economic liberalization, and the conversion of Bombay into "Mumbai," these criminal organizations focused on the "goods'" that continued to be illicit: arms and narcotics trafficking; extortion, protection money, and contract killings (supari commerce); and even illegal real estate and financial transactions—including "black money" that remains undeclared, untaxed, and unregulated. Many groups, including those affiliated with D-Company, have been accused of "fostering corrupt relationships with politicians, high-ranking government and police officials (netas), as well as with Mumbai's business leaders."[47] The urban attacks that took place throughout India in the late 2000s were carried out by SIMI, IM, and other affiliated outfits. As testimony by David Headley, the primary reconnaissance agent for the LeT attacks on Mumbai in November 2008, confirms, there is a great deal of cooperation between the LeT, the ISI, and D-Company's Karachi-based cell.

Incidentally, the November 2008 attacks are an illustrative example of the lapses of the Indian security apparatus as a whole. As early as September of that year, R&AW analysts had reportedly identified, through interrogations of suspects in Uttar Pradesh, that LeT operatives had planned an attack on luxury hotels along the south Mumbai coastline. By early November, an intelligence input was received from the United States detailing the sea-based nature of an imminent attack, while knowledge of LeT's maritime capacities were known even from information in the public domain. In essence, a more or less complete picture of the plot existed in parts across India months before its execution. Yet the information was not communicated to the prime minister's office, IB, NSG Command, Navy, or Coast Guard.[48] Preventative plans were not made, and India was hit by one of the largest-scale strategic surprises in its history, broadcasted in real-time on international television over the course of 3 days.

And yet, the weeks following the 2008 attacks on Mumbai did not involve a military buildup along or retaliatory attacks across the LOC, or other punitive

---

[47]Ryan Clarke, *Crime-Terror Nexus in South Asia: States, Security, and Non-state Actors*. New York: Taylor and Francis, 2011, p. 46.

[48]Prem Shankar Jha, "How a Plot Was Lost," in Hindustan Times, *26/11 The Attack on Mumbai*, Penguin Books India, 2009; See also, *Report of the High Level Enquiry Committee (HLEC) on 26/11*, December 2009, available at http://www.scribd.com/doc/23474630/Pradhan-Committee-Report-about-26-11

measures against Pakistan. Instead, for the first time in the wake of an urban terrorist attack, the Government of India's response was to address lapses within its domestic security system. As C. Christine Fair put it, "the nature of the attack and its media profile, the unprecedented mobilization of elites with business interests, India's growing capacity to manage national security affairs, the strategic regional context of the event," including the evolving Indo-Pakistan dynamic, "and, finally, the initiative of specific Indian leaders all contributed to these important innovations."[49]

The responsive capacities of the National Security Guards, India's elite rapid-reaction forces, have since been decentralized, with hubs in each major city. Prior to the Mumbai attacks, the NSGs were centrally concentrated outside of New Delhi, from where deployment to places like Mumbai followed nearly 10 hours of squabbling between municipal, state, and national authorities. Once in Mumbai, the commandos were forced to use a local public bus to travel from the airport in the city's north to the southern tip. Had they arrived during a peak traffic period, the time of deployment would have been even greater.

In the months following the attacks, the new home minister, P. Chidambaram, created a Coastal Command that was tasked with securing India's coastline and established 20 counterterrorism schools to train police and paramilitary forces, as well as a National Investigation Agency (NIA) to investigate suspected terrorist activities.[50] Legislation, including the "Unlawful Activities (Prevention) Act" gave security agencies the authority to hold suspects for 6 months without pressing charges. The Coast Guard, meanwhile, was set to add to its ranks 54 new vessels and 20 aircraft, and 168 speedboats, induct 3,000 new personnel, and create a 5-year plan to deploy a network of 46 coastal radars.[51]

In order to encourage information sharing, Multi-Agency Centers (MACs) have been instituted at the state and national levels to fuse intelligence across the Home, Finance, and Defense ministries. And domestic security, namely prevention, response, and investigation of terrorism, has been brought under the auspices of the MHA, headed until 2012 by Chidambaram. The Home Ministry now coordinates daily security meetings with the prime minister that

[49]C. Christine Fair, "Prospects for Effective Internal Security Reforms in India," Presentation at International Studies Association Meeting, February 2010, available at http://ssrn.com/abstract=1885488.
[50]Rama Lakshmi, "Indian Official Unveils Plan to Strengthen Security," *Washington Post*, 11 December 2008.
[51]Sandy Gordon, "India's Unfinished Security Revolution," IDSA Occasional Paper, No. 11, 2010, available at http://www.idsa.in/system/files/OP10_IndiasUnfinishedSecurityRevolution_0.pdf

include the national security advisor, home secretary, the secretary of R&AW, the director of the IB, and other principles.[52]

At the center of these reforms is the most recent proposal for a National Counter-Terrorism Center (NCTC) within the IB, which in turn falls under the purview of the Home Ministry. The purpose of the NCTC would be to integrate intelligence from the many national and state-level apparatuses, including the police forces that are at the forefront of all investigative and law enforcement work, into an integrated framework. The proposed NCTC would also have the power to make arrests throughout the Union.

A few caveats follow any large-scale overhauls, not least the ones described. The first is that much remains to be done. Funding of many of these reforms remains impeded by arcane defense procurement policies, as well as broader issues related to inefficiencies in Indian governance.[53] Center-state relations and politics, meanwhile, underlie any large-scale reforms of this nature. At the crux of this is the fact that, by design of the Indian Constitution, policing is left as a state issue, as erstwhile Home Minister Sardar Vallabhai Patel, who oversaw the phrasing of this article in the constitution, felt that states are most familiar and intimately connected with issues at the local, *thana*, or precinct level. Resistance to the implementation of the NCTC stems from the fact that the center did not consult with the state governments, whose involvement in the process is vital for the success of an institution with the express purpose of receiving and aggregating information from the state governments. Even at the local level, patronage politics, and funding and procurement issues, respectively hamper the de-politicization and upgrading of state-level police forces.

Meanwhile, many of the articulated and statutory reforms remain unfunded and unimplemented. This is due in part to center-state relations, but also due to broader issues of legality. Few of India's intelligence and security agencies have any legal grounding: the precursors of the IB and CBI were legacies of British colonial rule, established to counter erstwhile political organization by

---

[52]Personal communication with Amitav Mallik (Padmashri), former member of the National Security Advisory Board (India) and Defense Research and Development Organization; See also P. Chidambaram, "A New Architecture for India's Security," *Intelligence Bureau Centenary Endowment Lecture*, New Delhi, 23 December 2009; "Home Minister proposed Radical Restructuring of Security Architecture," 23 December 2009, available at http://www.in.com/news/current-affairs/fullstory-home-minister-proposes-radical-restructuring-of-security-architecture-12161215-131928-1.html
[53]C. Christine Fair, "Prospects for Effective Internal Security Reforms in India," Presentation at International Studies Association Meeting, February 2010, available at http://ssrn.com/abstract=1885488; See also Lant Pritchett, "Is India a Failing State? Detours on the Four Lane Highway to Modernization," *HKS Working Paper No. RWP09-013*, 13 May 2009.

Indian nationalists, while hasty postcrisis thinking brought about the ad hoc establishment of R&AW following the 1962 Sino-Indian war. Thus there has never been a legal basis for how intelligence is collected, shared, authorized, and overseen to ensure communication and against abuses. Particularly as the proposed architecture runs up against various legal norms—the ability of a central agency to dictate to state governments, the capacity of a clandestine institution to arrest citizens, and issues of secrecy and human and civic rights related to intelligence acquisition and aggregation—its legal basis may play a central part of the discussion.[54]

A final caveat is that the concentration of security systems within the Home Ministry may represent a specific idiosyncrasy of personalities within the Manmohan Singh UPA-II government. These can be contrasted with the government of Prime Minister Vajpayee, in whose government National Security Adviser Brajesh Mishra was responsible for most security issues. The post-Kargil Committee institution of the National Security Council, over which Mishra presided, remained intact under the UPA government, but its relative importance diminished considerably.[55] Thus, whether the modifications instituted by Chidambaram represent long-haul institutional changes to India's "steel frame," its government bureaucracy, remains to be seen.

# Structural Change?

Water management, notably of the Indus River System, is another issue that is central to the Indo-Pakistan dynamic. As the Indus starts in northwestern India, and runs through Pakistan's most populated areas, its flow is central to Pakistan's existence. Yet in the wake of massive population booms, increased industrial usage, climate change-induced melting of glaciers that source the Indus upstream, the drying up of the groundwater aquifers that feed the river downstream, and the encroachment of the saline Arabian Sea inland, that flow appears increasingly threatened. When an issue as central to daily life as water becomes imperiled, its politicization is inevitable.

The Pakistani media and leadership have lambasted India's management of the upper Indus, including construction of run-of-the-river hydroelectric

[54]Manish Tewari, "Legally Empowering the Sentinels of the Nation," *Observer Research Foundation,* ORF Issue Brief, No. 20, August 2009; "Enabling Intelligence in India: Autonomy, Accountability and Oversight," Conference held by the Observer Research Foundation, New Delhi, 29 July 2011.
[55]D. Shyam Babu, "National Security Council: Yet Another Ad Hoc Move?," in P. R. Kumaraswamy (ed.), *Security Beyond Survival: Essays for K. Subrahmanyam.* Sage Press, 2004.

dams (those that use natural river flow, without storing water) on the Indian-administered side of the border, such as the Baglihar and Kishanganga dams. The plans and parameters of these dams fell within the legal terms of the Indus Water Treaty but were nonetheless altered under Pakistani concerns.[56] In fact, many of the deleterious environmental issues affecting Pakistan owe more to population increase and water mismanagement, industrial waste of resources, glacial melt due to climate change, and even bilateral military activity on the northern glaciers, than to illegality or Indian malfeasance. Meanwhile, electricity generation and irrigation within and for Kashmir (the parts administered by both India and Pakistan) remains underdeveloped; the Kashmiris themselves remain victims of Indo-Pakistani strategic jockeying over the Indus.[57]

From an Indian perspective, the Indus Water Treaty has historically been among the greatest successes of both collective water management between any two nations, and of political cooperation between India and Pakistan. It has never been abrogated or broken to date. In the wake of the 2001 attack on the Indian Parliament by Pakistan-based militants, then Home Minister L. K. Advani had suggested rescinding the IWT in order to punish Pakistan, but the plan was never implemented. Yet even with the status quo, New Delhi is caught in an awkward place domestically: "If [India] adheres to the treaty, then it compromises development in Jammu and Kashmir. And if it builds hydro-electric dams, it risks facing rebukes and more from Pakistan."[58] As demands increase on the diminishing river system, Indo-Pakistani joint technical management and cooperation may be inevitable, perhaps in an expansion of the Indus Water Treaty. But given its politicization, joint management of the Indus River System may prove to be more difficult than any other regional plans.

"Virtual water," however, may assuage some concerns over the Indus.[59] Pakistan's primary uses of water from the Indus River System are not personal or municipal consumption or even industrial use—though the latter remains large and growing, with hydroelectric power accounting for 32 percent of total power generation. Instead, the primary usage of Indus River waters is agricultural irrigation, which accounts for nearly 94 percent of water demand in Pakistan. Agriculture, in turn provides about 21 percent of GDP, 50 percent

[56]Gitanjali Bakshi and Sahiba Trivedi, "The Indus Equation," *Strategic Foresight Group*, 2011.
[57]Sundeep Waslekar, "Final Settlement: Restructuring India-Pakistan Relations," *Strategic Foresight Group*, 2005.
[58]Ramananda Sengupta, "What every Kashmiri Jihadi should know," *Zee News*, 14 July 2011.
[59]Wendy Barnaby, "Do Nations Go to War Over Water?" *Nature*, 458 (19 March 2009): 282–3.

of employment, and 65 percent of Pakistan's exports.[60] Much of this irrigation involves rerouting natural river water and groundwater aquifers in order to provide water to food-producing farmlands that otherwise receive insufficient rain or groundwater. The end goal of this irrigation process is a reliable source of food crops.

Instead of spending money and resources to reroute water and reorganize its administration in order to irrigate farmland, the final products—food—can be traded directly. As part of broader commercial enhancements, trade of water-intensive agricultural goods ("virtual water") produced with comparative advantages on each side of the border, including staples like onions,[61] would lessen the need for politically sensitive reorganization of water-sharing mechanisms. As Charles Kenny has written, "whatever the spikes in agricultural prices, it remains far cheaper to grow crops where there is substantial natural rainfall than" to redistribute water to and attempt to grow crops "in places where there isn't" as much natural water. This is why, in many water-scarce areas, as much as three-fourths of countries' cereal needs are already imported. "The only reason that number isn't higher is because . . . of considerable subsidies" and other trade barriers.[62] As these trade barriers—including to water-intensive agricultural goods—are reduced, concerns over water management may follow suit.

Of course, given India's preponderance over Pakistan, any moves toward political and economic normalization would have to be unilateral. As the Pakistani politician Javed Jabbar has said, "The onus is on India. India has to reassure us continuously, and not just symbolically, which, to the credit of Prime Minister Vajpayee, he did that by going to the Pakistan monument in 1998 and 1999 and acknowledging that India recognizes the permanence of Pakistan. But it has to go beyond that."[63]

One place where this unilateral restructuring is beginning is in power trade. India is restructuring its western electricity grid in order to further integrate and trade electricity with Pakistan. A number of power generation and petroleum refinery facilities are currently based in Gujarat, on India's west coast and adjacent to Pakistan's southern and India's central regions. In the wake of Pakistan's energy crisis, Pakistan has agreed to import petroleum from Gujarat's Mudra port, which will service industries in Pakistan's Sindh Province.

---

[60]Akhtar Shaheen, "Emerging Challenges to Indus Water Treaty," Institute of Regional Studies, Islamabad. Vol. 28, 2010, available at http://www.irs.org.pk/PublFocus.htm

[61]"India urges Pakistan to resume onion exports," BBC News, 7 January 2011.

[62]Charles Kenny, "Trickle-Down Economics," Foreign Policy, 5 December 2011.

[63]Javed Jabbar, "Darkness Before Dawn? The Future of Pakistan," 2011 Carnegie International Nuclear Policy Conference, Carnegie Endowment for International Peace, 29 March 2011.

Meanwhile, further north, a trade corridor and integrated check post from Indian Punjab's Atari, adjacent to the Wagah border connecting India's Amritsar with Lahore in Pakistan, is being constructed to facilitate trade 24 hours a day and 7 days a week.[64] In March of 2012, Pakistan permitted Indian wheat to be transported from Kandla in Gujarat to Karachi port, onward to the Torkham trading post that facilitates trade between Pakistan and Afghanistan.[65] Port facilities along the Sindh–Gujarat maritime border are being upgraded, while financing mechanisms to facilitate trade as well as an upgraded visa process are currently being discussed by the Indian and Pakistani ministries of finance and external affairs.[66]

In fact, plans to develop an oil refinery in Jalandhar, in Indian Punjab, would provide surplus petroleum goods to northern Pakistan—notably Multan and Lahore—an area that consumes 65 percent of Pakistan's energy. A Punjab-based refinery infrastructure would come with far fewer transport costs than imports originating from Karachi and the Arabian Sea. Indian exports to Pakistan have increased from 25 items in 1988 to 1,771 items in 2008 and from 1,350 items in 2006 to 2,334 in 2011. Pakistani exports to India, meanwhile, have risen from 48 items in 1988 to 371 items in 2008 and to 333 in 2011. Pakistan's "positive list" of items it allows from India went from 600 items in 2000 to 1,934 in 2009. As Rahul Khullar, secretary of the Indian Ministry of Commerce, put it "colossal economic integration between the two Punjabs is in the offing."[67]

Many Pakistanis fear that much of this trade will be unidirectional, and that opening their country's borders to Indian trade will simply exacerbate their balance of trade deficit. Yet while power, electricity, and even some manufacturing may well be unidirectional—as India's refining and power generation infrastructure and financing capacities are superior to Pakistan's, and Indian investments in infrastructure within Pakistan come with prohibitive risks—these industries are only one leg of the full trade potential. Resources trade from Central Asia will be an important asset in Pakistan's favor: India needs access to iron from Afghanistan's Hajigak mine, not to mention the products of all the LNG and LPG plants and MOUs that India has been developing in Kazakhstan, Turkmenistan, and Uzbekistan. India may be able to access these resources through Iran, but in the long run,

---

[64]"Upgraded Wagah Check-Post Opens, to Boost Trade Ties," *The Indian Express*, 14 April 2012; "Trade Will Place Peace on Fast Track," *The Hindu*, 18 April 2012.

[65]"Pakistan Allows Indian Wheat to Pass through Karachi," *The Gulf Today*, 28 March 2012.

[66]"Power from India: Pak Sets Ball Rolling," *The Tribune*, 23 April 2012.

[67]Mr Rahul Khullar, secretary of commerce, Indian Ministry of External Affairs, "India-Pakistan Trade: Opportunities and Next Steps," New Delhi: Observer Research Foundation, 2 April 2012.

the pipeline-to-road-to-rail-to-sea-to-road shipment costs of the Chabahar road would be cut drastically if the trade were conducted across Pakistani territory instead. C. S. Verma, chairman of Steel Authority of India Limited and the head of a consortium of Indian industries invested in Afghanistan's Hajigak iron mine, told Reuters, "We are very bullish and believe that, over the longer term," transporting Afghan minerals over Pakistani territory "will be a productive investment. Not just for us, but others in the region including Pakistan. There are license fees, logistics, and so forth."[68] To that end, India has conferred with Pakistan specifically on trade from and joint investment in Afghanistan.[69]

Questions about India and Pakistan's competing strategic aims in Afghanistan, however, may prove to be a major hurdle in that arena. Afghanistan remains a central concern for Pakistan's national security: it serves to provide strategic depth from India, to ensure Pakistan's own domestic cohesiveness through the allegiances of the Baluch and Pashtuns, and more recently, as a source of threats from Islamist fighters and American bases in Afghanistan. Thus, a heightened Indian presence in Afghanistan would be seen as a challenge to Islamabad.

Yet for geographic reasons, India's influence could never match that of Pakistan, even with the existence of the Chabahar Road to western Afghanistan. In fact, India's aim is not to match Pakistan's influence. Today, India's goals in Afghanistan center on accessing resources, balancing China, and *defensively* minimizing the militant threat to India's own territory. Unlike the past, when India funded and trained Afghanistan's Pashtun and Baluch insurgents to oppose Pakistan—if not offensively, then certainly as retaliation for Islamabad's support for Punjabi and Kashmiri insurgents—today, India's strategic presence is predominantly economic.

In the security realm, perhaps the highest expectation between India and Pakistan should not be complete *cooperation*, which may be a pipe dream in the near future; indeed, even in early 2013, a series of vicious attacks and counterattacks between Indian and Pakistani armed forces along the Line-of-Control nearly threatened the decade-long ceasefire there.[70] More realistic, then, is an expectation of *mutual avoidance*: so long as each is focusing on another threat—for Pakistan, this means militancy and America to the west, and more consequentially, given larger India's defense reorientation, China

---

[68]Sanjeev Miglani, "India eyes Pakistan for access to Afghan mine bonanza," *Reuters*, 21 March 2012.
[69]"India invites Pakistan for investors' meet on Afghanistan," *Daily Times*, 10 June 2012.
[70]Praveen Swami, "Runaway Grandmother sparked savage skirmish on LoC," *The Hindu*, 16 January 2013.

and the east for India—and not on opposing one another, mutually beneficial futures in economic integration can move forward.

# The "Foreign Hand"

Another element of the Indo-Pakistan dynamic is, of course, that of extra-regional countries. In that realm, Pakistan's relations with the United States have taken a major hit. The United States feels that Pakistan is being duplicitous in its dealings in the nuclear nonproliferation and counterterrorism realms. The 2004 discovery of the A. Q. Khan nuclear proliferation network—in which elements of Pakistan's nuclear program were sold on a global black market to countries as diverse as North Korea, Iran, Libya, and the United Arab Emirates—demonstrated the insecurity, beyond mere vertical proliferation, of Pakistan's nuclear arsenal. And between 2006 and 2012, Pakistan's nuclear arsenal has expanded almost two-fold despite being an American ally. Meanwhile, from Washington's perspective, Islamabad is "not doing enough" in the War on Terror, selectively countering certain Al Qaeda-aligned militants that oppose the Pakistani state while enabling and even encouraging militants that do its strategic bidding in Afghanistan and Kashmir, particularly the Haqqani network and LeT. When Osama bin Laden, the leader of Al Qaeda who had been number one on the US Federal Bureau of Investigation's "Most Wanted" list for over 10 years for planning the 9/11 terror attacks on the United States in 2001, was discovered and killed in a raid by US Navy Seals in May 2011 in Abbottabad, a town known for its Pakistani military institutions, Washington was livid. Members of the US Congress threatened to cut relations with and aid to Islamabad, and some even entertained notions of limited military strikes against Pakistan.

Pakistanis, who are keen on securing military and civilian aid from the United States, including the 25 billion USD that the country has received since 9/11,[71] simultaneously feel that the United States has not sufficiently appreciated the strategic conundrum in which Islamabad has placed itself by supporting Washington in its "War on Terror." Pakistan has lost over 3,000 soldiers in military operations along the Afghan border, not to mention the hundreds of civilians killed as a result of the blowback from having

[71]Lawrence J. Korb, "Reassessing Foreign Assistance to Pakistan: Recommendations for US Engagement," *Center for American Progress*, 2 April 2009, http://www.americanprogress.org/issues/2009/04/pakistan_korb.html

supported Washington—from CIA unmanned aerial vehicle (UAV, or drone) strikes, from violent domestic groups opposing Islamabad's decision, and from the clandestine CIA presence in Pakistan. The use of drones by the CIA in Afghanistan to attack Al Qaeda militants across the Pakistani border have allegedly had massive civilian casualties, making cooperation with the United States a difficult domestic political sell for Islamabad and Rawalpindi. And perhaps the most notorious case of CIA involvement in Pakistan was the Raymond Davis Affair, in which the presence of a clandestine CIA contractor was not reported to Pakistani intelligence. When Davis was involved in the killing of three Pakistani civilians, the military, intelligence, and civil institutions in Pakistan felt the fall-out in the streets, and US-Pakistan relations arguably fell to their nadir.[72]

At the same time, while allegedly a "major non-NATO ally" tasked with executing Washington's War on Terror, Islamabad has watched America sign a nuclear assistance deal with its historical archenemy, New Delhi, while refusing to do the same with Pakistan (on the grounds that the A. Q. Khan network demonstrated the risk of Pakistan's nuclear arsenal). Pakistanis feel that Washington does not sufficiently understand its own domestic and strategic situation, and has not pressured India sufficiently on the issue of Kashmir.

As a result of these incongruities, what Pakistan perceives as America's fickleness in South Asia has earned the ire of many Pakistani officers, arguably making the Pakistani military a more anti-American than anti-Indian institution. In fact, many of Pakistan's strategic decisions over the last decade—from the expansion of its nuclear arsenal to the growing range of its nuclear missiles and even its links to some Al Qaeda-aligned militant groups—have Washington, rather than New Delhi, in mind. A common fear among Pakistani decision-makers, particularly in the decade since American advisers assisted Pakistan in the creation of a Strategic Plans Division to ensure the domestic security of its nuclear arsenal, is that the Pentagon seeks to seize control of Pakistan's nuclear arsenal.[73]

Since the 1980s, Pakistan has had a nuclear arsenal capable of deterring even a conventional Indian retaliation, even as India's military is expanding to meet the Chinese threat. Thus, Pakistan's strategic needs vis-à-vis India are already met and the country does not require further nuclear expansion to

---

[72]Mark Mazzetti, "How a Single Spy Helped Turn Pakistan Against the United States," *New York Times Magazine*, 14 April 2013.
[73]Mark Mazzetti, *The Way of the Knife: The C.I.A., a Secret Army, and a War at the Ends of the Earth*. New York: Penguin Press, 2013.

discourage an Indian offensive. This reality was tested in Kargil in 1999 and again after Operation Parakram in 2002 and following the Mumbai attacks of 2008. Yet to retain its autonomy and ensure against the prospect of an *American* seizure of its nuclear assets—and to increase its own ostensible utility, indispensability, and imperviousness vis-à-vis the United States— Islamabad has expanded and even dispersed its nuclear arsenal.[74] Former Indian Foreign Secretary Shyam Saran has written that

> the Pakistani military and civilian elite is convinced that the United States has also become a dangerous adversary, which seeks to disable, disarm or take forcible possession of Pakistan's nuclear weapons . . . Pakistan's suspicions of U.S. intentions in this regard did not diminish and have now risen to the level of paranoia. The American drone attacks against targets within Pakistani territory and, in particular, the brazenness with which the Abbottabad raid was carried out by U.S. Navy Seals . . . have only heightened Pakistan's concerns over U.S. intentions. These have overtaken fears of India, precisely because the U.S. has demonstrated both its capability and willingness to undertake such operations. India has not.
>
>   Thus the recent shifts in Pakistan's nuclear strategy cannot be ascribed solely to the traditional construct of India-Pakistan hostility. They appear driven mainly by the fear of U.S. assault on its strategic assets. The more numerous and compact the weapons, the wider their dispersal and the greater their sophistication, the more deterred the U.S. would be from undertaking any operations to disable them or to take them into its custody.[75]

A secondary reason for the expansion of Pakistan's largely Saudi-funded nuclear program may be the role of Pakistan's nuclear arsenal in Saudi Arabian strategic thinking: if Riyadh feels a need to nuclearize in response to an Iranian threat, it can easily obtain its own nuclear deterrent from Pakistan's expanded stockpile.[76]

The choice to support militant factions that are aligned with Al Qaeda but that do not necessarily serve Islamabad's own strategic interests in India,

---

[74]Bruce Riedel, "Pakistan and the Bomb," YaleGlobal, 21 February 2011.

[75]Shyam Saran, "Dealing with Pakistan's Brinksmanship," *The Hindu*, 12 December 2012. These views are echoed by Pakistani nuclear physicist Pervez Hoodbhoy in "The Evolution of Pakistan's Nuclear Posture," Presentation at Belfer Center for Science and International Affairs, Harvard University, 22 April 2013. See also Pervez Hoodbhoy, "The Flight To Nowhere: Pakistan's Nuclear Trajectory," in "Pakistan: Reality, Denial and the Complexity of its state," *Heinrich Boll Stiftung*, Vol. 16, 2009.

[76]See, for example, Bruce Riedel, "Enduring Allies: Pakistan's partnership with Saudi Arabia runs deeper," *Force Magazine*, December 2011.

Afghanistan, or domestically, similarly serves to give Pakistan the upper hand in its relationship, and strengthen Pakistan's bargaining position with Washington.[77] Because the Pakistani military has its own confrontation with the United States, which has military bases across Pakistan's western border in Afghanistan, Stephen Cohen argues that Rawalpindi may want "to normalize to some degree its relationship with India. It does not want to fight wars on two fronts."[78]

The question of China's own interests—keeping Indo-Pakistan enmity alive in order to keep India bogged down in South Asia—can certainly weigh on the emerging India-Pakistan dynamic. And Pakistani diplomats have repeatedly referred to Beijing as an "all-weather friend," in contrast to its "fair-weather friend," the United States. Former Pakistani Prime Minister Yousef Gilani recently described the Sino-Pak friendship as being "higher than the mountains, deeper than the oceans, stronger than steel, and sweeter than honey." To this end, it has been argued that Beijing will continue to financially and strategically underwrite Pakistan's military-economic complex. Particularly if Islamabad loses its American patron (in the wake of Washington's drawdown from Afghanistan and the political fallout from the bin Laden raid), many analysts anticipate that China will unconditionally fill the void.[79] And to this end, there has been chatter among Pakistani think tanks of an enhanced Chinese military presence in the Gilgit-Baltistan region of northern Kashmir, and indeed of leasing the territory to Beijing much as Islamabad did with the Shaksgam Valley after 1963.[80]

Yet China's own strategic calculations vis-à-vis Pakistan are increasingly being compromised by its own assessment of risk within Pakistan. Chinese nationals involved in infrastructure development projects—including the development of Gwadar Port and natural gas infrastructure in Baluchistan—have come under attack by militants in that region. The Lal Masjid incident also involved the kidnapping, by non-state Pakistani militants, of Chinese nationals working in Islamabad. The fallout of these attacks came with not only political risk, but also financial risk. Following the 2008 financial crisis that demolished foreign demand for Chinese goods, the economy of the People's Republic has

---

[77]See, for example, Dhruva Jaishankar, "The India-Pakistan Security Dilemma: Major Issues and Charting A Viable Role for the United States," *Atlantic Council of the United States*, 26 July 2011.
[78]Stephen P. Cohen, "Will India-Pakistan Relations Improve?," *Forbes India*, 26 December 2011.
[79]See, for example, Asim Yasin, "China to Support Pakistan through Thick and Thin," *The News*, 28 September 2011.
[80]Gilgit-Baltistan 50 saal keliye chin ko deney parghur, *Roznama Bang-e-Sahar*, 13 December 2011; Tufail Ahmed, "Urdu Daily: Chinese Military Taking Over Gilgit Baltistan, Pakistan Considering Proposal to Lease the Dispute Region to China for 50 years," *MEMRI*, 12 February 2012.

faced a number of problems associated with domestic underemployment. These problems have exerted pressure on Beijing to focus its investments domestically and, if they are international, to ensure a positive return.

The macroeconomic and security situation in Pakistan poses a major difficulty for Beijing to deliver those investment returns. With a debt-to-GDP ratio that went above 60 percent in 2010, massive trade and fiscal deficits, a tax base of less than 2 million people (in a country of 190 million) and power shortages that constrain investments, Pakistan does not appear to be an ideal place for a medium-term Chinese investment. As Evan Feigenbaum writes, "the bottom line is that China will not simply 'bail out' Pakistan with loans, investment, and new untied aid" that will "produce rapid, sustained, and balanced Pakistani growth. In the long term, economic interaction with India— the restoration of traditional regional ties and natural economic affinities in the subcontinent—will almost certainly be more decisive."[81]

---

[81]Evan Feigenbaum, "China's Pakistan Conundrum," *Foreign Affairs*, 4 December 2011.

# PART FIVE

# Conclusion

# 13

# Conclusion

**A**s India has awakened from its decades-long isolationism, many around the world have anticipated what its "expansion" beyond South Asia will mean. From China's perspective, India is part market for Chinese goods, and part strategic competitor. From America's perspective, India is a market and strategic partner in the challenge to hedge against Beijing. From the perspective of a number of smaller third and "second world" countries, India's growth has meant a credible diplomatic partner capable of negotiating the pulls of the west and east. So what exactly will India's "emergence" beyond South Asia mean for the world?

## Diplomatic Conduct

There has been much discussion about India's role in an expanded UNSC, namely, with a permanent position that includes veto power. The rationale is to use India's increasing clout—not only within South Asia but also further afield—toward the solution of problems in global governance, from nonproliferation to humanitarian issues to climate change. In spite of Prime Minister Jawaharlal Nehru's original insistence that the position be given to a much larger China in the immediate wake of the UN's establishment, New Delhi's political class has lobbied, if less than wholeheartedly, for such a position for generations.[1] The addition of India would be part of a more expanded United Nations, which would be more representative of shifting power structures in the world. In fact, many have argued that the Group of Twenty finance ministers and central bank governors (the G-20, or Group of Twenty) has begun that expansion on an economic front, in the wake of the 2008 economic crisis, replacing the more exclusive G-8.[2]

---

[1]Manu Bhagavan, "A New Hope: India, The United Nations and the Making of the Universal Declaration of Human Rights." *Modern Asian Studies*, 44, 2 (March 2010): 311–47.
[2]Peter Hajnal, *The G8 System and the G20: Evolution, Role, and Documentation*. London: Ashgate Publishing, 2013.

But in many ways, such power, and expectations of how it will be used, may *not* be in India's strategic interests. Abstention from critical diplomatic votes has been a central diplomatic tool of India's; doing so enables New Delhi to balance interests between conflicting parties—between Middle Eastern countries and the United States, for instance—by, paradoxically, fence-sitting. Indeed, the Indian Foreign Service and India's foreign policy actors in sum have preferred, and tended toward a diplomatic style that favors bilateral dealings in accomplishing policy-oriented goals rather than publicly engaging in multilateral forums. It has been able to deal diplomatically, for example, with the Iranian, Saudi, American, and Israeli governments independently in bilateral forums without entirely compromising its interests with any. And this is one of the reasons that the SAARC model has been insufficient in addressing South Asia's needs; from New Delhi's perspective, it has been a multilateral forum for many countries to badger India rather than one in which India can engage with its neighbors and the interests it shares with them individually.

That said, the 2000s and 2010s have brought shifts in the way New Delhi has interacted with the United Nations and multilateral system. One such incident is the diplomatic jockeying between Iran and the United States. A stipulation of the US-India nuclear deal of 2008 was that India would fully participate in efforts to "dissuade, isolate, and, if necessary, sanction and contain Iran for its efforts to acquire weapons of mass destruction."[3] To that end, New Delhi repeatedly voted to condemn Tehran's secret pursuit of nuclear enrichment in the International Atomic Energy Agency. Yet, because India also depends on Iran for energy supplies and for access to Central Asia, it has been unable to throw its hat into the American ring and condemn Iran fully. Indeed, in balancing these divergent interests, India has had little choice but to continue to juggle its ties with both blocs—to oscillate between siding with Washington (as in India's IAEA votes condemning Iran and decision to prohibit oil purchases through the Asian Clearing Union) and supporting Tehran (as in New Delhi's continued investment in Iran) as situations arise.[4]

That oscillation is largely in line with India's legacy of "nonalignment" and "strategic autonomy." Specifically in voting against international interventions in the domestic affairs of other countries—whether owing to human rights, nuclear proliferation, or other challenges—India's position has followed two traditional tenets of its realist-oriented foreign policy: nonintervention in the

---

[3]"Henry J. Hyde United States-India Peaceful Atomic Energy Cooperation Act of 2006," H. R. 5682.
[4]Neil Padukone, "Between Washington and Tehran," *Pragati: The Indian National Interest*, 10 April 2012.

internal affairs of countries outside of South Asia, and the view that strategic and economic interests alone ought to determine New Delhi's international actions. The former is, of course, a legacy of India's sensitivity to outside intervention in the Kashmir dispute, which New Delhi considers a domestic affair between Kashmiris and New Delhi, and at best a bilateral issue between India and Pakistan. If India were to vote to condemn another country for domestic transgression, or authorize international intervention therein, New Delhi fears that it leaves others open to do the same in Kashmir, where India's human rights record has been criticized by many outside observers.[5]

Yet this understanding of foreign intervention itself has changed with India's efforts to extend itself beyond South Asia, particularly in the economic realm. Investments in another country's economy, after all, are interventions in the internal affairs of that country. The growing presence of Indian nationals and investments in foreign countries—and thus, the goal of ensuring the security of, and a positive return on a foreign investment—changes the nature of a "strategic interest" that would influence foreign policy decisions. Moreover, the politics of multilateral forum votes will always play a part in India's voting decisions. In the wake of the 2011 Arab Awakenings, in which protestors and rebels rose up in opposition to the Khalifa and Mu'ammar Gaddafi regimes in Bahrain and Libya, respectively, prompting massive crackdowns and the deaths of hundreds of civilians, India abstained from a UN vote condemning Gaddafi. Despite this abstention, the United States and NATO launched an intervention supporting the rebels and toppling Gaddafi. (The same did not happen to the Khalifa regime.) In 2012, the Syrian Uprising, in which rebels rose up in opposition to the Ba'athist Bashar al-Assad regime, prompted a similarly massive crackdown, with the resulting violence killing tens of thousands of people in a year. At the time, New Delhi was on a rotating membership in the UN Security Council, and reluctantly supported a UN vote to condemn the Syrian government, while opposing the use of force and favoring political dialogue.[6]

An editorial in India's *Daily News and Analysis* stated that, "exercising diplomatic weight, pining for a UNSC seat by displaying uncouth rationalism, and taking the Indo-US strategic partnership to greater height" were factors influencing India's decision in the Syria vote.[7] Nonetheless, most of these votes have been largely symbolic: calling to condemn violating parties diplomatically

---

[5]See, for example, C. Raja Mohan, "Balancing Interests and Values: India's Struggle with Democracy Promotion." *The Washington Quarterly*, 30, 3 (Summer 2007): 99–115.
[6]Ted Piccone and Emily Alinikoff, "Rising Democracies and the Arab Awakening: Implications for Flobal Democracy and Human Rights," *Managing Global Order Series, The Brookings Institute*, January 2012.
[7]Alankrita Sinha and Abhijit Iyer-Mitra, "Decoding India's Syria vote," DNA, 9 February 2012.

or publicly reprimand them. Whether India would change its traditional stance enough to authorize a direct military intervention, however, remains to be seen. Pratap Bhanu Mehta writes that, "As India feels less pressure from the international community on issues such as Kashmir, New Delhi feels more willing to relax its dogmatic support for sovereignty."[8]

# Economic Diplomacy: Hard and Soft Power

In contrast with the days of socialism, closed-borders and import-substitution, India is increasingly economically linked with the rest of the world. While much of India's economy remains dependent on domestic consumption, this external linkage is of increasing consequence. Access to foreign resources, services, and goods—not to mention foreign access to India's own markets—increases the stake New Delhi has in the global economy, and in turn the correlation between foreign events and India's own domestic development and economic and even political stability. And this economic integration with the rest of the world raises opportunities as well as costs of India's engagement with the world beyond its borders. And in fact, India's business and economic interests, including those of key corporations, play a growing role in India's foreign policy.

It is with this in mind that trade delegations have begun to function as important tools of foreign policy. This involvement of trade delegations partly compensates for the relatively small—and arguably insufficient—size of the Indian Foreign Service's diplomatic corps, which ought to be any country's first line of political engagement with a foreign country. India, a country of 1.1 billion people, fields a foreign service the same size (less than 1000 people) as Singapore, a country with a population of 5 million. The Federation of Indian Chambers of Commerce and Industry (FICCI) and Confederation of Indian Industry (CII), two leading trade and business groups, have offices in regions around the world that facilitate diplomatic dialogues.[9]

With countries like the United States, Singapore, Myanmar, Japan, and even Pakistan, trade might be likened to a "flirtation" period that paves the way for deeper political or even military engagement, and indeed this speaks to a soft power inherent in Indian business practice. Many of the business arrangements into which India-based companies have entered have been facilitated by long established and often locally integrated Indian Diasporas.

---

[8]Pratap Bhanu Mehta, "Do New Democracies Support Democracy? Reluctant India." *Journal of Democracy*, 22, 4 (October 2011): 97–109.
[9]Jim Yardley, "Industry in India Helps Open a Door to the World," *New York Times*, 31 March 2012.

These Diasporas have brought with them cultural influence—including the popularization of Indian culture, food, film, and spirituality—which have often helped to smooth business and strategic ties thereafter. Indian businesses that invest abroad tend to employ local workers, contributing directly to the local economy and earning goodwill among local populations. The narrative of rising India as an emerging economic power also comes with soft power tangibles, such as the reputed Tata Nano car, technical assistance in facilitating elections, cultural products such as food and films, not to mention the very idea of the Indian nation: a pluralist amalgamation of different interests reconciled by a sometimes chaotic democracy. This is certainly the case with India's relations with the United States and much of Western Europe, Singapore and Southeast Asia, the Gulf Arab countries, and East Africa. In this sense, soft power is a *facilitator* rather than a pure enabler of India's influence. Indian Diasporas have existed in these places for decades, but without economic and strategic heft, India had thus far been unable to capitalize on their local presence.[10]

Yet questions of the potentially negative implications of these economic engagements will certainly remain. A question of the *local* strategic, political, and human rights consequences of India's economic investments applies to countries like Sudan, where India's own economic footprint has increased in recent years, and where external investment in resources are largely connected with local political and conflict dynamics. For instance, due in part to a desire to explore and excavate potentially oil-rich land, Sudan's capital, Khartoum, has cleared various regions of the country, displacing local populations in places like South Sudan, Abyei, Darfur, the Beja Mountains, and Nuba Mountains. These displacement campaigns have resulted in massive humanitarian crises associated with mass murder, internally displaced persons (IDPs), disease, malnutrition, civil strife, and worse.[11] Meanwhile, Khartoum has spent nearly 80 percent of the revenue it received from petroleum and other energy-based infrastructure—which makes up the majority of its international trade—on aircraft, weapons, and light arms so that indigenous militias can "protect" oil development projects from Sudan's own civilians.[12]

---

[10]Shashi Tharoor, "21st Century Leadership," *India Seminar*, #601, September 2009; Parag Khanna, "Bollystan: India's Diasporic Diplomacy," in Prasenjit K. Basu, Brahma Chellaney, Parag Khanna, and Sunil Khilnani (eds), *India as a New Global Leader*. London: Foreign Policy Centre, 2005.

[11]Human Rights Watch, *Sudan, Oil and Human Rights*, United States, 2003, available at www.hrw. org/reports/2003/sudan1103/sudanprint.pdt, accessed 20 October 2005.

[12]This was a primary tactic used in its campaign against the SPLM and the Southern Sudanese tribes through the 1990s, but continues today in different forms; David Shinn, Testimony before the US-China Economic and Security Review Commission: China's Approach to East, North, and the Horn of Africa, Dirksen Senate Office Building, 21 July 2005, available at: www.uscc.gov/hearings/2005hearings/ written_testimonies/05_07_21_22wrts/shinn_david_wrts.htm, accessed 22 October 2005.

Unlike Sudan's connection with China, which has supported Khartoum's questionable behavior in diplomatic forums such as the UNSC and even sold it weapons and developed weapons factories within Sudan, any link between violence in Sudan and New Delhi, which has invested largely in energy and other infrastructures, is certainly not direct. But India's investments have unarguably added to Khartoum's military coffers. When questioned about the human rights situation in Sudan vis-à-vis Indian investment in 2002, then-minister of Petroleum and Natural Gas of India Ram Naik said, "I know in the US or Canada these feelings are there. But we in India don't have such feelings on this issue. We feel the investments there are safe and . . . we are keen to have [them]."[13] Many years and two ministers of Petroleum and Natural Gas later, however, ONGC realized that the political situation had become precarious enough to merit a little concern, and took out political risk insurance for its second phase of investment in Sudan.[14]

The Indo-Sudanese dynamic is in many ways emblematic of India's traditional realist-oriented engagement in other countries: engaging based on India's economic and strategic interests alone without intervening in the internal affairs of other countries. When a key tenet of India's foreign policy worldview was a form of isolationism, this may have been enforceable. But when foreign investments became a central tenet of India's global engagement, that worldview necessarily shifted. Investments in a foreign country's economy—that is, an intervention in that country's internal affairs—require the stability of that investment. This in turn, changes the nature of a "strategic interest" that would influence foreign policy.

Following a referendum in 2011, Sudan was bifurcated into two countries—Sudan and South Sudan. Indian investments in the region's oil and energy sectors, which exist in both countries, may come to play central roles in how the two new countries develop. Indeed, in 2012, India saw that diplomatic and military spats between Sudan and South Sudan were affecting the stability of its own investments, and sent a special envoy to mediate between Khartoum and Juba. The decision to send an envoy was made *after* Beijing announced its own decision to intervene and negotiate between the two sides.[15]

This notion of stake-holding driving intervention or "moral attention" is not exclusive to India: the United States and other countries have only intervened in humanitarian crises in which they have commercial or strategic interests at

---

[13]Politics Trump Human Rights in Sudan, National Post, 24 June 2002, available at http://www. article13.com/A13_ContentList.asp?strAction=GetPublication&PNID=180 accessed 22 October 2005.
[14]Anupama Airy, ONGC seeks political risk cover for 2nd phase of Sudan Investment, New Delhi, The Financial Express (India), 27 April 2005.
[15]Sachin Parashar, "Indian Envoy in South Sudan on Oil Mission," *Economic Times*, 2 April 2012.

stake; the deaths of eight thousand people were sufficient to merit American military intervention in Libya, for example, while the deaths of nearly 6 million in the Democratic Republic of Congo were not. In fact, such interventions may only be effective if the intervening country has a stake in—and thus leverage over—the country of intervention.

India's particular calculations regarding economic engagement are driven by an assessment not only of economic opportunity, in that any shock to India's energy supply or market access could threaten its growth, but also of strategic opportunity cost: New Delhi worries that if it drops Sudan, Iran, Myanmar, or any other politically contentious country, Beijing could easily pick up the pieces under preferential financial terms. India feels that, at the end of the day, its own engagement or disengagement is relatively inconsequential to events on the ground in any extra-regional country, given China's usually larger presence.

And yet, India's "soft power" edge may give it a strategic advantage in places like Africa and the Middle East. The United States and Europe have limited credibility due to their imperial legacies, while China, despite its hands-off reputation, effectively sides with status quo interests. For this reason, the South Sudanese have a relatively poor view of Beijing, which has long supported their oppressors in Khartoum. In East Africa, Indian businesses tend to employ local workers, in contrast with the modus operandi of Chinese firms, which tend to import their own workers from China to do local construction jobs. The presence of integrated Indian Diasporas in regions like East Africa and Southeast Asia and the influence they bring, meanwhile, has facilitated New Delhi's ensuing economic engagement. As South Sudan, for one, endeavors to integrate with the countries of East Africa—including with an oil pipeline to Kenya's Lamu port to reduce its dependence on Khartoum and Port Sudan—India's cultural presence may give it a strategic advantage.[16]

## The Politics of Energy Consumption

Another dilemma India faces is increased and increasing dependence on hydrocarbon-based energy and its suppliers, particularly Saudi Arabia and Iran. India faces a particular challenge in this respect, having been caught in the crossfire of a highly consequential "civil war" in the Islamic World: between Shi'as, represented by Iran and its proxies, on one side, and Sunnis,

---

[16]Neil Padukone, "India's Involvement in the Sudan," *Pragati: The Indian National Interest*, 17 September 2012.

represented by Saudi Arabia and its proxies, including Pakistan and militant groups therein, on the other.[17] Tension between Iran and its western neighbors may be more rooted in geopolitics than in religion, as similar conflicts stem as far back as ancient Babylon and Persia, Arabs and Persians before the Safavid Empire that turned Iran into a Shi'a nation, and the Iran-Iraq and larger Iran-Arab conflict in modern history. Yet it has taken on an increasingly religious character in recent years.

India is not only caught in this geostrategic tussle in the international political realm, but is also feeling the effects of this tussle domestically. Starting from the 1970s, both Shi'a Iran and Sunni Saudi Arabia began to flex their religious muscles throughout the Islamic world. Shi'a organizations and parties, from Hizbullah in Lebanon to (Sunni) Hamas in Gaza, to Shi'a groups in Iraq and Afghanistan, and even Shi'as in India have been part of political networks cultivated by the Islamic Republic of Iran. India's Shi'a clergy in particular maintain close ties with and monitor theological developments in the Shi'a religious center of Qom, Iran. While most of these contacts are purely spiritual in nature, the Iranian government has turned many of these cultural ties with Indian Shi'a institutions into political clout.[18] In fact, Tehran often has a hand in Shi'a riots that occur in India, particularly Uttar Pradesh.[19]

The same goes for Saudi Arabia and Islamist organizations affiliated with its Wahhabi and Ahl-e-Hadith strains of Sunni Islam. From the 1980s, Zia ul-Haq's Pakistan became a major South Asian conduit of disseminating Saudi Arabian Sunni doctrine. Zia originally used the JeI, which had extensive links through much of the Gulf, for political and religious mobilization within the country. These networks have extended further into other denominations and sects, both religious and militant, including the local South Asian Deobandi Movement and even organizations such as the SIMI, which has been connected with Pakistan's LeT and which has carried out bombing attacks throughout India. As the host of Islam's two holiest sites, Mecca and Medina, and of millions of South Asian migrant workers, Saudi Arabia is an important transit point for many South Asian Muslims, many of whom "subsequently return home with Wahhabi views. Wahhabi funding from the Gulf Arab region has also enabled Wahhabi missionaries to convert Sunni Muslims to their interpretation of Islam."[20] The Indian embassy in Saudi Arabia itself has openly

[17]See, for example, Vali Nasr, *The Shia Revival: How Conflicts within Islam with Shape the Future.* New York: W. W. Norton and Company, 2006.
[18]Bharat Karnad, "US Wrong on India's Iran Policy," *The Diplomat*, 19 March 2012.
[19]Personal communication with member of Indian National Security Council Secretariat, 29 June 2009.
[20]Husain Haqqani, "The Ideologies of South Asian Jihadi Groups." *Current Trends in Islamist Ideology*, 1 (April 2005): 23–4.

expressed concern that "Saudi funding for religious schools and organizations has contributed to extremism in both India and Pakistan."[21]

This influence from the Gulf is weakening India's—and South Asia's—own narrative of Islamic syncretism. The interaction between Islam and Hinduism from the twelfth century on produced a syncretic, subcontinental spiritual identity, influenced by Hindu sects and Sufi Islam that emphasized the mystical, aesthetic, and spiritual dimensions of religion over rigid exoteric dogmas. This brought about a shared cultural space in which practitioners of different religions worshipped at the same shrines, revered the same saints, and even performed the same rituals. While partition compelled fundamentalist Muslims in Pakistan and extremist Hindus in India to try to define their new national identities in opposition to what had been, thus weakening this syncretic identity, these tensions on both sides of the border are being worsened by the influence of Saudi and Iranian Islamist doctrines that have contributed to a rise in not only sectarian polarization within the subcontinent, but also in its violent manifestations.[22]

Yet this influence is not driven by geopolitics and religion alone: the capacity of both Iran and Saudi Arabia to engage in this extra-regional Islamist activism is underwritten by the hydrocarbons trade. There is little coincidence that this activism from both countries rose steeply in the wake of the 1970s oil crisis, after which investments in Gulf energy infrastructures caused massive booms in Saudi and Iranian coffers, as well as the 1979 Islamic Revolution in Iran and seizure by Wahhabi militants of the Grand Mosque in Saudi-administered Mecca, which compelled Iran, and in turn, Saudi Arabia, to strengthen and export their respective Shi'a and Wahhabi religious doctrines. With India increasing its dependence on hydrocarbon resources from both countries, New Delhi is caught in another dilemma that its own investments are coming with strategic blowback. Indeed, this is a political dilemma that the entire hydrocarbon economy faces.

Of course, a second consequence of increased hydrocarbon usage is its connection to anthropogenic climate change. Between the economic development trajectory that was established in 1990 and 2006, India experienced an 88 percent increase in its carbon dioxide emissions, emitting over 1,742,698 metric tons of $CO_2$ per year, which amounted to 5.78 percent (and growing) of the world's carbon dioxide output.[23] India's diplomatic line on

[21]Wikileaks, Cable 224156: Indian charge in Riyadh on Saudi-India relations, dated 9 September 2009, cited in Hasan Suroor, "Indian 'concern' over Saudi funding for extremists," *The Hindu*, 17 March 2011.
[22]Neil Padukone, "The Case for Indian Islam," *Pragati: The Indian National Interest*, 30 November 2012.
[23]World Bank, Little Green Data Book 2007, Development Data Group of the Development Economics Vice Presidency and Environment Department, 2008, available at http://siteresources.worldbank.org/INTDATASTA/64199955-1178226923002/21322619/LGDB2007.pdf

the issue had held steadfast to the notion of differentiated responsibility: that it will not act until the western, developed countries make larger, unilateral reductions. Yet, certain actors in New Delhi—most notably Jairam Ramesh, minister for rural development and minister (additional charge) of drinking water and sanitation, and a former minister of state for environment and forests in the UPA-II government—recognize that climate change, regardless of the source of emissions, not to mention hydrocarbon-based pollution from locally consumed energy, will have some of the most disastrous consequences within South Asia itself. This is not only on the bilateral or international level, as discussed in Chapters 6 and 11, but also domestically. River recession, enhanced flooding, and diminishing agricultural supplies are not issues that can only be dealt with on the international level; they also have profound domestic and local consequences.[24]

Capital-intensive farming techniques, new methods of managing farmland, and globalization—including the vulnerability of rural agriculture to global competition and displacement of traditional lifestyles—have put rural areas in a tight bind. These are exacerbated further by environmental changes that can salinate, desiccate, flood, or otherwise render arable land unusable. In turn, domestic competition over scarce land for farming or industrial projects would rise as well; rifts between rebels in Jharkand and Arcelor-Mittal Steel[25] or between Essar Steel mineral extraction and adivasi farmers in Chhattisgarh[26] may be just the tip of the iceberg. As people are forced to migrate to cities, competition over finite resources therein—land and water in particular—will increase.

Even in the short-term, pollution from growing energy consumption has blanketed many Indian ecosystems, both human and ecological. According to the Environmental Performance Index released by Yale and Columbia universities, India ranks last in air pollution measures in a survey of 132 countries around the world. And in rankings of overall environmental health, India came at number 125.[27] The implications of these conditions for public health are profound. Stemming from Minister Jairam Ramesh's understanding of the issue, in anticipation of the Copenhagen discussions on climate change in 2010, New Delhi unilaterally announced plans to reduce India's carbon intensity—a measure of energy efficiency related to the amount

---

[24]"India announces energy intensity target," *Policy Brief*, India Climate Portal, December 2009.

[25]Moushumi Basu, "Arcelor-Mittal in Jharkhand." *Economic & Political Weekly*, 43, 48 (29 November 2008): 22–3.

[26]Devyani Srivastava, "Mining War in Chhattisgarh," Institute for Peace and Conflict Studies, Article # 2577, 23 May 2009, available at http://www.ipcs.org/article_details.php?articleNo=2577

[27]"India," Environmental Performance Index, Yale University, 2012, available at http://epi.yale.edu/dataexplorer/indicatorprofiles?ind=eh.air

of carbon emitted per unit of energy consumed—by 20 to 25 percent below 2005 levels by 2020.[28]

To that end, natural gas has been seen as a cleaner intermediary—and alternative—energy source to petroleum and coal. The 2003 large-scale (but certainly not complete) conversion to compressed natural gas (CNG) for transport technologies in New Delhi, where transport had accounted for over 70 percent of carbon emissions,[29] was visible soon after implementation. Visible pollution diminished markedly, and after the implementation of CNG, emissions of Nitrous Oxide, Particulate Matter, Carbon Monoxide, and Volatile Organic Compounds decreased by 5.5 percent, 5 percent, 8.5 percent, and 3.5 percent, respectively.[30]

Yet increased reliance on natural gas comes with two caveats. The first, of course, is that access to it comes with profound geopolitical consequences, including dependence on gas terminals and pipelines and on the countries that supply them. The second is that natural gas, as a fossil fuel comprised of hydrocarbons such as methane, does little in the realm of climate change mitigation: though carbon monoxide and certain other pollutants are reduced compared with emissions from coal and oil, they do remain, while other unhealthy and climate change-inducing pollutants, such as carbon dioxide, are still emitted in large quantities. In fact, increased dependence on natural gas, and investments in the infrastructures that explore, extract, liquefy, and refit technologies to exploit it, will come with a massive opportunity cost: delaying necessary investments that make environmentally sustainable renewable fuels such as solar, wind, and geothermal sources available and at a price that is scalable.[31]

# Foreign Military Intervention

Commentators within India and outside of the subcontinent have spoken of India's "deeply ingrained tradition of strategic restraint." Stephen Cohen and

---

[28]"India announces energy intensity target," *Policy Brief*, India Climate Portal, December 2009, available at http://www.indiaclimateportal.org/component/option,com_policybrief/view,policy briefdetail/id,20

[29]"White Paper on Air Pollution in Delhi with an Action Plan," Ministry of Environment & Forests, Government of India, 1997.

[30]Ragini Kumari, Luc Int Panis, Rudi Torfs, "Assessment of Transport Emissions in Delhi after CNG Introduction," Flemish Institute for Technological Research (VITO), Belgium, 2006.

[31]Personal communication with Jannette Barth, Senior Economist at Pepacton Institute LLC in New York City, 24 April 2012; John Deutsch, "The New World of Natural Gas," Forum on Global Energy, Economy and Security, Energy and Environment Program, The Aspen Institute, 2010.

Sunil Dasgupta cite New Delhi's use of force "mainly in response to grave provocation and as an unwelcome last resort." Even after the military victory in East Pakistan in 1971, "New Delhi did not press its military advantage in the west to resolve the Kashmir problem [on its own terms]. Similarly, India's nuclear weapons program, the military capacity that could have transformed India's strategic position, remained in limbo for twenty-four years after India tested its first atomic device in 1974."[32] Conceding that Pakistan and India's other neighbors have never been persuaded of Indian restraint, Cohen and Dasgupta argue that strategic restraint "has not served India poorly thus far, nor will it be an ill-conceived choice for the future. In a region characterized by many conflicts and an uneasy nuclear standoff, restraint is a positive attribute."[33]

Yet, as India faces a new strategic environment, "restraint is not seen as a virtue by those who want India to be a great power, a counterbalance to a rising China, and a provider of security in the international system rather than a passive recipient of the order created and managed by others."[34] Given the fact that India has become the largest global importer of arms over the last decade, and not only faces, but also creates for itself a new strategic landscape, questions arise over whether this doctrine of restraint may change. If India has a quest to become a "global superpower," with strategic and economic interests extending far beyond its conventional borders, will it be inclined to militarily intervene abroad, should its interests be threatened? Will this new strategic horizon mean the end of its "strategic restraint"?

There are, of course, distinctions between the concentric theaters of Indian influence. As Indian strategists, both in and out of government, have described, there is (i) India itself; (ii) India's "neighborhood," which includes the countries of South Asia with whom India shares borders; (iia) Afghanistan and Myanmar, which fall between the "neighborhood" and "near-abroad", and depending on the frame of reference, can be referred to as a "near neighborhood"; (iii) the "near abroad," that includes the adjacent countries of the Indian Ocean littoral of Central Asia, Southeast Asia, the Gulf, and the southern Indian Ocean; and (iv) further afield.[35]

As explored in Part Four, India's strategic restraint vis-à-vis its neighborhood not only remains intact, but has also been expanded in the light of New Delhi's

---

[32]Stephen P. Cohen and Sunil Dasgupta, *Arming without Aiming: India's Military Modernization.* Washington, D.C.: Brookings Institution Press, 2010, p. 1.

[33]Stephen P. Cohen and Sunil Dasgupta, *Arming without Aiming: India's Military Modernization.* Washington, D.C.: Brookings Institution Press, 2010. See also Bharat Karnad, "Habit of Free Riding," *India Seminar*, No. 599, July 2009.

[34]Ibid.

[35]C. Raja Mohan, "India and the Balance of Power," *Foreign Affairs*, July/August 2006.

efforts to reach conciliation with its South Asian neighbors. This is compelling India to eschew military intervention even in the wake of "grave provocation" such as the 26 November attacks on Mumbai, or even where it feels its security interests are being threatened owing to instability in Nepal and Sri Lanka. Extending its military power within South Asia—as it sought through its Monroe Doctrine—only resulted in failure and invited instability throughout the subcontinent.

In its "near neighborhood," Afghanistan was the host of a few hundred ITBP soldiers, who were brought to western Afghanistan to secure the area around the Zaranj-Delaram highway that India was constructing. Taliban attacks on the project resulted in the deaths of 129 Afghans and 6 Indians, which included two Border Roads Organization employees and four ITBP officers.[36] This was the first extra-regional deployment of Indian troops outside of United Nations auspices, but served only to ensure the safety of India's own development workers and did not have a mandate outside of that. The ITBP forces were withdrawn and returned to Indian soil following the completion of the road's construction, while others remained to provide security for India's diplomatic consulates around the country.[37] None of the troops, however, have engaged in combat with local forces. Sections of India's strategic community have suggested deploying Indian troops to Afghanistan as part of the broader American-led International Security Assistance Force mission, with the option of an extended presence after the withdrawal of American troops. This suggestion has been downplayed, however, partly because Washington has been wary of encouraging India's presence in Afghanistan, citing Islamabad's fear of encirclement. India's current strategic partnership with Kabul limits India's military presence to trainers for the Afghan National Army and Police.[38]

In its "near abroad," India's deployment of naval forces beyond its maritime boundaries—aside from joint naval exercises in the South China Sea and port calls as far as Japan—have thus far been restricted to humanitarian relief and combating piracy. Immediately after the 2004 tsunami, the Indian and American navies joined to form a rescue and relief operation between India and southern India. The complex disaster relief operation was a tactical success between the potential quadripartite partners—the United States, Australia, Japan, and India—and paved the way for further maritime

---

[36] "India hands over strategic highway to Afghanistan," *The Hindu*, 23 January 2009.
[37] "India to send more ITBP troops to Afghanistan," *Rediff News*, 12 March 2010; "Centre mulls more Afghan security," *The Telegraph – Calcutta*, 2 March 2010.
[38] Neil Padukone, "India and Pakistan's Afghan Endgames: What Lies Ahead?," *World Affairs Journal*, 175, 4 (November/December 2012).

integration between those countries' services for humanitarian purposes. The arrangement notably excluded China. New Delhi learned from the experience and stockpiled deployable emergency supplies and rations, which were valuable when India evacuated hundreds of its own and other countries' citizens from the Levant during the war between Hizbullah in Lebanon and Israel in the summer of 2006.[39]

In 2002, debates took place within the ruling National Democratic Alliance (NDA), led by the Bharatiya Janata Party, over the role of India and Indian troops in the forthcoming American invasion of Iraq. The idea to contribute Indian troops was entertained with an eye to the burgeoning US-India partnership, and the NDA had sought to use the issue as a way to demonstrate its bona fides to Washington. The decision was rejected, largely on the suggestion of nongovernmental analysts, owing to India's erstwhile alliance with Baghdad, a fellow "secular" country in the Arab world whose military India had trained and which had supplied India with petroleum, as well as the perceived imperialistic nature of the invasion both domestically and globally: if Islamic Pakistan had not contributed troops, why should a country led by a Hindu nationalist party? From this perspective, the decision to contribute troops would have come with great costs, but would have brought few strategic payoffs for India.[40]

The nature of India's military expansion and potential intervention abroad— particularly in its "near-abroad" and further afield—is largely contingent upon an assessment of India's own interests compared with the potential consequences, both positive and negative, for India. As India's experiences in Sri Lanka and even Pakistan demonstrated, the exercise of conventional military strengths can prompt asymmetric responses, that is, terrorism, that have disproportionately large consequences. In this respect, the idea of military overreach makes it such that "few Indians can muster enthusiasm to send an expeditionary force anywhere."[41] Cautiousness in the realm of extra-regional (and even regional) military deployment prevails.

That said, a domestic debate on the nature of India's military buildup and power projection is underway between "Great Power Realists," typified by Brahma Chellaney, Bharat Karnad, and a handful of serving and retired military personnel on the one hand, and the so-called "Nehruvians," characterized by

---

[39]C. Uday Bhaskar, "Tsunami Reveals Indian Military's Humanitarian Response Capability," *IDSA Comment*, 8 January 2005, available at http://www.idsa.in/idsastrategiccomments/TsunamiRevealsIndianMilitarysHumanitarianResponseCapability_CUBhaskar_080105

[40]"Troops to Iraq: Manmohan Clarifies Natwar's Remark," The Hindu, 8 July 2004; Sudha Ramachandran, "India rules out its troops for Iraq," *Asia Times*, 15 July 2003.

[41]Stephen P. Cohen and Sunil Dasgupta, *Arming Without Aiming: India's Military Modernization.* Washington, D.C.: Brookings Institution Press, 2010, p. 183.

the authors of one highly noted 2012 study on Indian foreign policy, entitled *Nonalignment 2.0*, on the other.[42] The former argue in favor of a massive defense modernization program that would impose greater "jointness" across the three services in order to enable greater military power projection capabilities across and even beyond the Indian Ocean region. The latter, comprised of economists, former diplomats, national security and military specialists, business leaders, and political analysts, see "strategic autonomy" as the primary guiding principle of India's foreign policy, enabled by a combination of economic, diplomatic, military, and soft power assets, and are cautious in the exercise of force and even of bold strategic decisions.

The views of the "Nehruvians" have perhaps held greater sway across Indian popular opinion and decision-making, owing largely to the state of civil-military relations in India, in which the military has long been subordinate to the elected civilian leadership and bureaucracy. While even the "Great Power Realists" have appreciated the democratic nature of this arrangement—particularly when contrasted to civil-military dynamics in which the civilian government is subordinate to the military, as in Pakistan, for example—they simultaneously lament the consequences this ironclad subordination has on military planning and arguably, effective preparedness.[43]

Yet, while the views of the "Great Power Realists" may not have been mainstreamed, and "India beyond its borders is fundamentally a status quo power,"[44] their influence has not gone unheeded. It is largely due to their influence that China has come to the fore of Indian military and strategic planning, that India's naval and air forces have been expanding at unprecedented rates (greater than that of the Army), and that India has become the largest importer of arms and weaponry in the world.

## (Cold) War with China?

Indeed, China and its military undoubtedly influence India's evolving strategic worldview. New Delhi is largely reorienting its defense alignment in anticipation of an enhanced Chinese presence in the region. Meanwhile, many of New Delhi's bilateral and multilateral ties in the Indian Ocean region are

---

[42]Sunil Khilnani, Rajiv Kumar, Pratap Bhanu Mehta, Lt. Gen. (Retd.) Prakash Menon, Nandan Nilekani, Srinath Raghavan, Shyam Saran, Siddharth Varadarajan, "Nonalignment 2.0: A Foreign and Strategic Policy for India in the Twenty First Century," *Center for Policy Research*, 2012.

[43]Anit Mukherjee, "The Absent Dialogue," *India Seminar*, No. 599, June 2009.

[44]Stephen P. Cohen and Sunil Dasgupta, *Arming Without Aiming: India's Military Modernization*. Washington, D.C.: Brookings Institution Press, 2010, p. 185.

underwritten by a shared aversion to Beijing's military strategy. One bilateral relationship in particular—between the United States and India—appears to be of greatest consequence to Chinese threat perceptions in the "Asian century." All of this raises a question among Asia watchers: will a Sino-Indian war erupt? If so, where, when, and over what?

In contrast to the bipolarity of the Cold War, India is unlikely to relinquish its autonomy and throw its hat in the ring fully with the United States in any Sino-US conflict. Teresita Schaffer, a former US ambassador in South Asia has written that

> strong Indo-U.S. relations do not imply hostility toward China, and an effective U.S.-China relationship does not suggest animosity toward India. In the past . . . the increasing attention that high-level U.S. officials have directed toward India has encouraged China to respond with high-level visits to India and occasional overtures toward the United States . . . a kind of "virtuous cycle." A good relationship with the United States is likely to enhance China's willingness to play a constructive role in South Asia, for example, by encouraging Pakistan's leaders to lay a foundation for peace. By contrast, ineffective or stormy relations between the United States and China could tempt Beijing to look to South Asia for ways to make life more difficult for the United States, as China has done in the past.[45]

This view is perhaps overly sanguine, as, certainly from the perspective of the US Department of Defense, China lies at the center of much of its strategic planning. This is evinced by the Pentagon's Defense Planning Guidance of 1992, which defined potential peer competitors—notably the Chinese in East Asia—as successors to the Soviet Union in American strategic thinking. If not in letter, the White House's "Strategic Pivot" of 2011–12 is an affirmation of this spirit, acknowledging that Beijing's economic and military rise could challenge the American-backed order of the western Pacific and ignite a major conflict; the Taiwan Strait could be the Fulda Gap of the twenty-first century. Meanwhile, India has become the world's largest importer of arms, accounting for 10 percent of global arms imports between 2007 and 2011, according to the Stockholm International Peace Research Institute (SIPRI). It is difficult to deny that this military expansion and modernization has at its source concerns over China's strategic expansion. Moreover, China would outpace India by the same metric, but for the fact that many of China's arms have come to be produced domestically and indigenously—and even exported. Beijing's *rate* of

---

[45]Teresita Schaffer, "Building a New Partnership with India." The Washington Quarterly, 25, 2 (Spring 2002): 41.

military expansion, including both imported and indigenous sources, certainly outpaces that of India.[46] Do these realities, then, signify that a military confrontation is inevitable?

Strategic competition between New Delhi and Beijing is taking root in a few theaters: (i) along the Indo-Tibetan border in the northeastern sector at Arunachal Pradesh, (ii) to a lesser extent along the Indo-Kashmiri-Xinjiang border in the northwestern sector by Himachal Pradesh and Kashmir, (iii) in the Bay of Bengal littoral, extending to the South China Sea, (iv) arguably into Central Asia, and (v) along the southern Indian Ocean.

China's military buildup along the Tibetan border has ignited an escalating conventional-arms race along the McMahon Line that demarcates the de facto Sino-Indian border; an Indian military expansion that is largely supplied by Western defense firms. Tibet is more accessible from Han (eastern) China than it is from India. The Brahmaputra Valley in India's "seven sisters" states is militarily accessible only from the south. But from there, the Himalayan Mountains and Tibetan Plateau restrict India's northward movement. In that sense, Beijing would have an upper hand in that theater: even a massive Indian military buildup in Arunachal or Himachal Pradesh would have great difficulties launching an *offensive* against Chinese forces there, in part because of the geographic advantage of the Tibetan Plateau.

Whether New Delhi would risk an air assault that it would most likely lose (and provoke a greater Chinese military presence) over land in Tibet that is, strategically speaking, relatively useless to India and that it is unable to occupy is not a likely course of action. This is particularly true because it remains unclear what support, if any, India would receive from the United States. Indeed, Washington has not made its position on Arunachal Pradesh clear: would it side with India or intervene on India's behalf in the case of a confrontation in Arunachal Pradesh? In fact, it may not be in America's interest to do so and involve itself in another conflict in which it has little directly at stake. Washington's own commitments to intervene in conflicts that its military *allies*—such as the Philippines, Japan, and even Taiwan—have with China remain largely uncertain. Thus, an Indian buildup along the McMahon Line serves more to reduce India's disadvantage rather than expose any Chinese vulnerability. Meanwhile, because Tibet is largely seen as a buffer and not as core a strategic vulnerability to Beijing as the Pacific, it is unlikely that China would divert resources from the Pacific to Tibet just to maintain superiority in

---

[46]"Rise in international arms transfers is driven by Asian demand, says SIPRI," Stockholm International Peace Research Institute, 19 March 2012.

that theater, which it would likely retain regardless given its geographic and economic advantage over India.

Though Beijing would prefer to maintain military superiority over India along the McMahon Line, China's biggest vulnerability in Tibet is not an Indian military offensive, but local internal stability. Beijing's strategic concerns are the few mountain passes along the Arunachal border, which India could use to infiltrate and try to destabilize China's control of Tibet from within, as it has in the past. That New Delhi would undertake such operations in the currently evolving bilateral environment is a separate, and unlikely scenario. Regardless, the existence of an evolving nuclear missile program (the Agni-V series), which has a 5000-km (3100-mile) range that can reach Shanghai and Beijing, demonstrates that credible deterrence will likely remain intact along the Sino-Indian border.

Beyond the Sino-Indian land borders, the area along the Indian Ocean littoral is another point of contention between New Delhi and Beijing. For its own purposes of securing Sea Lines of Communication for its own trade, and also to resist China's regional presence, the expansion of India's navy and air force—the key tools of power projection beyond its traditional land orientation—has been occurring at a far greater relative rate than its army modernization.[47]

The maritime realm is where any Indian advantage over China might be most pronounced, given India's naval presence at Port Blair in the Andaman Islands, just at the mouth of Malacca Strait. Malacca is, of course, one of the most trafficked waterways on the Indian Ocean, as it connects the Indian Ocean to the Pacific, and China to energy, raw materials, and consumer markets. Even if Beijing's plans to circumvent Malacca—through the Strait of Lombok, Myanmar-based road, rail, or pipelines, or a canal through Thailand—materialize, India would, in the case of a confrontation, be able to use its presence at Port Blair to interdict the trade or activities of China's other assets in the Bay of Bengal, and push back against Beijing's presence in the region. Moreover, this is only possible if Beijing is capable of eluding the massive American military presence—as well as the regional navies of Japan, the Philippines, Taiwan, and Vietnam—in the East and South China Seas.

As for China's longer-term plans to develop a roadway, further west, through Xinjiang, Kashmir, the Karakoram Mountains, and Baluchistan that links to Pakistan's port of Gwadar on the Gulf of Oman, it would appear that India's shrinking naval capacity on its western command would leave it exposed. Yet

---

[47]Stephen Cohen and Sunil Dasgupta, *Arming without Aiming: India's Defense Modernization.* Washington, D.C.: Brookings Institution Press, 2010.

even with China's potential naval base at Seychelles, India's remaining western command, though reducing out of a perceived need to focus on the south and east and to diminish Pakistani threat perceptions, would enable it to maintain supremacy against China in the Arabian Sea. Meanwhile, the Chabahar Port and road to Afghanistan that India has developed not only serve New Delhi's interests vis-à-vis resources and militancy in Central Asia, but also with regard to China. The Chabahar Port was foremost a response to Pakistan's disallowing transit trade to India, but it serves the additional purpose of counterbalancing China's developments at Gwadar, should they come to bear. India's Ayni Air Base in Tajikistan similarly provided a counterpoint to China's South and Central Asian presence.[48]

In the end, the political issues that divide India and China are insufficient to merit war. Tibet is the closest thing to a politically emotional source of conflict between the two countries. Though Tibet shares cultural links with South Asia (an issue many conservative Hindu strategists in particular seek to flag) and ethno-linguistic links with Han China, both India and China have historically been geographically separated from Tibet, and from each other by Tibet. From China's perspective, Beijing ought to retain control over Tibet to ensure that it is not used as a base from which to attack Han China. From India's perspective, Tibet's existence as an autonomous buffer between Han China and the Gangetic Plain ought to have been enshrined. Yet ultimately, Tibet is not an existential issue for either country: its status can enhance either country's security, but threatens them only marginally.

In fact, war would go against the interest of both countries. India, though it holds certain strategic and geographic advantages, remains militarily inferior to China, would have more at stake in a conflict, and would likely be militarily—though not necessarily strategically—defeated in the case of an actual combat. China, meanwhile, hopes for a *stable* South Asia and Indian Ocean, for it is that region on which much of its trade and economic vitality depends, particularly the Sea Lines of Communication over which India, with its growing naval power, has increasing influence.

With regard to China, India faces a classic security dilemma: even as Beijing expands its arsenal to defend itself against more credible threats from countries like the United States, the same weaponry and military doctrines can be deployed against India, which in turn feels it must expand its own military. The developing strategic ties and military expenditures and infrastructures are largely intended as means of restricting what the other *can* do—that is, maintaining military balances—that ensure that one country does not overstep

---

[48]Neil Padukone, "The Elephant and the Dragon," *The National Interest*, 3 May 2012.

and actually ignite military combat: they exist to deter an outbreak of hostilities initiated by either side.[49] And ultimately, China's maritime geography places it in a precarious position that will limit how far any major regional arms race could go.

# Domestic Developments, Foreign Stagnation

Another important question regarding India's "rise" is whether India's economic growth and increasing global profile will be stymied by domestic developments. Some of the issues that have not been addressed in the preceding sections are discussed in the following pages.[50]:

## *Left-wing Extremism*

In the central and eastern corridor of India, Tribals or *adivasis* have been more marginalized in modern India than even *dalits* (or "untouchables"), with higher poverty rates, lower healthcare access, and at greater risk of caste, corporate, and government-sponsored oppression—particularly displacement by minerals-extraction firms from the resource-rich forests in which they live. As Ramachandra Guha writes, Maoist

> revolutionaries identify with the tribals in the short-term, fighting for better wages for forest work and against their harassment by petty officials. Their long-term goal, however, is the capture of political power by armed struggle. In this the tribals are merely . . . cannon fodder. The Maoists use violence regularly and recklessly. Policemen are slaughtered . . . civilians killed by land mines. Their treatment of dissenters is especially savage; these are tried in "peoples courts" and then sentenced to amputation or death.[51]

According to the Home Ministry, over 150 districts across Chattisgarh, Jharkhand, Andhra Pradesh, and the rest of eastern India are affected by

---

[49]Personal Communication with General (Ret.) Michael Hayden, Former Director of the United States Central Intelligence Agency, 31 March 2012.

[50]This organization of this section is influenced by a series of essays written by historian Ramachandra Guha around the theme of why India will *not* or should not become a superpower. See, for example, Ramachandra Guha, "Will India Become a Superpower?," *Outlook India*, 30 June 2008; Ramachandra Guha, "Superpower Fantasies: India Should Seek other goals than joining a global race," *Telegraph India*, 12 September 2009; Ramachandra Guha, "Will India Become a Superpower," in *India: The Next Superpower?*, LSE Ideas, *London School of Economics*, 2012.

[51]Ramachandra Guha, "Will India Become a Superpower?," *Outlook India*, 30 June 2008.

Naxalite violence. While these account for even stray *incidences* of Maoist violence, and the reality is closer to about 40 or 50 districts in which there is a substantial presence, the issue speaks to a larger challenge that may be more expansive in absolute and relative geographic reach than even the Taliban insurgency in Pakistan that has received global attention. Meanwhile, as India urbanizes, the Maoist and Naxal movement (named after the Naxalbari village in West Bengal where, in 1967, the first major leftist uprising began), has targeted those at the receiving end of urban inequities through its "Urban Perspective Plan."[52]

## Religious Fundamentalism

The narrative of religious syncretism that existed in South Asia was weakened when the subcontinent was partitioned into religious sectors in 1947. Extremist Muslims in Pakistan and radical Hindus in India tried to define their new national identities in *opposition* to what had been. In India, post-partition accusations of being a fifth column for Pakistan—along with demands from right-wing Hindus that Muslims in India behave a certain way (as "*Hindu Muslims*")[53]—have often amounted to large-scale breaches of public safety and human security, in which thousands of innocent civilians have been killed in communal riots.

Electoral democracy has absorbed some of those strains by ensuring political rights and representation, but exacerbated others through vote-banks that empower conservatives who purport to represent their communities. Yet the end result has been often violent anti-Muslim rioting, largely with electoral gains to be reaped by religiously oriented political parties in India in the ensuing polarization: the deaths of thousands of Muslims in the riots following the demolition of the Babri Masjid in Uttar Pradesh in 1992 and the Godhra Train fire in Gujarat in 2002, resulted in relative impunity—and even electoral victories—for the largely Hindu perpetrators.[54] Meanwhile, certain strands of Islam in India have become less tolerant and increasingly violent, as

---

[52]P. V. Ramana, "Maoists' Tactical United Front (TUF) and Urban Movement," Paper Presented at IDSA Weekly Fellows Seminar Series, Institute for Defence Studies and Analyses, 10 July 2009, available at http://www.idsa.in/reports/MaoistsTacticalUnitedFrontandUrbanMovement100709.html

[53]See, for example, Pratap Chandra Swain, *Bharatiya Janata Party: Profile and Performance*. New Delhi: APH Publishing, 2001, p. 93.

[54]Paul R. Brass, *The Production of Hindu-Muslim Violence in Contemporary India*. New Delhi: Oxford University Press, 2003. See also Steven I. Wilkinson, *Votes and Violence: Electoral Competition and Communal Riots in India*. Cambridge: Cambridge University Press, 2004.

the growth of the Indian Mujahideen and Students Islamic Movement of India and their militant activities attest.[55]

## Systemic Political Corruption

Guha refers to the corruption and corrosion of the democratic center and the instability engendered by multi-party coalition governments. He specifically laments the turn, in the 1970s, of the INC party from the vehicle of a freedom struggle to one of a single family and its nepotistic tendencies. Meanwhile, the 1990s saw the rise of coalition politics in New Delhi, in which single parties could only govern with full majorities with great difficulties. Other, often regional parties, meanwhile, have also converted their parties into family firms—including the "DMK in Tamil Nadu, the Shiv Sena in Maharashtra, the Akali Dal in Punjab, and the Samajwadi Party in Uttar Pradesh, all of which are controlled by a single family, with the leadership passing from father to son."[56]

## Superficiality of the Mainstream Media

Mass media in India, while decentralized away from government control is increasingly falling prey to a "propaganda model." Private media outlets, once held as a pillar of competitive democracy that challenges the status quo, are increasingly business models interested in the sale of a product—readers and audiences—to advertisers, rather than in delivering quality, investigative, and critical journalism to the public.[57]

## Economic Inequality

While the opening of India's markets has increased the strength of the middle class—somewhere between 100 and 300 million depending on the

---

[55]Husain Haqqani, "The Ideologies of South Asian Jihadi Groups." *Current Trends in Islamist Ideology*, 1, (2005): 23–4. As mentioned in the previous chapter, however, much of this *violent* militancy is related to both the dynamic with Pakistan, as well as with the state of organized crime within India.

[56]Ramachandra Guha, "Will India Become a Superpower," in *India: The Next Superpower?*, LSE Ideas, *London School of Economics*, 2012.

[57]"Social and Political Challenges to Indian Security," Conference at the Observer Research Foundation, New Delhi, 30 March 2010. See also Edward Herman and Noam Chomsky, *Manufacturing Consent: The Political Economy of the Mass Media*. New York: Pantheon Books, 2002 (1988).

definition—many have been left behind. Admittedly, trickledown economics in India is not entirely negligible; the technology revolution has enabled even the poorest to engage in the financial sector, while more capital has brought about a rise in even informal sectors, the income of which often makes its way back to the rural villages that need it most. As a result, from the period of 1993–94 to 2004–05, the incidence of poverty fell from 35.8 percent to 27.5 percent in the entire country, from 36.8 percent to 28 percent in rural areas, and from 32.8 percent to 25.8 percent in urban areas.[58] Yet, as the economist Amartya Sen has written, the current vision of India is "half California and half sub-Saharan Africa." In fact, much of sub-Saharan Africa ranks *higher* in some human development indicators than India, where over 50 percent of children under the age of 5 are malnourished. These economic schisms exist at different levels of Indian society: between regions, among states, between metropolitan and rural areas, and between economic classes within single locales. Indeed as Sen and Jean Dreze have written, India has undoubtedly experienced massive levels of economic growth, but "economic growth is not constitutively the same thing as development."[59] In the period of 1993–94 to 2004–05, the GINI coefficient that measures wealth inequality increased from 0.303 to 0.325 in the entire country, from 0.285 to 0.298 for rural areas, and from 0.343 to 0.378 for urban areas.[60]

## Un-reconciled Borderlands

In Manipal, Nagaland, and Kashmir, local populations have long been wary of New Delhi's control. Concerns over insurgencies in those regions have often compelled New Delhi to use massively overhanded techniques in dealing with them, including human rights abuses enabled by the Armed Forces Special Powers Act, which gives India's military a largely free writ against populations in those regions. Yet these regions have long, arguably since before independence, fallen outside of the writ of the modern Indian state, owing partly to the economic geography of border regions, where ethno-linguistic ties and economic linkages span rather than terminate at political borders.

---

[58]Petia Topalova, "India: Is the Rising Tide Lifting All Boats?," International Monetary Fund, IMF Working Paper 08/54, March 2008, available at http://www.imf.org/external/pubs/ft/wp/2008/wp0854.pdf

[59]Amartya Sen and Jeane Dreze, "Putting Growth In Its Place," *Outlook India*, 14 November 2011.

[60]Petia Topalova, "India: Is the Rising Tide Lifting All Boats?," International Monetary Fund, IMF Working Paper 08/54, March 2008, available at http://www.imf.org/external/pubs/ft/wp/2008/wp0854.pdf

## A "Flailing State" Apparatus

Deficits in governance and the shocking incapacity of public institutions, as manifest in the malfunctioning of universities, law courts, hospitals, civil services, public safety, and national security have become national headlines, to say nothing of daily inconveniences if not threats to Indian citizens. With a large and growing economy, strong electoral democracy, and relatively cohesive polity, it is difficult to argue that India is a failed or even failing state. The economist Lant Pritchett, however, has aptly described India as a "flailing state," in which the head (policies, plans, laws, commissions, government apparatuses) works appropriately, but the body and limbs (institutions, governance, bureaucracy, and processes of implementing the mandates of the head) are either paralyzed or flailing.[61] Multitudes of well-intentioned and brilliantly planned commissions, laws, legal statutes, policies, and bureaucracies abound in India to serve justice, provide public services, ensure social stability, and reduce poverty—that is, to govern effectively. But while these institutions exist, the processes of governance and how their mandates are implemented remain questionable at best. Corruption, cronyism, inefficiency, and work ethic are among the issues that afflict policy implementation in realms as diverse as security, health, poverty alleviation, and infrastructure. Entire books can be—and have been, and will be—written about inadequacies in various facets of Indian governance and their consequences for Indian development.[62] India's flailing state, meanwhile, is also related to its poor infrastructure, from transportation to electricity- and power-generation, to the delivery of even basic goods such as clean, potable water.

## Economic Instability

The reforms that opened India's economy to foreign trade and investment and to domestic deregulation and privatization increased foreign investment in India, as well as Indian investment abroad. But questions remain over

---

[61]Lant Pritchett, "Is India a Flailing State? Detours on the Four Lane Highway to Modernization," Harvard University Kennedy School of Government, 19 September 2008, available at http://ksghome.harvard.edu/ lpritch/Papers/Is%20India%20a%20Flailing%20State_v1.pdf

[62]See, for example, Julius Court, "Assessing and Analysing Governance in India: Evidence from a New Survey," World Governance Survey, July 2003; Goran Hyden and Julius Court, "Governance and Development: Sorting Out the Basics," United Nations University, World Governance Assessment Project Working Paper No. 1, February 2001.

whether the factors that contributed to this growth can be sustained over the medium term. Following the 2007–11 financial crisis, global demand for Indian services plummeted, accompanied by a rise in unemployment and inflation. The attendant decrease in national revenue shined a spotlight on failures in Indian governance, namely tax avoidance and havens, and the broader issue of "black money," that which has been earned in India but has not been declared to the government or taxed. To narrow the gap, the UPA-II government attempted to implement a General Anti-Avoidance Rule (GAAR), which would cut down on tax havens abroad—notably Mauritius— and implement retroactive taxation measures for foreign corporations. These measures, along with a string of corruption scandals and government tepidness on rapid liberalization—brought on by concerns of exposing the Indian economy to the risk of foreign markets—caused investor confidence to fall: FII inflows dropped to 3 billion USD in 2011 while even Indian companies focused their investments abroad, and projections of 8 to 9 percent growth slowed to only 6 percent in 2011, with inflation hitting nearly 10 percent in 2012–13.[63]

Overexposure to international markets, however, may subject the Indian economy to systemic risks caused elsewhere that reverberate domestically. The decision of the Reserve Bank of India, under Governor Y. V. Reddy, to remain bearish and retain high lending standards—in the face of a bullish global market—largely insulated the Indian banking system from the sub-prime and liquidity crisis of 2008.[64] Should the Indian economy come under pressure to hyper-liberalize under similar circumstances, India may fall victim to economic overreach and perhaps foreign vulnerability. Yet this dilemma—of limiting its own growth versus falling prey to the instability or predatory nature of foreign markets on the other—will undoubtedly influence India's development, and raises important questions about the sustainability of the country's economic growth trajectory.

## Managing Tensions

In many senses the confluence of these challenges threatens a return to India's immediate post-independence nationalist thinking: that internal division would fragmont the country and keep it ripe for external manipulation. And in fact,

---

[63]Sachin Kumar, "FII inflows to hit 3-year low," *Hindustan Times*, 21 December 2011.
[64]See, for example, Joe Nocera, "How India Avoided a Crisis," New York Times, 19 December 2008.

these factors may restrict India's internal stability, economic growth trajectory, and its ensuing strategic expansion.

For better or worse, democracy has absorbed some of these internal strains. From one perspective, it has meant that even the downtrodden have a greater say, via elections and political organizing, in the political process and economic outcomes of the country's development. From another perspective, electoral democracy absorbs people's revolutionary fervor, displacing it into a ballot box, rather than actually channeling it into substantive structural change that may come more efficiently through violence.

Questions remain, of course, about the state of democracy in many Indian states and districts, namely the deep-ranging patronage networks between political parties and their often ethno-linguistic, caste, or sectarian vote blocs: members of a group vote for, and often run as candidates of certain parties, ensuring the party's control of state institutions. In exchange for their political support, clans, families, businesses, and individuals from those groups are given primary access to contracts, jobs, and investments in and from state agencies. In one sense, this is representative democracy at its essence: voters elect those people who will represent and *deliver* on some of their interests. But more often, these patronage networks amount to massive corruption: the use of public office for private and sectarian gain. And indeed many Indian political party leaders have used these contracts to amass large personal fortunes and buy off any opposition, while contributing to the rigidity of the ethnic identities they purport to represent.[65]

The nature of these patronage networks may evolve along with the economic development of the country. The Maharashtra-based Shiv Sena, for example, was initially a nativist, pro-Maharashtrian party that targeted its ire at Tamil and other South Indian migrants to Bombay who were, nonetheless, Hindu. When Bombay's textile mills began to close down in the 1970s and led to an employment void for many of the city's Maharashtrian workers, the patronage networks of the Shiv Sena focused on the dispossessed Maharashtrians and turned that party into a formidable electoral force in the city and state.[66] Yet over the years, as additional migrants came to Bombay from northern states, and religious nationalism came to the fore of national politics,[67] the Shiv Sena

---

[65]Kanchan Chandra, *Why Ethnic Parties Succeed: Patronage and Ethnic Head Counts in* India. Cambridge, UK: Cambridge University Press, 2007.
[66]See, for example, Juned Shaikh, "Worker Politics, Trade Unions and the Shiv Sena's Rise in Central Bombay." *Economic and Political Weekly*, 40, 18 (30 April 2005).
[67]Arvind Rajagopal, *Politics after Television: Religious Nationalism and the Reshaping of the Indian Public.* Cambridge, UK: Cambridge University Press, 2001; Thomas Blom Hansen, *The Saffron Wave: Democracy and Hindu Nationalism in Modern India.* Princeton, NJ: Princeton University Press, 1999.

evolved into an increasingly Hindutva fundamentalist party, focusing their violent anger on the Muslim presence in the city.[68]

Indeed a change that will affect not only India's democracy, but also its very political and economic character, is urbanization. Today, just over 30 percent of India lives in urban areas. By 2030 that number is anticipated to rise to 40.6 percent and by 2050, India's urban population is expected to overtake the proportion in rural areas, according to the United Nations.[69] This is due in part to investment cycles that encourage investment in, and migration to metropolitan regions without a concomitant, sufficiently scaled development strategy for rural areas.[70]

Rural areas, meanwhile, have undergone structural changes that complicated life for farmers. These include shifts associated with the 1970s Green Revolution that induced "high-yield" crops that altered irrigation and farming techniques,[71] as well as socioeconomic changes in farm management. Historically, farms were bequeathed to their owners' eldest son under what were largely considered feudal arrangements. Yet following independence and Indian land reforms, Indian farms were more commonly split up among children in the name of equity. This was not an ignoble intention, but as a result, each plot became further divided and increasingly smaller. After even one or two generations, a single plot would not be large enough to produce a sufficient agricultural output to be economically viable—or even to produce enough for a farmer's family to sustain itself.[72] Being unable to produce and compete economically, farmers were often forced to abandon or sell their plots for more financially lucrative opportunities in cities.

---

[68]Jayant Lele, "Saffronisation of Shiv Sena – Political Economy of City, State, and Nation." *Economic and Political Weekly*, 30, 25 (24 June 1995): 1520–8.

[69]"World Urbanization Prospects: The 2007 Revision Population Database," Population Division of the Department of Economic and Social Affairs of the United Nations Secretariat, available at http://esa.un.org/unup/

[70]"In rural areas, economic opportunities are scant. . . . This lack of development and infrastructure deters further investment in rural areas, compelling people to migrate to urban areas in search of employment. As there are fewer people in rural areas, there is even less of an incentive to invest in them, compelling still more people to migrate to cities. This has the end effect of keeping rural areas stagnant and underdeveloped while their residents emigrate. Alternately, in urban areas, economic opportunities and investment exist, compelling people to migrate to urban centers. A greater population, in turn, drives more investment in urban centers, continuing the cycle." Neil Padukone, *Security in a Complex Era: Emerging Challenges Facing India*. New Delhi: Knowledge World Press, 2010.

[71]Vandana Shiva, "The Green Revolution in the Punjab, *The Ecologist*, 21, 2 (March–April 1991); Vandana Shiva, *The Violence of the Green Revolution: Ecological Degradation and Political Conflict in Punjab*. New Delhi: Zed Press, 1992, pp. 57–60.

[72]See, for example, Doug Saunders, *Arrival City: How the Largest Migration in History is Reshaping our World*. New York: Pantheon Press, 2011.

This bifurcation of Indian polity between urban and rural areas will have stark consequences for Indian development, both for the better and for the worse. For instance, the space for political patronage networks itself is diminishing. As Kanchan Chandra writes, "since the economic reforms of the 1990s, two parallel processes are transforming the Indian state: shrinking opportunities for patronage in the urban economy and expanding opportunities for patronage in the rural economy." In rural areas, the reforms have been accompanied by an expansion of the state's presence through such programs as the National Rural Employment Guarantee (NREG), the Rashtriya Swasthya Bima Yojana (the National Health Insurance Program), and the Gram Sadak Yojana, a plan to provide the all-weather road access to villages.

> However . . . loopholes in implementation . . . have expanded opportunities for patronage in the rural economy; and since [these programs] promise an expansion of rural state-led schemes through expanded subsidies on food, credit schemes, state-provided rural infrastructure, and a revamped public distribution system, among others, rural patronage opportunities are only likely to further expand. [On the other hand,] the urban economy is dominated by the industrial sector, where government no longer sets quotas, and licenses are fewer and more transparently allocated. The state does remain involved in land transactions, in regulatory activity and in a large public sector; but it is smaller now in the urban, industrial economy than ever since independence, and it will probably continue to shrink.[73]

Of course, the specific evolution of India's urbanization will be a key determinant of how India develops.[74] Since the 1990s, India's urban development model has reserved high-density living for informal settlement by the urban poor, while medium-density settlements—in the form of the satellite city and exurb—follow the approach to urbanism taken by American planners in the wake of World War II. Suburbs like Gurgaon and Noida, Navi Mumbai, and Yelahanka have become satellite towns connected to Delhi, Mumbai, and Bangalore, respectively, by car commutes. Thus it is perhaps more appropriate to refer to Indian urbanization as "metropolitan regionalization," which includes the development of the densely populated urban core with its less-populated

---

[73]Kanchan Chandra, "Caste in our social imagination," *India Seminar*, #609, September 2009.
[74]Meanwhile, urbanization may provide an answer to the question of India's population explosion. Many urban families produce fewer children, since large families with many children have less economic utility in densely settled areas than they do in rural, agricultural areas, where children provide labor for farming and for taking care of elders in sparsely populated areas. See, for example, David Owen, "Sustainable Cities," *Business Day*, 8 October 2009.

surrounding areas, in contrast to rural areas. These concentric circles of dense urbanism, in turn, will affect the political fabric of India's settlement—for better and worse.

Meanwhile, governance reform efforts have taken place for decades and continue to. Democratic decision-making mechanisms were decentralized in 1993 with the 73rd Amendment to the Constitution, which granted constitutional status to the Panchayati Raj institutions, giving village councils the authority to develop local economic and social justice plans, and to levy taxes for their implementation. Parliament and State Legislative Assemblies have instituted various commissions to explore issues of public concern, from the status of Muslims, Dalits, and Adivasis, the state of the national security, intelligence, and defense procurement systems, to certain manifestations of poverty, to specific incidences or events, such as terrorist attacks. Often—though certainly not unconditionally—these commissions have led to major reforms in governance based on the commissioners' clout, reputation, and personal and public interest in the proposed reform. This includes some of the national security reforms undertaken after the Pradhan Committee of 2009 discussed in Chapter 12,[75] as well as the institution of the National Security Council and the expansion of the Port Blair naval base following the Kargil Review Commission of 1999.[76]

In 2011, corruption charges were leveled at various public figures in the central government and across bureaucracies, regarding the Commonwealth Games and other public expenditures. In response, millions of Indians took to the streets throughout the country in support of a national anticorruption movement. The protests featured acts of civil disobedience, hunger strikes, marches, rallies, and the use of social media to organize and raise awareness of what was fundamentally a nonpartisan movement. This movement found mainstream political representation in the *Aam Admi Party*, or Common Man's Party, led by Arvind Kejriwal, which is expected to be a formidable force in national and urban electoral politics.

In dealing with insurgencies, a combined strategy of military force and compromise has traditionally served India well strategically, and continues to. On the one hand, as part of its broader reform of its national security apparatus, New Delhi is upgrading its policing capacities at the national, state, and local levels, as described in Chapter 12. On the other hand, as Rajesh

[75]*Report of the High Level Enquiry Committee (HLEC) on 26/11* December 2009, available at http://www.scribd.com/doc/23474630/Pradhan-Committee-Report-about-26-11; C. Christine Fair, "Prospects for Effective Internal Security Reforms in India," Presentation at International Studies Association Meeting, February 2010, available at http://ssrn.com/abstract=1885488
[76]Kargil Review Committee, *From Surprise to Reckoning: Kargil Committee Report. Sage Publications,* 2000.

Rajagopalan writes, the essence of New Delhi's counterinsurgency strategy has been shaped by the fact that,

> short of secession, the Indian state has been willing to compromise [with rebellious sub-nationalities] on most other political demands. New states have been carved out to satisfy demands for local government and under the Sixth Schedule of the Indian Constitution some ethnic communities have been allowed to create autonomous regions and districts to allow for a measure of self-rule. Those rebels who were willing to give up the demand for secession and work within the Indian Constitution have been welcomed into the political order, becoming important regional leaders.[77]

These caveats—notably the fact that corrective functions do exist and are built into the system, irrespective of the large opportunities for improving them—considered, domestic challenges have not necessarily stymied the growth of regional or even global powers on the international realm. In its rise to and reign as a global imperial power, Great Britain, for example, faced Scottish and Irish revolutions on what it considered its own territory, while transforming its agricultural economy into one dominated by industry, which brought about urban poverty that was, until then, unseen anywhere in the world. The United States, meanwhile, hosted corrupt patronage networks through most of its metropolitan areas, de facto and even de jure oppression of nearly a quarter of its population through a deep-rooted system of racial segregation, abounding yellow journalism that ultimately gave way to a propaganda model of media management, and a current population with a Gini coefficient, a measure of economic inequality, of 0.45, which is even greater than India's 0.36 throughout the "American" century.

Nevertheless, all of these domestic issues will undoubtedly implicate India's development, and they are issues that Indian policymakers, citizens, as well as foreigners dealing with India will have to contend with and, ideally work to resolve. Yet the focus of Ramachandra Guha and others on New Delhi's hypothetical quest to become a "superpower" says little about the contours of its strategic doctrine—of its capabilities, intentions, perspectives, or actions. India's worldview explains how New Delhi views and hopes to engage with those outside its borders. Its reorientation *within* the subcontinent and how it

---

[77]Rajesh Rajagopalan, "Insurgency and Counterinsurgency," *India Seminar*, #599, July 2009; See also, Rajesh Rajagopalan, *Fight Like a Guerrilla: The Indian Army and Counterinsurgency*. London: Routledge India, 2008.

increasingly deals with the countries of South Asia in particular is undergoing a long-term shift that is of most profound consequence.

India's strategic reorientation is just that: a recalibrated *vision* and ensuing strategy rather than a concrete prognosis. That reoriented vision may not encompass global "leadership" in the sense that Indian statesmen often aspired to—a permanent seat on the UNSC, the ability to command people on distant shores, economic domination of the world economy. But it will come with profound consequences for the twenty-first century world, the "Asian century," and perhaps most importantly, India and the subcontinent themselves.

## Toward a South Asian Union?

India's attempt to reverse 60 years of enmity with its neighbors and work toward political conciliation and economic reintegration in South Asia harkens back to the pre-independence period in the subcontinent. One very radical departure from New Delhi's traditional foreign policy doctrine is the notion of external intervention in South Asia. Not only has India not opposed these interventions by foreign companies, banks, and even countries in South Asian markets and politics, but it has also welcomed and expanded upon them. Particularly with Pakistan, New Delhi has realized that America's influence in Pakistan can even be beneficial to India. And in the process of accessing markets, limiting China's presence, and maintaining stability, India's efforts to reach conciliation with its neighbors is leading India to temper its own engagement with the other countries of the Indian subcontinent.

These shifts in strategic worldview that have been occurring since the 1990s have extended across political party lines. The INC-led government of Narasimha Rao was the first to articulate the "Look East" policy that began the abrogation of India's Monroe Doctrine and the country's movement beyond South Asia in the early 1990s. The Janata Dal Party's I. K. Gujral, who led the Foreign Ministry from 1989 to 1990 and from 1996 to 1998, and the country as prime minister from 1997 to 1998, enunciated his "Gujral Doctrine," which stated that

first, with its neighbors. . . . India does not ask for reciprocity, but gives and accommodates what it can in good faith and trust. Second, we believe that no South Asian country should allow its territory to be used against the interests of another country of the region. Third, that none should interfere in the internal affairs of another. Fourth, all South Asian countries must respect each other's territorial integrity and sovereignty. And finally, they should settle all their disputes through peaceful bilateral negotiations.[78]

Prime Minister Atal Bihari Vajpayee, though head of the opposition Hindu nationalist Bharatiya Janata Party, practically applied these words to Pakistan, with his 1999 visit to the Minar-e-Pakistan in Lahore, where he signed the *Lahore Declaration* signifying India's acceptance of Pakistan's right to exist and commitment to peace. Vajpayee and, later, his successor Prime Minister Manmohan Singh of the Congress Party underwrote these symbols with actions such as the inauguration of bus service between Delhi and Lahore, and between Srinagar in Indian-administered Kashmir and Muzaffarabad in Indian-administered Kashmir, to say nothing of the additional steps toward conciliation and integration undertaken by both governments, outlined in Chapter 12. Going forward, even BJP President Rajnath Singh has said that, under a BJP-led government, there would be "no major changes in foreign policy. . . . As far as changes in the foreign policy is [sic] concerned, there is not likely to be a basic change in its fundamental principles. . . . Our foreign policy would be to have cordial relationship [sic] with our neighbors."[79]

Yet, even if these efforts are successful, this certainly does not mean that the smaller countries of South Asia will be vassals of New Delhi, that they will sublimate their autonomy into India's, or that the subcontinent would be a perfectly harmonious region. Part of the drive for India to temper its engagement with its neighbors has often been the very real concern over (a) anti-Indian sentiments and instability in its neighboring countries, (b) a Chinese presence in these countries, and (c) local economic nationalism that would restrict India's full economic potential. As much as India is taking pains to limit these scenarios, there is no guarantee that the capitals will not seek to retain their absolute sovereignty and oppose New Delhi, either to reap personal political gain or to appease the "huge anti-India constituencies" that remain in all of India's neighboring countries.[80] Yet New Delhi's own changing approach to its neighborhood may, over time, cause those anti-India constituencies themselves to diminish in size and strength.

Of course, this recalls the natural economic and political geography of the subcontinent, unimpeded by political borders, which traditionally had a highly

[78]Inder Kumar Gujral, "Aspects of India's Foreign Policy," Speech at the Bandarainake Center for International Studies, Colombo, Sri Lanka, 20 January 1997.
[79]Vikas Kumar, "India's economic, foreign policies unlikely to change under new government," *East Asia Forum,* 24 August 2013; "BJP rules out major foreign policy shift, if voted to power," *The Hindu,* 25 July 2013.
[80]C. Raja Mohan, "Beyond India's Monroe Doctrine," *The Hindu,* 2 January 2003.

decentralized political culture. Instead of seven nation-states and 28 provinces under the dominance of New Delhi, as was the goal of India's Monroe Doctrine, there might be more than 40 local divisions under a new patchwork of sovereignty. With the decentralization of Indian political decision-making to the provincial level—with state chief ministers and even panchayati raj leaders exerting greater influence at the local level—and coalition governments of different regional parties sharing political power in New Delhi,[81] India may be seeing a return to the layered, shared sovereignty model that typified its geography for centuries. With strengthening democratic institutions in Bangladesh, Nepal, Bhutan, and potentially Sri Lanka and the Maldives, and with a Pakistan renegotiating its own identity and model of federalism, this layered, shared sovereignty may be seen across the subcontinent.

Throughout history, these local political divisions have remained fundamentally decentralized politically, but nonetheless economically integrated based on geographic and economic features such as river systems, trade corridors, mountain ranges, and resource bases. Today, these would include routes retracing the Grand Trunk Road from Kabul to Lahore, through Delhi, onto Dhaka (via road, rail, electricity grids, or even natural gas pipeline); plantations in one country whose produce is processed or manufactured in a second; trade of goods such as onions, tea, and other agricultural products, technology, and manufacturing products, as well as services like finance, low-skilled labor, and information technology across the borders of South Asia; more open borders to encourage the flow of people, migrants, services, and labor throughout the region; and joint water management projects along the rivers that flow throughout the region that manage climate change, provide irrigation and transfer electricity to multiple countries.

The painful historical legacies of the past once led to regional deadlock, military confrontation, and worse. Yet India's strategic evolution, centered on offsetting China's influence and connecting with the world beyond South Asia, aims to diminish tensions among its subcontinental neighbors. This new atmosphere of political conciliation will enable the countries of the region to set the foundations for the intra-regional infrastructures that economically reintegrate the subcontinent, and undo the economic partition of South Asia.

---

[81] "The bottom-up federalization of India's politics [since 1989] . . . means that the lives of the vast majority of Indians will be shaped by the dominant feature of India's decentered democracy in the early twenty-first century: regionalization and regionalism(s)." Sumantra Bose, *Transforming India: Challenges to the World's Largest Democracy*. Cambridge, MA: *Harvard University Press*, 2013.

# Index